100
HIKES in

W9-CNA-952

THE
GREAT SMOKY
MOUNTAINS
NATIONAL PARK

RUSS MANNING

THE
MOUNTAINEERS

For Grace and Al, who have enriched so many lives

Published by
The Mountaineers
1001 SW Klickitat Way, Suite 201
Seattle, WA 98134

Published simultaneously in Great Britain by Cordee, 3a DeMontfort Street, Leicester, England, LE1 7HD

Manufactured in the United States of America

Edited by Kris Fulsaas
Maps by Russ Manning
All photographs by the author unless otherwise noted
Series cover and book design by Jennifer Shontz
Layout by Alice C. Merrill

Cover photograph: *Sunrise from Myrtle Point on Mount LeConte*
Frontispiece: *Mountain Farm Museum at Oconaluftee Visitor Center*

Library of Congress Cataloging-in-Publication Data
Manning, Russ.
    100 hikes in the Great Smoky Mountains National Park / by Russ Manning —
2nd ed.
        p. cm.
    Updated ed. of: The Best of the Great Smoky Mountains National Park, ©1991.
    Published simultaneously in Great Britain.
    Includes bibliographical references (p.   ) and index.
    ISBN 0-89886-636-7 (pbk. : perm. paper)
    1. Hiking—Great Smoky Mountains National Park (N.C. and Tenn.)—Guide-
books. 2. Trails—Great Smoky Mountains National Park (N.C. and Tenn.)—Guide-
books. 3. Great Smoky Mountains National Park (N.C. and Tenn.)—Guidebooks. I.
Jamieson, Sondra. II. Manning, Russ. Best of the Great Smoky Mountains National
Park. III. Title. IV. Title: One hundred hikes in the Great Smoky Mountains National
Park.
    GV199.42.G73 M36 1999
    917.68'89—dc21   99-6456
                                                                                      CIP

Originally published under the title *The Best of the Great Smoky Mountains National
Park* by S. Russell Manning and Sondra K. Jamieson, ISBN 0-9625122-2-2.

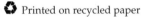

CONTENTS

NORTH CAROLINA DISTRICT

ACKNOWLEDGMENTS

I am grateful to the National Park Service staff of the Great Smoky Mountains National Park for taking the time to supply information and answer questions during the preparation of this book. I appreciate Howard McAnnally and Buck Lambdin, volunteers in the Backcountry Reservation Office, for reviewing part of an early draft and making valuable suggestions.

I also appreciate Allen Coggins kindly supplying a prepublication draft of *Place Names of the Smokies*, which I found useful in determining and confirming various place names.

Key to Map Symbols

——	Paved Road
– – –	Unpaved Road
········	Trail
········	Connecting Trail
——	Stream
–·—·—	Park Boundary
⌒□□	Parking Areas/Overlooks
) (	Pass/Gap
▲	Mountain Peak
60	Hike Number
17	Connecting Hike Number
ⓢ	Start (Trailhead)
AT	Appalachian Trail
△70	Backcountry Campsite
⏶	Campground
⛾	Ranger Station
■	Building
75	Interstate Highway
441	US Highway
28	State Highway

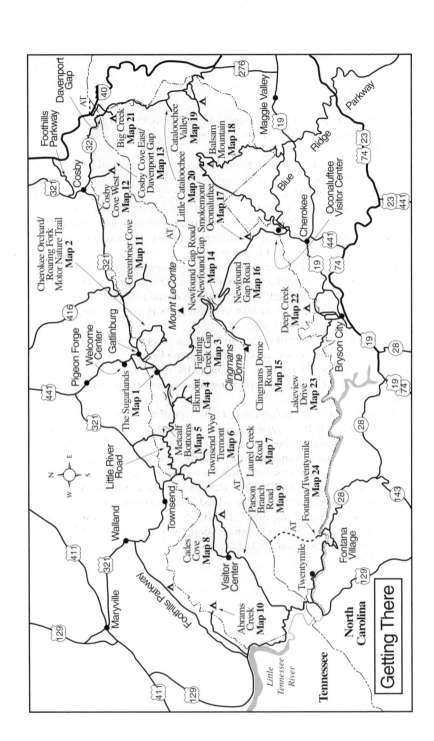

Getting There

PREFACE

I grew up in the coastal plain of southern Alabama. In such a monotonous place, the horizon is a straight line, more likely punctuated by a tall tree than a hill.

On my first encounters with mountains, I saw the hills and peaks rising to mysterious heights, creating hidden coves and valleys. I felt the allure of elevation and defile. When I came to live in this mountainous region of eastern Tennessee and western North Carolina, I experienced a certain excitement because of the proximity of mountains—always another region to explore, another peak from which to gaze across the land, another cove in which to rest beside a trickling stream.

The Great Smoky Mountains are the best of this region, an 800-square-mile national park in the Southern Appalachians where some of the highest peaks in the eastern United States gather to create a highland citadel. In time it has become the most visited national park in the country, with nearly 10 million visits each year.

In spite of the number of visitors to the Great Smoky Mountains National Park, you'll find many backcountry trails, some long, some short, that get you away from the crowds. You can wander the mountain ridges and investigate the isolated coves, experiencing for yourself the attraction of the mountains.

As you explore the Smokies, you'll have a particularly rich experience if you pay attention to the natural community around you. The vast deciduous and coniferous forest of these mountains is the special attraction—the trees, the birds, the mammals and reptiles, the shrubs and wildflowers, the mushrooms and mosses that in season provide a special enjoyment.

In this book, I describe 100 hikes that get you out to explore the mountains. With this new edition, I have added hikes covering more trails, suggested more backpacking and day-hike loops, and introduced more background and natural history information. I hope this book will help you more easily find what you are looking for in the Great Smoky Mountains National Park.

Russ Manning

INTRODUCTION

The Great Smoky Mountains National Park lies amid the Southern Appalachian Mountains, straddling the border between Tennessee and North Carolina, virtually half in one state and half in the other. The Appalachians are a long mountain range running northeast to southwest, from Canada to the coastal plain of Alabama. The range was named by the Spanish explorer Hernando de Soto, who may have been the first nonnative to see these mountains. He called them the "Appalachians," after an Indian tribe he had encountered along the Gulf Coast.

The Southern Appalachians divide into two mountain ranges—the Blue Ridge to the east and the Unakas to the west. At the widest part of the Unaka range stand the Great Smoky Mountains. The Smokies are also the tallest part of the Unakas, with sixteen peaks above 6,000 feet along the crest from the Pigeon River on the northeast to the Little Tennessee River on the southwest. The waters that gather on the sides of this Smokies crest run north and south and then west to eventually join the Tennessee River that flows westward to the Mississippi River.

Native Americans once wandered through the mist of the Great Smoky Mountains. By the time white settlers came to the Smokies, Cherokees were the dominant tribe. They called themselves *Ani-Yunwiya,* "the Principal People," Cherokee being the white man's name for them. Their lands covered

Deep Creek Valley from Newfound Gap Road

40,000 square miles that included the Great Smokies, or, as the Indians called it, *Shaconaqe*, "place of blue smoke." The Cherokees lived by the thousands in villages along streams and rivers; many concentrated along the Little Tennessee River that flows along the southeastern boundary of the present national park. But they ranged far across their lands, following ancient paths, including a transmountain route that crossed the Smokies at what is now called Indian Gap, just west of Newfound Gap.

When European settlers came to the region, they could not abide such vast lands being left unused, although from the perspective of the Cherokees, the land left in a natural state was well used. Continuous encroachment of white settlers onto Cherokee lands led to numerous battles between the two groups and to treaties forced on the Cherokees in which their lands were lost. With the Treaties of 1798 and 1819, the Cherokees were forced to give up the Great Smoky Mountains, thereafter living to the south and west.

But treaties were short-lived in those days. With the Indian Removal Acts of 1828 and 1830, pushed through Congress by President Andrew Jackson, the Cherokees were told to relinquish all lands and move west of the Mississippi River. In 1838, the U.S. Army received orders to capture those who remained and force them to move to Oklahoma; 4,000 Cherokees died along the route that became known as the "Trail of Tears." But before they could all be rounded up, some from the remote villages escaped into the mountains and hid in the coves and hollows of the Smokies. The Army knew it could never capture these Cherokees and so gave up pursuit. In addition there were about 70 Cherokee households who had earlier ceded their lands and so were not included in the eviction orders. These exempt households, along with the escapees, coalesced to become the Eastern Band of the Cherokees, while those who had moved to Oklahoma became the Cherokee Nation, or the Western Band.

During the next ten years, a white man, William H. Thomas, who had been adopted by Chief Yonaguska, worked to secure the monetary compensation due the Eastern Band under the treaties. With this compensation, Thomas, who had become de facto chief, purchased some of the Cherokees' former lands to form the Qualla Boundary, named after the principal town in the area (today it's known simply as the Cherokee Reservation). In 1866, the North Carolina Legislature passed an act formally recognizing the right of the Cherokees to live in the state and to no longer be subject to removal. They were recognized by the U.S. government in 1868 and officially referred to as the Eastern Band in 1870. Today the Cherokees remain on their reservation at the foot of the Smokies in North Carolina.

With the Cherokees gone from the interior of the Smokies, the mountains were open to settlement. It was still a wild, undeveloped region. The pioneers who had already begun to settle the mountains were primarily "Scotch-Irish," a term applied to Scots who relocated to Ireland in the early 1600s and whose descendants then began a migration to America in the early 1700s. They first settled the Pennsylvania region, then moved south through Virginia into the Carolinas, where they joined with Germans and English to penetrate the mountains. These mountains were first officially referred to as the "Smoaky Mountains" in the Act of 1789, when North Carolina offered to cede to the federal government its western lands, which became the Southwest Territory and eventually the state of Tennessee. The mountain range was also at one time called the "Great Iron Mountains."

The settlers moved up the coves and into the river valleys of the mountains. They cut trees to build log cabins and open fields. This was still a primeval forest with trees so large many could not be cut, so the settlers often girdled the trees to kill them and thus let the sun reach the forest floor where the farmers then planted corn, the primary crop. They were a self-sufficient people who gathered nuts and berries and hunted wild game while cultivating crops and raising hogs and chickens.

Many of these early families lived alone in their coves, widely separated from their nearest neighbors. But in places, communities grew along watercourses and in fertile coves. Oconaluftee and Cades Cove were settled first; there were large concentrations in Greenbrier Cove and the Sugarlands and Cataloochee Valleys. In such places, the people banded together to form communities with schools and churches. Apart from this settlement by hardy mountaineers, the mountains remained essentially undisturbed.

But it was inevitable that the forest resources would attract the attention of the outside world. Lumber companies learned of the mammoth trees and unending forests of the Smokies. The companies moved into the mountains, bought land, and began cutting roads and laying rail lines to haul out the trees. Among the several companies, the Little River Lumber Company on the Tennessee side and the Champion Fibre Company on the North Carolina side were the largest. Company towns, places like Smokemont, Tremont, Elkmont, and Proctor, were built to house the workers. With the felling of the trees, some so massive a single tree filled a railcar, the mountains were devastated by erosion and fire.

From the perspective of the late twentieth century, it's easy to characterize these companies only as exploiters and despoilers of the land. And perhaps the lumber barons can be blamed for their "cut and get out" attitude. But from the perspective of the early part of the century, the loggers were hard workers who supplied a needed resource for the building of homes, towns, and cities in a fast-growing country. Whatever the view, virtually everyone now agrees it was fortunate that the movement to create a national park began at a time when approximately 20 percent of the primeval forest could be saved.

A NATIONAL PARK IS CREATED

In the 1920s, when the Great Smoky Mountains National Park was proposed, it was a unique venture. All previous national parks had been formed out of lands already owned by the U.S. government in the western part of the country. To create a national park in the eastern United States, the land would have to be purchased.

While there had been talk since the 1890s of establishing a national park in the southern Appalachians, the idea for a national park in the Smokies originated in 1923 with Willis and Anne Davis. Willis Davis was then manager of the Knoxville Iron Company, and Anne Davis was a member of the Tennessee State Legislature. In 1923 a Great Smoky Mountains Conservation Association was established with Willis Davis as president. Col. David C. Chapman, a wholesale druggist in Knoxville, Tennessee, was later made chairman of the board.

At the same time, there was renewed talk in Washington, D.C., about the need for a national park in the South. A Southern Appalachian National Park Committee was sent to investigate potential sites. The Great Smoky Mountains Conservation Association met with the group in Asheville, North Carolina, and some members of the committee visited the Smokies in August 1924; they were taken to the top of Mount LeConte, where the Conservation Association had established a camp. On December 13, 1924, the committee recommended the establishment of two parks, Shenandoah in the Blue Ridge Mountains of Virginia and the Great Smoky Mountains in Tennessee and North Carolina.

In anticipation of a national park being established in the Smokies, Anne Davis introduced a bill into the Tennessee legislature authorizing purchase of land owned by the Little River Lumber Company, the largest lumber operation on the Tennessee side of the mountains. An amended bill called for the city of Knoxville to pay one-third of the purchase price. Knoxville agreed, and the bill was signed in April 1925. But the actual purchase awaited the intentions of the federal government.

In 1926, a bill passed by the U.S. Congress called for lands to be taken over by the federal government when the states of North Carolina and Tennessee had purchased at least 150,000 acres, and for a national park to be established when a major portion of the land had been secured. The bill was signed by President Calvin Coolidge on May 22, 1926. The Little River Lumber Company property was then purchased, the first property to be secured for the park.

The two states created park commissions possessing authority to purchase land. Chapman was named chairman of the Tennessee commission, and State Senator Mark Squires headed the North Carolina commission. The two faced a monumental task. The established boundaries encompassed more than 6,000 separate tracts of land, including large ranges owned by eighteen lumber companies, more than 1,000 small farms, and something like 5,000 small lots, some of which had summer homes on them. In 1926, there were 7,300 people living in the designated area. In addition to overseeing the survey, appraisal, and purchase of the land, the commissions had to raise the necessary money. The funds came from private contributions, including $1,391.72 given by schoolchildren; from federal and state government appropriations; and from the Laura Spelman Rockefeller Memorial—John D. Rockefeller Jr. donated $5 million from this fund established by John D. Rockefeller Sr. as a memorial to his wife.

By 1930, purchased land in both states totaled 152,000 acres, surpassing the minimum needed for the federal government to accept stewardship. Maj. J. Ross Eakin was named the park's first superintendent. In 1933 the Civilian Conservation Corps (CCC) began building trails, bridges, and park facilities. On June 15, 1934, the U.S. Congress authorized full establishment of the national park. On September 2, 1940, the Great Smoky Mountains National Park was dedicated by President Franklin D. Roosevelt as he stood along the curved wall of the Rockefeller Memorial, built at Newfound Gap for the dedication ceremonies.

By 1959, 508,000 acres had been purchased for $12.7 million for the park. The volunteer efforts of hundreds of citizens of Tennessee and North Carolina resulted in a vast forestland preserved for the enjoyment of all Americans for generations to come.

GEOLOGY OF THE GREAT SMOKY MOUNTAINS

At least three mountain ranges have occupied the region where the present Unaka range (Great Smokies) stands today. More than a billion years ago, the oldest rocks were laid down as sediment in a great trough in the earth's crust. After the sediment had accumulated to several thousand feet, the trough closed, possibly because of an early collision of the continental plates that make up the earth's surface. The sedimentary rocks were compressed, broken, and folded; molten rock from the earth's interior invaded and added heat to the process. The rocks were eventually converted to a hard crystalline mass.

Afterward this area was uplifted, probably due again to plate tectonic forces. The land immediately began to erode, with rocks and soil deposited as sediment in a large marine basin just to the west. This new deposit solidified about 600 million years ago into rock that became known as the Ocoee Series, which consists of the Snowbird, Great Smoky, and Walden Creek Groups.

The Great Smoky Mountains are made up of this Ocoee Series, with the main part of the mountains being the Great Smoky Group within the series. This group is a mass of clastic sedimentary rocks, pebble conglomerate, sandstone, and silty or clay-containing rocks. No fossils are found, primarily due to the ancient age of the rocks. Three formations make up the Great Smoky Group—the fine-grained Elkmont Sandstone on the bottom, the coarse-grained Thunderhead Sandstone in the middle, and the dark silty and clay-containing Anakeesta Formation that has been altered to slate, phyllite, or schist. The hard, resistant Thunderhead Sandstone erodes slowly and so forms rounded mountain peaks when it nears the surface. But the slaty Anakeesta fractures into thin, jagged pieces; this rock forms the steep-sided ridges and pinnacles of the Smokies.

The Great Smoky Mountains from Andrews Bald

About 450 million years ago, folding and faulting pushed the rocks of the Ocoee Series up and over younger rock to the northwest, creating a second mountain range. About 375 million years ago, there followed a period of heat and pressure, and then later more folding and faulting with masses of rock once again being pushed northwest. About 250 million years ago, in the last episode of great mountain building, the whole region rose high above sea level, most likely due to the collision of the African and North American continental plates.

The present look of the Great Smoky Mountains was not created by the folding and faulting episodes, but by the subsequent erosion that swept away countless tons of rock to leave the mountains you see today. The Smokies were once much higher, perhaps higher than the Rocky Mountains, which are younger formations. The erosion was accelerated with the additional uplift caused by isostatic adjustment, a process in which the weight of overlying layers is removed by erosion and less dense rock below is forced upward by surrounding dense rock. Erosion has lowered the Smokies to a level at which there is no tree line, as there is in the Rockies; trees grow on the crest of the Smokies because these mountains no longer stand above the elevation at which trees cannot grow.

Part of the erosion process involved cold temperatures. From 500,000 to 20,000 years ago, glaciation in the north created colder-than-usual temperatures in the Great Smokies region. During this period, alternate freezing and thawing caused rock to crack and split into huge boulders that slid and tumbled down to the valley floors. You'll find these boulders sitting along streambeds, too big to have been carried there by the action of present or past streams. Once the glaciers retreated and the climate warmed, boulder creation slowed and it now happens infrequently.

Although the Smokies have in the past experienced great faulting and folding and boulder formation, and though occasionally you'll see a rock slide along one of the roads, the mountains today are more settled. They have had millions of years in which to age to rounded mountains clothed in a rich biological diversity.

THE SMOKIES' FLORA AND FAUNA

The great attraction of the Great Smoky Mountains area is its community of plants and animals. Within this vast forest have been found 1,500 species of flowering plants; 100 kinds of trees; 600 mosses, liverworts, and lichens; 2,000 different fungi; 61 species of mammals; 80 species of snakes and amphibians, including 30 salamanders; 70 kinds of fish; and 200 different bird species. This is probably the most biologically diverse region in all of North America, a feature recognized by its designation as an International Biosphere Reserve under the UNESCO Man and the Biosphere Program.

Pink Lady's Slipper

These numbers notwithstanding, it's estimated that only 10 percent of the species living in the Great Smoky Mountains National Park have been identified. In 1998, the National Park Service launched an All-Taxa Biodiversity Inventory that over a period of ten to fifteen years will attempt to list every living thing in the park. With insects, fungi, and other small organisms included, there could be more than 100,000 species that need to be identified. In the process, new species will surely be discovered, like Rugel's ragwort and the red-cheeked salamander, which exist nowhere else.

This biological diversity has an ancient origin. During the last ice age, northern species of plants gradually seeded southward, moving ahead of advancing glaciers, eventually invading as far south as the Smokies. When the ice age ended, the glaciers retreated and the northern plant species followed, reseeding themselves northward. But all the northern plants did not leave the Smokies region. As the temperatures rose to their original levels, these northern species also seeded up the slopes to the higher, and thus cooler, elevations. As they vacated the lower levels, the southern plant species returned to take their place. As a result, the Great Smoky Mountains have both northern and southern plant species, and a hike from the lowlands to the Smokies crest is often described as a hike from Georgia to Canada because you pass the same plant species along the way.

Today, this great forest can be viewed as five communities of tree associations, mostly due to differences in elevation, from 840 feet at the lowest point at the mouth of Abrams Creek to 6,643 feet at Clingmans Dome. With elevation change comes climate differences—60 inches of rain per year in the valleys compared to 88 inches per year on the mountain peaks, and a decrease of 3.6 degrees Fahrenheit for each 1,000 feet in elevation gain.

The **Cove Hardwood Forests** occupy the valleys between the mountain ridges. The trees include basswood, magnolia, white ash, sugar maple, American beech, and silverbell; also present may be buckeye, holly, yellow birch, hemlock, oaks, hickories, red maple, and yellow poplar or tuliptree. This forest produces the spectacular fall color for which the Great Smoky Mountains are famous.

Along stream banks and on moist, shady slopes stand the **Hemlock Forests**—cool, dark evergreen forests with a shrub layer of rhododendron and doghobble. The hemlocks are occasionally interspersed with red maples, birches, holly, sugar maples, and silverbell.

The **Pine-Oak Forests** with mountain laurel shrubs grow on exposed ridges, which are typically dry. Huckleberry and blueberry grow below the laurel.

Protected slopes at the higher elevations are occupied by **Northern Hardwood Forests,** dominated by beech and yellow birch, which contribute color during the fall season. Basswood, mountain and striped maples, and yellow buckeye also occur with the shrubs hydrangea and viburnum.

At the highest elevations stand the northern **Spruce-Fir Forests,** which consist of red spruce and Fraser fir. Found mainly in the national park, the Fraser fir is an allied species of the balsam fir that grows farther north.

Occasional open areas, called "balds," occur along some ridges. These can be heath balds, which are covered in shrubs, or grassy balds, consisting of a carpet of thick grass, scattered shrubs, and small trees.

The forests of the Smokies are the cause of a blue haze that typically hangs over the mountains and gives them their name. Through transpiration, the trees give off *terpenes*. These hydrocarbon molecules break down in sunlight and recombine to form molecules that are large enough to refract light, and that react with each other and various pollutants to create the smokelike haze.

Ferns and mosses cover the floor of the forest, and flowering plants sprinkle the forest with color in spring. Shrubs create an intermediate level;

White-tailed deer

three of these—rhododendron, mountain laurel, and wild azalea—bloom in late spring and early summer to create a forest wonderland. The ubiquitous rhododendron occurs primarily in two varieties, the rose-purple Catawba and the white Rosebay.

The forest is inhabited by a profusion of wildlife. The chickadee, Carolina wren, wood thrush, yellow-throated vireo, hooded warbler, red-breasted nuthatch, tufted titmouse, and winter wren—and a multitude of other birds—rest in the trees and flit among the bushes. You'll occasionally also see owls and other raptors, woodpeckers, wild turkey, and ruffed grouse.

Streams harbor rainbow and brown trout and the native brook trout. Other fish include sculpins, dace, hogsuckers, chubs, shiners, stonerollers, bass, and darters. These live in association with numerous insects, aquatic beetles, spiders, crayfish, leeches and worms, snails, salamanders, and frogs.

Mammals occupy both the land and the trees—squirrels, chipmunks, rabbits, bobcat, mice, skunks, fox, raccoons, opossums. Numerous white-tailed deer are most easily seen, but the black bear symbolizes the park. The bear population fluctuates around 1,500 individuals that can occasionally be seen by visitors hiking trails or driving one of the park roads.

The park is also inhabited by the wild boar, or hog, an exotic that invaded the park after escaping from a hunting preserve in North Carolina. The boars are prolific but have been reduced in recent years; the park staff would like to eradicate the animal because of the damage it does while rooting for food.

Several animal species that once lived in the park region are no longer here. Bison, elk, and wolves are all gone. The cougar may be extinct in the Smokies, but there have been sightings, which convinces some that cougars still live in the park.

A reintroduction program is underway to return several species to the Great Smokies. River otters, peregrine falcons, Smoky madtoms, yellowfin madtoms, and spotfin chubs have been brought back. Elk have been proposed for reintroduction. Red wolves began to be reintroduced the summer of 1991, but the effort was unsuccessful because of high mortality among the young, and the adult wolves apparently had difficulty establishing home ranges in the mountains. The decision was made to abandon the program in 1998; the remaining wolves were captured and transferred to other reintroduction sites.

The Smokies are one of the last wild areas in the country that is large enough and diverse enough to support such reintroduction programs. At the time the park was established, a fifth of the forest remained, nearly 120,000 acres, one of the largest stands of old-growth woods in the eastern United States. These trees are hundreds of years old; researchers have found a 327-year-old pignut hickory, a 390-year-old tuliptree, a 380-year-old red spruce, a 390-year-old chestnut oak, a 344-year-old white oak, a 451-year-old eastern hemlock, and the oldest, a 564-year-old black gum. National champions in size that stand in the park include yellow buckeye, striped maple, black cherry, chestnut oak, red hickory, Fraser magnolia, Carolina silverbell, devil's walking stick, red maple, northern red oak, eastern hemlock, Allegheny serviceberry, sourwood, bitternut hickory, and red spruce. The largest known tree in the park is a yellow poplar (tuliptree) that is 7 feet, 8 inches in diameter, and the tallest is a 187-foot white pine. While these trees are relatively old, they are not necessarily the oldest; growing conditions in a specific locale cause many trees more than 300 years old to be not so large. In the intervening years, areas that had been severely damaged by farming and logging operations have now recovered with second-growth timber.

Although the Smokies are protected from development and abuse with designation as a national park, these forests of the Smokies are threatened. The demise of the chestnut tree is perhaps a harbinger.

The chestnut was once the primary tree of the Great Smoky Mountains. It comprised 20 percent to 30 percent of the trees in the park. A parasitic fungus that attacked the chestnut was unintentionally introduced into this country around 1904 and spread throughout the eastern forests. In the 1920s and 1930s, the blight killed the chestnut trees in the park. All that remain are the rotting trunks of fallen trees and occasional saplings sprouting from roots that are still alive; these saplings eventually also die from the blight infestation.

Also at the turn of the century, the balsam woolly adelgid, an aphid that attacks fir trees, was unintentionally introduced into this country. The adelgid feeds through cracks in the bark of the mature trees, injecting saliva that damages the plant cells, eventually killing the trees. The young trees, which have relatively smooth bark, survive until their bark develops cracks; they too are then attacked by the insect. In the Smokies, the adelgid has killed nearly all of the adult Fraser firs. As the trees die, other plant species also go; eight species of mosses and liverworts that live in association with the firs are also declining.

The adelgid is thought to have been introduced from Europe on nursery stock in 1908. The insects spread south after their arrival, infecting other fir and balsam trees, but wreaking havoc in the South where relatively mild winters allow many adelgid larvae to survive. The adelgid arrived in the Great Smoky Mountains in 1963 and began attacking the park's mature Fraser fir. The Park Service has tried to save some trees by spraying a soap solution that removes the larvae's woolly covering and exposes them to the elements. But this can save only a few trees. Research continues on how to control the insect, and seeds have been collected and preserved so the genetic strain will not be lost. Also, seedlings are grown for planting out of the adelgid's range and at a location in the park where the trees can be treated.

Other exotic pests threaten park trees. The dogwood anthracnose, a fungus that is capable of killing the dogwood tree, has now infected 60 percent of the park's flowering dogwoods. The gypsy moth, not yet in the park, has destroyed oak forests to the north and is rapidly moving south; one day it will invade the park. The hemlock adelgid is also on its way and has already devastated the hemlocks of Shenandoah National Park to the north. The beech scale insect, which can destroy mature beech trees, arrived in 1993. The European mountain-ash sawfly is already at work on the mountain ash that grow on the crest of the Smokies.

In addition, air pollution is causing damage to the park's vegetation. So far, thirty plant species show signs of damage from ozone, caused by the reaction of sunlight with pollution in the air. Acid rain, the result of sulfur and nitrogen oxides released from burning fuels, is suspected of causing damage to the red spruce of the higher elevations, in addition to reducing visibility by 60 percent and acidifying the mountain streams; rainfall in the Smokies is five to ten times more acidic than normal rain.

The park staff, especially through its Twin Creeks Natural Resources Center, is working to lessen the effects of these threats to the forests of the Great Smokies. And at least to the extent that they will save a few of each species, they will succeed. But ultimately, while the park staff tries to limit and eradicate exotic pests and works to prevent environmental pollution, we look to nature to adapt. Although the park lost all its chestnut trees seventy years ago, the forest returned with an increase in other species. The biological diversity ensures that as one species disappears, another will take its place, and thus the forest of the Smokies will never disappear. The forest that our descendants will see may be different from the forest we know today, but in the Great Smoky Mountains there will always be a forest, for nature will prevail in this last large preserved remnant of the great Southern Appalachian forest.

WILDERNESS PRESERVATION IN THE PARK

The approximately 20 percent of the primeval forest that remained when the Great Smoky Mountains National Park was formed now makes up the old-growth stands in the Smokies. In the years since the park was created, the remainder of the forest has regenerated in the logged areas so that now a half million acres of forest clothe the mountains. Except for some park staff and a caretaker or two, no one lives in the Great Smoky Mountains any longer, other than in the surrounding valleys and on the opposing hillsides beyond the park boundaries. Yet this is a place many people visit and then return to time and again, drawn back by some sense of belonging. Millions come each year to find their stamina challenged, their minds cleared, and their spirits replenished in an act many characterize as "coming home." This home place for so many must be protected and preserved for future generations.

In 1965, the director of the National Park Service recommended a second transmountain road through the Great Smoky Mountains National Park. Conservationists worked to defeat the proposal and to discourage proposals for other roads that would destroy the integrity of the park. Although there are no current road proposals and the present park administration is dedicated to preserving parklands, there is no guarantee that a new road through the park will not be proposed again someday.

To permanently protect the Great Smoky Mountains, conservationists for more than thirty years have called for wilderness designation under the National Wilderness Preservation System. Approximately 478,000 acres of the park qualify for wilderness protection. These are the lands of deep forest and high mountain, crossed only by the trails described in this book. All parklands with current development are excluded from the wilderness proposal, so the wilderness designation of these acres would not change existing use by visitors; it would only prevent damage to the park by further development. The park administration currently manages this area as if it had this wilderness designation.

Although legislation has twice been introduced to the U.S. Congress to designate most of the national park as wilderness, the effort has stalled over a 1943 agreement in which the Park Service accepted a 44,000-acre addition to the park in trade for the promise to build a road within the park along the north shore of Fontana Lake. An additional 1,920-acre inholding within this area was purchased from Cities Services Oil Company in 1983. The Northshore Road was never built, and now most people are opposed to building this road. A payment to Swain County, North Carolina, the principal body involved, has been proposed in lieu of a road, but there are some who still want the road built. In addition, there are those who simply oppose wilderness status for the parklands, especially the Fontana Lake north shore area.

Conservationists persist in the work for official wilderness designation to protect for all time this last great mountain wilderness in the eastern United States. If you want to add your voice to the call for wilderness, contact the Conservation Committee of the Smoky Mountains Hiking Club (see Appendix, Addresses and Phone Numbers, at the back of this book).

GETTING THERE

The Smokies are surrounded by Knoxville to the northwest and Chattanooga to the southwest, in Tennessee, and by Atlanta, Georgia, to the south, Greenville, South Carolina, to the southeast, and Asheville, North Carolina, to the east. Knoxville and Asheville are the closest, so if you are flying in from another part of the country, you will probably arrive at one of these two cities.

From Knoxville, the drive to the park is about 30 miles. Take I-40 east, get off at the Hwy. 66 exit (you'll see signs for the park), and head south through Sevierville where you'll pick up US 441, which leads through Pigeon Forge and along a spur of the Foothills Parkway to Gatlinburg. To reach the Sugarlands Visitor Center, continue straight through Gatlinburg to enter the park. A bypass takes you around Gatlinburg, but it can be closed in winter. Just before the bypass, you'll find a Gatlinburg Welcome Center, where you can get preliminary information and where you may, if you choose, leave your car and take a trolley in to the Sugarlands Visitor Center and, during the summer and fall, on to Fighting Creek Gap and Elkmont.

The drive from Asheville is about 60 miles; take I-40 west and get off at the US 23 exit headed southwest. In 4 miles bear left on US 23/74, the "Great Smoky Mountains Expressway." The highway eventually joins US 441 headed north. Stay on US 441 when it leaves the expressway and pass through Cherokee into the park, where you'll find the Oconaluftee Visitor Center. You can also get to the North Carolina side of the park along the Blue Ridge Parkway, a 469-mile national scenic highway that connects the Smokies with Shenandoah National Park in Virginia. Sections of the parkway are often closed in winter because of snow and ice.

The two main visitor centers, Sugarlands and Oconaluftee, are connected by 29 miles of US 441, which bisects the park. Locally, it is called the "Newfound Gap Road" because it crosses the crest of the Smokies at Newfound Gap. At times during the winter, this road is closed due to snow. On the way from Oconaluftee Visitor Center north to Newfound Gap, you'll pass the Smokemont Campground. In Newfound Gap, you can take the Clingmans Dome Road west to the Forney Ridge Parking Area and the paved trail to the top of Clingmans Dome, the highest peak in the park. This road is closed in winter, usually beginning in mid-November after the first snow falls and ice forms. At the height of the visitor seasons in the spring and fall, and even in summer, the Newfound Gap and Clingmans

Dome Roads can be clogged with traffic. In this case, you may want to visit the park at one of the other access points described later in this book.

Other routes around the park provide access to various campgrounds and trailheads. You will probably want to use one of these routes if you do not need to go by a visitor center at one of the two main entrances.

From US 321 at Townsend you can enter the park on Hwy. 73 to the Townsend Wye. There you can turn right on Laurel Creek Road to reach the Tremont area and the Cades Cove Campground; the Cades Cove Visitor Center lies halfway along the 11-mile one-way Cades Cove Loop Road. At the Wye, you can also turn left on Little River Road to reach Metcalf Bottoms Picnic Area, Elkmont Campground, and Fighting Creek Gap before reaching the Sugarlands Visitor Center at Newfound Gap Road.

In Gatlinburg, you can take Cherokee Orchard Road to the Roaring Fork Motor Nature Trail for trailhead access to Mount LeConte. US 321 east from Gatlinburg takes you to a turnoff into the Greenbrier Cove area and, farther east, to the town of Cosby and a turn southeast on Hwy. 32 to Cosby Campground.

On the east side of the park, from I-40 you can take the Maggie Valley/ Waynesville (US 276) exit to Cove Creek Road, which leads into Cataloochee Valley to the Cataloochee Campground. Farther north, take the Waterville exit to reach the Big Creek Campground.

Just south of the Oconaluftee Visitor Center on Newfound Gap Road, turn northeast on the Blue Ridge Parkway to reach the Heintooga Ridge Road that leads north to Balsam Mountain Campground.

From the town of Cherokee on the southern boundary of the park, turn west on US 19 to Bryson City, where you can reenter the park to reach the Deep Creek Campground. North of Bryson City, Lakeview Drive leads to remote trailheads.

Fontana Village lies on Hwy. 28 on the southwest edge of the park; trailheads are found at Fontana Dam and Twentymile Ranger Station. Abrams Creek Campground lies off Hwy. 129 on the western side of the park near the Foothills Parkway.

The Foothills Parkway, a proposed 72-mile road along the northern park boundary, is also under the jurisdiction of the Great Smoky Mountains National Park. There are currently two completed sections, in addition to the spur that connects Pigeon Forge and Gatlinburg. A section to the northwest runs from US 129 at Chilhowee Lake on the Little Tennessee River along the crest of Chilhowee Mountain to US 321 near Walland. Along this stretch you'll find the Look Rock observation tower and a picnic area and campground; from the tower, you'll have long views southeast into the park. At US 321, the Foothills Parkway continues east for a few miles, but this section is still under construction and so is closed to traffic. The other completed section is on the other side of the park and runs from US 321 near Cosby to I-40. This 6-mile section of the Foothills Parkway, closed in winter, has high mountain vistas and offers grand views of the Cosby area in the park and English Mountain to the northwest outside the park. Construction has been proposed to link these two sections of the Foothills Parkway. The right-of-way for the road constitutes around 9,000 acres of the park's 521,000 acres.

VISITING THE GREAT SMOKY MOUNTAINS NATIONAL PARK

Around 850 miles of trails wander through the Great Smoky Mountains National Park. In addition, quiet walkways scattered along the main roads are short hikes into the forest where you can walk as far as you'd like and then turn around. Of the 172 designated trails in the park, some are both horseback-riding and hiking trails, but many are just for walking. From this large number of trails, this book offers the best 100 hikes; some of these are routes that include more than one trail.

The best times to visit the Great Smoky Mountains are spring and fall, when the temperatures are mild and special attractions include either abundant wildflowers or a forest of red and yellow and every shade between. Yet in winter, you can experience the snow-covered mountains, and even at the height of summer, you can find cool coves in the depths of the forest and lower temperatures on the mountain crest.

You might want to time your visit to coincide with festivals held in the park. The last weekend in April is the Great Smoky Mountains Spring Wildflower Pilgrimage, in which you can join guided walks for flower identification and other natural-history topics. Cades Cove has gatherings at the Cable Mill area—Old-Timers Day, storytelling, quilt shows. Fontana Village sponsors both a spring wildflower hiking week and a fall-color hiking week. A Mountain Life Festival is held at Oconaluftee Visitor Center in the fall. For more information, see Appendix, Addresses and Phone Numbers, at the back of this book.

Preparations

Even if you are out for only a short time, wear walking shoes or hiking boots. Carry drinking water, a lunch or snacks, a hat, toilet paper, and rain gear. Also take along a first-aid kit, sunglasses, and a map and compass, and just in case you get lost or injured, bring along a whistle, extra clothes, a knife, a flashlight, a lighter or waterproof matches plus firestarter, and a plastic sheet or emergency blanket. Many of these items are among the recommended Ten Essentials that should be taken on every outing in the wilderness.

If you are camping in the backcountry, you'll need everything for surviving overnight in the open for however many days you choose to be out. Basics include a good backpack, a sleeping pad and bag, a waterproof tent, and a backpacking stove and fuel. If you are inexperienced in backpacking, the park rangers or your local outfitters can give advice on the equipment needed.

The maps this book provides for each region's hikes can be supplemented with topographical maps for the area. These are available from your local map supplier and at the park visitor centers. At the minimum, obtain the inexpensive "Great Smoky Mountains Trail Map," available at park visitor centers; the map gives you an overall view of the trails and their connections. The park rangers will be glad to give you additional information about a trail's current conditions.

Precautions

At virtually every trail junction, you'll find wooden signs inscribed with trail information. Study a trail map (see Preparations, earlier) and read the information at each junction, and you should be able to find your way around. Still, pay attention to where you are going so you can at least retrace your steps to get back out if you lose your way. You have full responsibility for knowing where you are going and not getting lost. Be aware that, with the exception of the Appalachian Trail, the trails in the Smokies are not blazed, although it's usually easy to see where the paths go. Always let someone know where you are going. And if you get lost, do not leave the trail; search parties will always look for you first on the trail.

You'll occasionally see horses on trails designated as both hiking and equestrian trails; hikers should step to the side and let horseback riders pass.

Pets, bicycles, motorized vehicles, and guns are not allowed anywhere in the park.

Do not pick wildflowers, and leave historic and archaeological sites undisturbed.

Boil all water in the backcountry at least one minute to destroy bacteria and other microorganisms, including *Giardia lamblia*, a flagellate protozoan causing an intestinal disorder called giardiasis. Filters and water purifying tablets can be used, but ask for ones that remove or kill *Giardia*.

Many trees in the park have died in the past few years from insect infestation, disease, and air pollution; watch for falling trees and limbs, and do not set up camp under a dead tree.

If you stay to the trails, you'll probably not come into contact with poison ivy. If you venture off-trail or reach an overgrown section of trail, avoid the three-leaf clusters. You might also encounter stinging nettle, a 1- to 2-foot-high plant with stinging hairs; if you brush against it, you'll feel the stinging for several minutes, but with no lasting effects.

Be especially careful climbing on rocks, walking along the edge of bluffs, and crossing streams. Even when you are crossing a footbridge over a creek, use caution. Some of the bridges are long and narrow and can be wet, slippery, and, in winter, covered with ice. Always test a handrail before leaning against it; some may need repair and may not hold your weight. Don't even think of climbing on waterfalls.

Stream crossings can be easy or difficult. After a heavy rain, a stream can be swollen with rushing water. Do not attempt to cross such a stream unless you are sure you can make it; hikers have died trying. When the water level is down, you'll find that you can rockhop most streams, but this can also be hazardous if the rocks are wet; use caution and be prepared if your feet slip. If you decide to wade across, wear your shoes to protect your feet; some hikers carry along old tennis shoes or sandals to slip into for stream crossings. Find a branch to use for balance if you're not carrying a walking stick. If you are strapped into a pack, release the hip belt so you can easily slip out of the pack if you fall in the water. If you take a dunking and the water carries you away, float on your back with your feet pointed downstream so you can ward off rocks until you have a chance to stop yourself and get out.

Weather in the mountains is unpredictable, so dress appropriately, preferably in layers that you can adjust as you warm up or cool down. It rains frequently, and so you should always have rain gear. It can also be quite cold; you may find snow on the ground and/or freezing conditions in the higher elevations when the temperatures are relatively mild in the lowlands. In cold and wet weather, you face the danger of hypothermia, the lowering of core temperature beyond the point at which the body can maintain its own heat. The symptoms are uncontrolled shivering, slurred speech, memory lapse, stumbling, fumbling hands, and drowsiness. Hypothermia can occur in any season and can result in death. If you are wet and cold, get under some shelter, change into dry clothes, and drink warm fluids. Get in a sleeping bag, if available. To prevent hypothermia, stay dry, eat even if you are not hungry, and drink water even when you are not thirsty.

You must take responsibility for your own safety, keeping in mind that hiking in a wilderness setting far from medical attention is an inherently hazardous activity. It is best to travel with someone; if one of you is hurt, the other can care for the injured and go for help.

Don't let all these warnings discourage you from taking these hikes. Many people have walked these mountains before you, and only a relative few have suffered injuries. Just be prepared and use common sense.

Animals and Insects

Black bears inhabit the Great Smoky Mountains National Park. These animals are not extremely dangerous; even so, take precautions to not attract or irritate the bears.

A mother bear is very protective of her cubs. If you encounter a mother with cubs, or a cub alone whose mother is surely nearby, back off. Do not advance on the bears and do not place yourself between the mother and her cubs. If you see a bear cub climbing a tree, the mother has probably scooted it up the tree thinking you are a danger; move on.

If you face a bear, observe from a distance; do not turn and run, which might cause the bear to run after you. But back off slowly, if you must, to avoid an encounter.

Under no circumstances should you feed a bear or leave food for a bear, which could become conditioned to humans and pose a threat to hikers that come after you.

In the backcountry overnight, all food and trash must be hung to keep it away from bears. Recommended minimums are to hang the food so that it's 4 feet from the nearest tree trunk and 10 feet off the ground. Almost all backcountry campsites now have cables with rigging stretched between trees that makes this an easy task. Also to avoid encounters, keep cooking and sleeping areas separate, except at shelters. Keep your tent and sleeping bags free of food odors by not putting food in them. If your pack is free of food odors, you may hang only your food and trash bags and keep your pack inside the tent with you; also keep your boots in the tent when you retire.

The wild boar is a nonnative species in the park. The park has an active eradication program that includes capture and shooting; maybe 600 remain in the park. Because they are nocturnal, these wild hogs are seldom seen by hikers. If you do encounter a herd of boar, simply stand still. The boars will probably be more afraid of you than you are of them. In their frenzy to run away, they will scatter in all directions; if you also try to run away, the two of you might collide.

The northern copperhead and the timber rattlesnake live here. Always watch where you put your feet and hands, and give snakes a wide berth.

On warm spring and summer days, gnats, black flies, and mosquitoes might be a bother, so carry along insect repellent. Before starting off on a hike, apply repellent to your shoetops, socks, and pants to discourage ticks; the deer tick can transmit a spirochete that causes Lyme disease. Remember to check yourself after a hike.

Camping

There are several established fee campgrounds in the park that are accessible by automobile. Reservations are recommended from spring through fall for the Cades Cove, Elkmont, and Smokemont Campgrounds (call 800-365-CAMP or, on the Internet, access http://reservations.nps .gov). You can just show up and be given an open site, but it's not likely there will be one. All other campgrounds (Cosby, Abrams Creek, Big Creek, Cataloochee, Balsam Mountain, Deep Creek, and Look Rock) are first come, first served. The Cades Cove and Smokemont Campgrounds are open all year; during the winter and early spring, they are also first come, first served. All other campgrounds are closed in winter.

In addition, LeConte Lodge provides meals and lodging in the backcountry at the top of Mount LeConte. The only access to the lodge is a hike of several miles. You must have a reservation.

You may camp for free in the backcountry at eighty-seven designated campsites (each has a number, shown inside a triangle on maps in this book) and at sixteen established shelters; camping in the backcountry is not allowed anywhere else. You must register for a campsite prior to beginning your hike. You are subject to a fine if caught camping without a registration or if you are found in an undesignated site. For most campsites, you may self-register at any of the ranger stations, visitor centers, and campgrounds around the park and also at Fontana Dam and the Great Smoky Mountains Institute at Tremont. You may also register in person with a ranger. Some of the campsites (Nos. 10, 13, 23, 24, 29, 36, 37, 38, 47, 50, 55, 57, 61, 71, and 83) and all shelters are rationed, so you must contact the Backcountry Reservation Office (423-436-1231; www.nps.gov/grsm) to reserve a place at one of these areas. You may call up to a month in advance.

When you are staying at a shelter, you must use the shelter so you will be protected from bears by the fencing. You are subject to a fine if found in a tent beside a shelter, except for Appalachian Trail "thru-hikers" who arrive at a shelter where all bunks are taken.

You may use down and dead timber for campfires. Keep any fires small; build only in existing fire rings at campsites and only where fires are legally permitted. Consider using a camping stove even where wood fires are permitted.

For water, you'll find a spring or creek near most campsites, but at least within half a mile. Some high mountain springs, though, can be dry during summer droughts, so be prepared by carrying some water with you. Boil or treat all drinking water.

Bury your waste at least 6 inches deep and well away from trails and campsites; bury waste at least 200 feet from all water sources. Do not bury sanitary napkins, tampons, or toilet paper; instead add them to your trash and carry them out. Do not wash dishes or bathe in a stream; take water from the stream to do your washing and let the waste water drain onto the ground at least 200 feet from all water sources. Pack out all trash and litter.

Appalachian Trail

The Appalachian Trail covers 2,100 miles from Mount Katahdin, Maine, to Springer Mountain, Georgia. The "AT," as it is commonly referred to, is the longest completed trail in the country and one of the longest in the world.

For 71 of those many miles, the AT passes through the Great Smoky Mountains National Park, for the most part following the crest of the Smokies, which is also the dividing line between the states of Tennessee and North Carolina. The trail enters the park at Davenport Gap at the northeast end of the park and travels the mountain ridge until Doe Knob, where it turns down the mountain to exit at Fontana Dam on the southwest. Because the AT follows the Smokies crest, it offers some of the best views in the park.

The hikes in this book take you to some of the more interesting spots on the AT, such as Mount Cammerer, Charlies Bunion, Silers Bald, Thunderhead Mountain, and the Shuckstack. Along these sections of the AT, you'll often see "thru-hikers," those headed north to Maine in the spring or south to Georgia in the fall, or as far as they can walk.

If you intend to hike the entire AT through the park, you'll need the *Appalachian Trail Guide to Tennessee–North Carolina*, available from the Appalachian Trail Conference (see Appendix, Addresses and Phone Numbers) and the park visitor centers.

Adopt-a-Trail Program

If you live in the area of the Great Smokies or visit frequently and would like to participate in maintaining the park's many trails, you may want to join the Adopt-a-Trail Program. In this volunteer program, participants hike a specific trail several times a year to perform routine minor trail maintenance and to report to the park staff on trail conditions, hazards, signs, and any emergency actions needed.

If you are at least eighteen years old and in good physical condition, and would like to adopt a trail, contact the park headquarters at the address and phone number listed in Appendix, Addresses and Phone Numbers, at the back of this book.

Bicycling

Bicycles are not allowed on trails in the park, with the exceptions of the Gatlinburg Trail, the Oconaluftee River Trail, and parts of the Indian Creek and Deep Creek Trails that are old roads. You may ride bicycles anywhere motorized vehicles are allowed, although many park roads are unsuitable for bicycling because of the traffic and the lack of a shoulder to ride on.

Some back roads that see less traffic are the roads in Greenbrier off US 321, the one-way Balsam Mountain Road, the roads into Cataloochee Valley, the road into Elkmont off Little River Road, and the road into Tremont just west of the Townsend Wye. Most of these are all or partially gravel, and so you should use a mountain bike or an all-terrain hybrid. Always wear a helmet.

A special treat is to bike the 11-mile Cades Cove Loop Road, but the volume of traffic can often be intimidating. Fortunately, the park staff has set aside Wednesday and Saturday mornings until 10:00 A.M. (May to September) for bikers; the road is closed to motorized vehicles until that time.

HOW TO USE THIS BOOK

In this book, the hikes are divided into Tennessee and North Carolina Districts. Within each district, the hikes are grouped by access point. When you arrive at a trailhead, you'll find the hikes from that area grouped together in this book.

The maps that accompany each access point are designed to help you find the trailheads and to see the general route of the hikes and the trail connections. The hike numbers in the text correspond to the hike numbers on the maps.

Each hike begins with a summary that lists the overall **distance,** indicating "one-way" whenever the hike is not a loop, and sometimes also lists the intermediate distance to attractions along the way.

There is also a **difficulty** rating of easy, moderate, or strenuous. This rating is a subjective judgment. *Easy* hikes are usually shorter with little elevation gain. *Moderate* hikes are longer and have some elevation gain and more challenging terrain. *Strenuous* hikes are usually long, with plenty of elevation gain and difficult terrain.

The **elevation gain** or **loss** indicates a difference in elevation between a one-way hike's highest and lowest points, but note there could be several ups and downs along the way. **Elevation change** is given for a loop hike or when the hike is one way but the highest or lowest point is along the hike, rather than at the beginning or end.

You'll also find **cautions** about what you might encounter on the hike, such as creek crossings, rocky footing, steep climbs, and steep descents. Take these into account. The numbered campsites that occur along a given hike are listed both in the hike description and on the map in case you plan on camping in the backcountry.

Trail **connections** are included so you may combine hikes for longer outings.

After the summary, an **attractions** paragraph highlights the hike's best aspects, followed by directions to the **trailhead.** Then the hike **description** details what you'll encounter on the hike. The mileages given are almost always cumulative. If you intend to hike the route in the reverse direction, it will probably be useful to calculate the reverse mileages.

The sections at the back of the book include selected references for further reading/information, a list of useful addresses and phone numbers, and a general index.

A Note About Safety

Safety is an important concern in all outdoor activities. No guidebook can alert you to every hazard or anticipate the limitations of every reader. Therefore, the descriptions of roads, trails, routes, and natural features in this book are not representations that a particular place or excursion will be safe for your party. When you follow any of the routes described in this book, you assume responsibility for your own safety. Under normal conditions, such excursions require the usual attention to traffic, road and trail conditions, weather, terrain, the capabilities of your party, and other factors. Keeping informed on current conditions and exercising common sense are the keys to a safe, enjoyable outing.

The Mountaineers

Ramsay Cascades

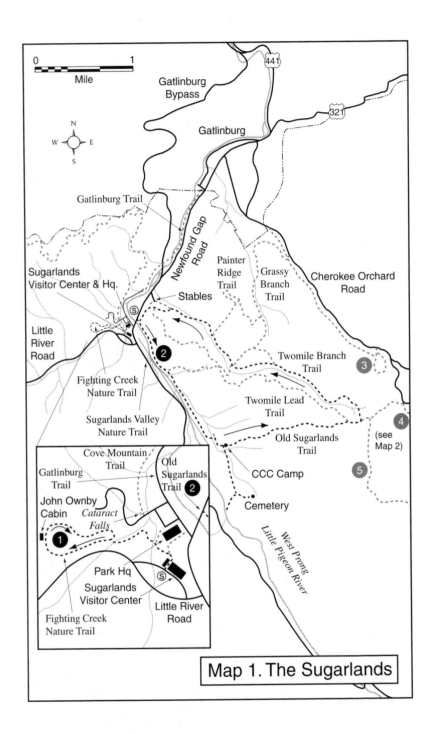

Map 1. The Sugarlands

THE SUGARLANDS

The Sugarlands was named for the numerous sugar maple trees that once grew in the valley. The settlers tapped the trees for the sweet sap they turned into maple syrup. Though many of the trees were cut during the years of lumbering, maple is still a common tree in the park. The nearby visitor center took the name "Sugarlands."

Getting there: The Sugarlands Visitor Center on the Tennessee side of the park is the first stopping place for most visitors. (If you enter the park on the North Carolina side, you can get information at the Oconaluftee Visitor Center, and head across the park on Newfound Gap Road to Sugarlands Visitor Center.) From US 441 (Newfound Gap Road) in Tennessee near Gatlinburg, drive into the park. Cross a bridge over the West Prong of the Little Pigeon River and pass a right turn to the park headquarters. Then turn right at the junction with Little River Road and immediately turn right into the parking area for the visitor center.

Cataract Falls

Side trips: In addition to the trails described in this chapter, there are a few short side trips available in the vicinity of The Sugarlands. The parking area beside the park headquarters building is also the beginning of the *Gatlinburg Trail*, which continues down the road and then veers off on a trail to end up in Gatlinburg in 2.0 miles, passing a scenic cascade at 0.7 mile, where a branch of the West Prong rejoins the creek. Also, just down the road from this parking area, past a cemetery on a knoll, turn onto the second road on the left, which takes you across a bridge over Fighting Creek to reach the *Cove Mountain Trail* on the right; walk this trail for 0.1 mile to Cataract Falls, where Cataract Branch drops 40 feet over a rock ledge on its way to Fighting Creek. The universally accessible *Sugarlands Valley Nature Trail* begins 0.4 mile up Newfound Gap Road from the visitor center. This 0.5-mile trail loops by the ruins of some early twentieth-century resort cabins and along the West Prong of the Little Pigeon River.

1 | FIGHTING CREEK NATURE TRAIL

Distance: 1.0-mile loop; to John Ownby Cabin, 0.5 mile one way
Difficulty: Easy
Elevation change: 100 feet
Season: Year-round
Cautions: Some uphill, footbridges
Connections: None

Attractions: Many of these lowland valleys of the Smokies were settled in the 1800s by hardy immigrants to the mountains: Scotch-Irish, English, Germans. They knew, or learned, how to live off the land. They cleared the trees, built cabins, raised crops, gathered nuts and berries, hunted the surrounding forests. Their descendants were here when the national park was established. After these people gave up their land for the park, the forest began the work of reclamation. Roads became mere depressions in the ground. Fields grew up in trees. Houses tumbled down and decayed, or were dismantled. Rock fences and foundations became lost in weeds and bushes. On this short nature hike, settled land reclaimed by forest and a restored log cabin introduce you to the Great Smoky Mountains National Park.

Trailhead: From the Sugarlands Visitor Center parking area, walk down the sidewalk between the visitor center and the rest rooms on the left to the beginning of the nature trail.

Description: The trail leads down into a lowland woods. Soon a side path to the right leads to the park headquarters; stay left on the main trail,

John Ownby Cabin

which crosses a bridge over Ash Hopper Branch, a tributary of Fighting Creek. Bear left along Fighting Creek, a tributary of the West Prong of the Little Pigeon River. A depression between the trail and the creek is an old roadbed that led to the farms along this valley that made up the Forks of the River Community. The name of Fighting Creek originated with an argument between two landowners who both wanted to donate land for a new schoolhouse; later when court was held in the school, cases were sometimes settled outside, further justifying the name.

At 0.2 mile, at an ancient sycamore tree, the trail turns to cross a long bridge over Fighting Creek, leading to a junction of the loop, with the trail going both left and right; turn left. At 0.3 mile, a pile of stones marks a house site on the right with nonnative yuccas, boxwoods, and daffodils. Noah McCarter's clapboard-sided house stood here in the 1920s. The open area to the right was likely a garden or field. A spring flows down from the slope behind the site.

The trail then tops a rise where you'll see the remains of a stone fence on the left. Descending, the path crosses a footbridge over a small creek. Then at 0.5 mile, cross another footbridge over a stream and walk up to the John Ownby Cabin. This single-room log cabin was restored by the Park Service in the 1960s. Enter the back door and walk through the house, and out the front door onto the porch; then follow the path in front up to the spring. There would have been a small structure over the spring, called a "springhouse," to keep debris out of the water and for storing food in the cool confines of the spring enclosure.

The trail turns uphill to the right behind the house (the side you first approached) to cross the slope above the Noah McCarter house site and then settle into the lowlands again, swinging to the right and closing the loop at 0.8 mile at the bridge over Fighting Creek. Across the bridge, turn left and return to the visitor center.

2 OLD SUGARLANDS AND TWOMILE BRANCH TRAILS

Distance: 6.4-mile loop; to Cherokee Orchard Road, 4.0 miles one way
Difficulty: Moderate
Elevation change: 1,080 feet; to Cherokee Orchard Road, 1,100 feet
Season: Year-round
Cautions: Short section of highway walking, long ascent, mud holes and rocky in places, may encounter horseback riders
Connections: Grassy Branch Trail, Twomile Lead Trail, Bull Head Trail, Rainbow Falls Trail, Trillium Gap Trail, Painters Ridge Trail

Attractions: This loop follows the old Sugarlands Road into The Sugarlands valley and visits the site of one of several CCC camps that were established throughout the mountains in the early 1930s. The trail then ascends to Cherokee Orchard and returns along a cascading stream.

Trailhead: From the Sugarlands Visitor Center parking area, walk down the sidewalk past the Fighting Creek Nature Trail to pass in front of the park headquarters building and emerge onto a side road. (You can also drive to this side road and park beside the headquarters; from Gatlinburg, the road is on the right before the turn to the visitor center.) From this side road, walk out to the highway and turn left, back toward Gatlinburg. Cross the bridge over the West Prong of the Little Pigeon River and in 0.1 mile reach the trailhead for the Old Sugarlands Trail on the right. Take care crossing the highway.

Description: Head into the woods on an old roadbed. Almost immediately, the Twomile Lead Trail comes in from the left; this is your return route, so here stay to the right. The old roadbed heads upstream along the West Prong. At 0.7 mile, the road turns left, away from the West Prong (it continues up as the Grassy Branch Trail, not to be confused with the Grassy Branch Trail, hike 66, on the North Carolina side of the mountains), and the Old Sugarlands Trail then leaves this roadbed by heading to the right.

Descend into the lowlands along the West Prong and at 0.9 mile ascend onto a raised roadbed beside the river, which is the old Sugarlands Road, one of the early roads that crossed the mountains. Later it became Hwy. 71 but was abandoned when Newfound Gap Road was constructed. At 1.1 miles, the road crosses Bullhead Branch on a concrete bridge. Watch for stone piles and rows of rock that mark settlement areas. The trail swings left, crossing a small tributary of Bullhead Branch, and ascends to

Old Sugarlands Cemetery

a junction with an abandoned road on the left at 1.5 miles; turn right. Soon the trail swings left to pass through an old CCC camp.

In the camp, a side road to the right passes by a small rock-walled building and leads on up the valley of the West Prong into The Sugarlands, where a farming community existed. A short side trip up this road takes you past signs of civilization—rows of rocks to mark roadways and fence lines, rocks piled on boulders from once-cleared fields. At a junction in 0.4 mile, a path to the left leads 0.1 mile up to a large cemetery where McCarters, Huskeys, Reagans, and Ogles are buried. The road to the right is the continuation of the Sugarlands Road, which leads to the edge of the West Prong in 0.2 mile where a bridge once spanned the stream; the rock abutment is all that remains. When you've finished exploring, return to the Old Sugarlands Trail.

Back at the main trail, continue up the graveled road, which once led over the mountain to Cherokee Orchard. Ascend steadily until you reach a junction with the Twomile Lead Trail to the left at 3.3 miles; continue straight. Reach another junction, with the Twomile Branch Trail, at 3.4 miles. (The Old Sugarlands Trail continues straight up the road to Cherokee Orchard Road in 0.6 mile near the Rainbow Falls parking area; see hikes 4 and 5.)

Turn left onto the Twomile Branch Trail, which descends on a wide path that's muddy and rocky in places. At 3.8 miles, the trail crosses the upper reaches of Twomile Branch with small flows of water crossing the trail or flowing under in culverts. At 4.5 miles a connector trail to the right leads up to the Grassy Branch Trail; continue to the left downhill to make a sharp right and reach a junction with the Grassy Branch Trail itself at 4.9 miles. (This trail leads both to the left, to cross Twomile Branch to the Twomile Lead and Old Sugarlands Trails, and to the right, toward Cherokee Orchard Road.)

Continue straight, still descending, to reach a junction with the Painter Ridge Trail to the right at 5.3 miles. The ridge is named for mountain lions, or cougars, that once wandered the Smokies. The locals called the large cat a "panther," which was corrupted to "painter." (On the Painter Ridge Trail, in 0.4 mile, a side loop at the top of the ridge takes you out to a view of Gatlinburg.)

Continue straight on the Twomile Branch Trail, which drops into a cove and makes a hairpin turn across a side stream in a culvert. Ford Twomile Branch at 5.5 miles, and reach a junction at 5.9 miles. (The Twomile Branch Trail leads straight ahead to the McCarter Stables in 0.1 mile.)

Turn left on the Twomile Lead Trail. Ascend above the stables to a fork where the Twomile Lead Trail heads both left, up the mountain to reach the junction with the Old Sugarlands Trail in 2.9 miles, and right; take the right fork. Shortly, a side trail on the right leads 0.1 mile back to the stables; stay to the left to close the loop at the junction with the Old Sugarlands Trail at 6.3 miles. Turn right to walk out to Newfound Gap Road and back to where you parked.

CHEROKEE ORCHARD/ ROARING FORK MOTOR NATURE TRAIL

Pigpen at Ephraim Bales Place

Cherokee Orchard is a tract of land that once included an apple orchard and a nursery. The owners resisted condemnation when the park was established but eventually sold the land in 1931. This area contains the Twin Creeks Natural Resources Center, which conducts studies on the park's ecosystems, and the 5-mile Roaring Fork Motor Nature Trail, a scenic drive that is closed in winter.

Getting there: Take Airport Road southeast out of Gatlinburg at traffic light No. 8. At an intersection, stay straight on Cherokee Orchard Road. Cross the national park boundary, and very soon after you'll see the Twin Creeks Trail (which connects with the Noah "Bud" Ogle Place Nature Trail, hike 3, in 1.8 miles). You'll also pass the Grassy Branch Trail on the right. At 1.1 miles from the park entrance, a road on the right leads to the Twin Creeks Natural Resources Center. Parking for the Noah "Bud" Ogle homesite is reached at 1.7 miles from the park entrance. At a fork soon after passing the Noah "Bud" Ogle Place Nature Trail (hike 3), bear right on a one-way loop through Cherokee Orchard. The Rainbow Falls parking (hikes 4

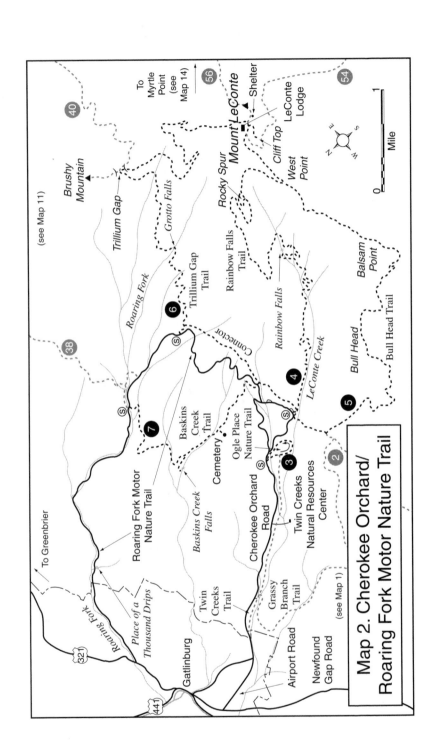

Map 2. Cherokee Orchard/
Roaring Fork Motor Nature Trail

and 5) lies on the right at 2.4 miles from the park boundary. At 2.8 miles, you will reach the Roaring Fork Motor Nature Trail on the right. From this junction, Cherokee Orchard Road goes left back down the mountain to close the loop in another 0.8 mile near the Noah "Bud" Ogle Place.

From Cherokee Orchard Road, the Roaring Fork Motor Nature Trail winds its way 5 miles to US 321 on the east end of Gatlinburg. In 1.7 miles from Cherokee Orchard Road, the Trillium Gap (hike 6) parking is on the left and in 3.1 miles a paved pullout on the left gives access to the Baskins Creek Trail (hike 7). The Grapeyard Ridge Trail (hike 38) joins the road just beyond the nearby bridge over Roaring Fork Creek at the Jim Bales Place. The Roaring Fork Motor Nature Trail continues another 2 miles, passing the Ephraim Bales Cabin and the Alfred Reagan Place and crossing Cliff Branch, where water spills down a rock face on the left called "Place of a Thousand Drips." The road then emerges in Gatlinburg. Due to frequent snow and ice, the Roaring Fork Motor Nature Trail is closed in winter, but trails along it are open year-round; it is possible to walk in to these trails along connecting trails.

3 | NOAH "BUD" OGLE PLACE NATURE TRAIL

Distance: 0.75-mile loop
Difficulty: Moderate
Elevation change: 160 feet
Season: Year-round
Cautions: Footbridges, rocky in places
Connections: Twin Creeks Trail

Attractions: On this hike, you'll see the home and barn of the Ogle family. When Bud Ogle and his wife, Cindy, came to this 400-acre farm in 1879, they lived in an old single-pen (one-room) cabin that stood nearby. They soon built and moved into a newer cabin, but then it was just the downhill half with a chimney. The birth of children required more room, and so they added the uphill half of the cabin on the other side of the chimney, creating a "saddlebag" cabin; the two halves appear to hang on either side of the chimney like saddlebags lying across a horse's back.

The Ogles were likely descendants of the original settlers of White Oak Flats, the forerunner of Gatlinburg. In town at traffic light No. 5, you'll find the original Ogle Log Cabin, built in 1807 by the five sons of Martha Ogle. The log cabin was moved a short distance to its present location beside the Southern Highland Craft Guild's Arrowcraft Shop. White Oak Flats was

Noah "Bud" Ogle Cabin

later named for Radford Gatlin; as postmaster, he likely named the town for himself.

Also on this hike is a tub mill on LeConte Creek. The mills were used to grind corn into meal. Tub mills were brought to the United States by Swedes when they settled in Delaware. A vertical shaft had millstones on top; on the bottom, paddles formed a waterwheel that was enclosed in a tub, which increased the efficiency by about 10 percent because of the weight of water that was carried around inside the tub before spilling out a hole in the bottom. Hundreds of these mills were scattered throughout the Smokies; there were at least thirteen on LeConte Creek.

Trailhead: From the park entrance, continue on Cherokee Orchard Road to find parking for the Noah "Bud" Ogle homesite at 1.7 miles.

Description: Walk down the old roadbed that leads to the log home of the Bud Ogle family. A barn stands above the house, but it's on the return part of this loop. Turn down to the right on the lower side of the cabin to enter the woods. Rockhop a small stream and cross a footbridge over a larger stream. At 0.2 mile, the Twin Creeks Trail comes in from the right; stay straight. Pass the site of the "weaner" cabin on the left, where each Ogle son lived for a year after they married until they found places of their own. A path to the right leads to the site of a second barn.

At 0.3 mile, the old tub mill sits beside LeConte Creek. The stream was once called "Mill Creek" for all the grist mills that were located along its banks. From the mill, the trail weaves among a rock maze and a tangle of rhododendrons so thick that the farm site was once called "Junglebrook." As the trail signs become faint, bear left along a stream to finally emerge at the barn above the Ogle cabin. The barn is a four-pen construction, a pen at each corner with all four covered by a gable roof. The pens served as stables; hay and other kinds of feed were kept in the loft. The spaces between the pens served as hallways that allowed entrance from all four sides of the barn. Walk on down to the house to close the loop.

RAINBOW FALLS TRAIL

Distance: 6.5 miles one way; to Rainbow Falls, 2.6 miles one way
Difficulty: Strenuous; to falls, moderate
Elevation gain: 4,000 feet; to Rainbow Falls, 1,750 feet
Season: Year-round
Cautions: Continuous ascent, narrow footbridges
Connections: Bull Head Trail, Trillium Gap Trail, Alum Cave Trail, The Boulevard Trail

Attractions: This trail leads past Rainbow Falls, where LeConte Creek spills 80 feet over the descending ledges of a rock bluff and then maneuvers through a boulder field and under the trail's two nearby footbridges. If you catch the afternoon sun just right, a rainbow appears in the mist of the falls. In an especially cold winter, you will find a column of blue-white ice. Hardy hikers can continue to the summit of Mount LeConte and LeConte Lodge. At 6,593 feet the third-highest peak in the national park, Mount LeConte was an attraction in the region even before there was a park. The mountain is named for John Le Conte, who assisted Samuel Buckley, one of the first naturalists to study the mountains, in measuring the elevation of the peak. During the movement to establish the national park, the Great Smoky Mountains Conservation Association enlisted a young Paul Adams, later a well-known naturalist, to establish a camp on the

LeConte Lodge

summit of Mount LeConte in 1925. The camp was at first just a tent and then a cabin that Adams built near the spring that gives rise to Roaring Fork Creek. Adams guided visitors, including members of the federal Park Commission, through the mountains and forests of the Smokies. He chronicled his experiences in a journal, *Mt. LeConte*, published in 1966. The camp was taken over in 1926 by Jack Huff and Will Ramsey. Huff eventually built a lodge with several cabins.

Today, LeConte Lodge is operated as a park concession providing meals and lodging from the end of March through mid-November; reservations must be made months in advance. Camping is also available at Mount LeConte Shelter; reservations required. If you intend to walk to the top and back in a day, start in the morning and allow all day for the hike.

Trailhead: From the park entrance, continue on Cherokee Orchard Road 2.4 miles to parking for the Rainbow Falls Trail on the right.

Description: Walk to the right into the woods to a trail junction. To the right is a connector to the Old Sugarlands Trail (hike 2); take the left-hand trail, the Rainbow Falls Trail. Just after turning up the Rainbow Falls Trail, pass another a connecting trail on the left that leads east to the Trillium Gap Trail (hike 6).

The Rainbow Falls Trail ascends the flank of Mount LeConte while paralleling LeConte Creek. The path soon swings away from the creek, but then loops back to cross the creek on a footbridge at 1.7 miles. Climb through several switchbacks to a second footbridge over the creek just before reaching Rainbow Falls at 2.6 miles. Another footbridge crosses the creek just below the falls, with the waterfall back in a cove. After viewing the falls, continue on up Mount LeConte (or you can retrace your steps for a round trip of 5.2 miles).

The trail continues the climb, recrossing LeConte Creek above the falls. As you gain the higher elevations, the trail switchbacks through a series of sandstone chutes lined with mountain laurel, rhododendron, and sand myrtle, blooming pink, purple, and white in May, June, and July. Ascend onto Rocky Spur, a ridge running down from Mount LeConte. (At 5.4 miles a side trail takes you up onto the myrtle-covered ridge for outstanding valley views to the north and then loops back into the main trail.)

Enter the spruce-fir zone near the top of the mountain where the path becomes rocky. At 6.0 miles the trail reaches a junction with the Bull Head Trail (hike 5) to the right; turn left to climb the remaining 0.5 mile to LeConte Lodge. Pass a junction with the Alum Cave Trail (hike 54) to the right 0.1 mile before the lodge. Past the entrance to the lodge on the left, the Trillium Gap Trail (hike 6) turns down to the left. Straight ahead, The Boulevard Trail (hike 56) passes the Mount LeConte Shelter and rises over High Top, the highest peak on the mountain.

Two points on the Mount LeConte summit offer spectacular views— Cliff Top for sunset and Myrtle Point for sunrise. The trail up to Cliff Top lies on the right just before the entrance to the lodge. Myrtle Point is off The Boulevard Trail on the other side of the mountain.

From the summit of Mount LeConte, you can descend by five different routes: the way you came, for 13 miles round trip; the Alum Cave Trail (hike 54) to Newfound Gap Road; The Boulevard Trail (hike 56) and then along the Appalachian Trail to Newfound Gap; the Trillium Gap Trail (hike 6) to the Roaring Fork Motor Natural Trail; or the Bull Head Trail (hike 5) to Cherokee Orchard. The Bull Head Trail is the only one that descends to a point near the trailhead parking area where you began this hike; it makes for a round trip of 13.3 miles.

5 | BULL HEAD TRAIL

Distance: 6.3 miles one way; to LeConte Lodge, 6.8 miles one way
Difficulty: Strenuous
Elevation gain: 4,000 feet
Season: Year-round
Cautions: Continuous ascent, rough footing
Connections: Old Sugarlands Trail, Rainbow Falls Trail, Alum Cave Trail, Trillium Gap Trail, The Boulevard Trail

Attractions: Bull Head is a heath-covered bald on a spine running northwest from Balsam Point, which lies on a ridge to the west of the Mount LeConte summit. From a distance, Bull Head is thought to resemble a bison's head. As you climb Bull Head toward Mount LeConte, you have increasingly spectacular views. In addition to rooms at LeConte Lodge at the summit, camping is available at Mount LeConte Shelter; reservations required.

Trailhead: Park at the Rainbow Falls trailhead (hike 4).

Directions: From the parking area, head to your right into the woods on the Rainbow Falls Trail. At an intersection of trails, turn to the right down an old asphalted roadway on what is considered part of the Trillium Gap Trail (hike 6) to reach the edge of Cherokee Orchard Road. Here, you'll intersect with the Old Sugarlands Trail (hike 2), where you'll turn left past a gate to walk down an old road.

Pass an abandoned section of trail that was the old route of the Trillium Gap Trail, where some old signs may still stand. Bear left to a split-log footbridge across LeConte Creek. In a forest of mixed hemlock and hardwood, small watercourses lined with rhododendron are the last water until the summit of Mount LeConte. At the top of a rise at 0.4 mile, the Bull Head Trail begins on the left. (The Old Sugarlands Trail continues down the old roadway to emerge on Newfound Gap Road.) Turn left onto the Bull Head Trail and ascend through a canopy of young hemlock. As you climb through a second-growth forest, views appear on your right through the rhododendron and laurel.

The trail passes below Bull Head. At 2.5 miles traverse a boulder bowl with an open-end view of the valley. Then switchback above Bull Head and follow the ridge, ascending toward the summit of Mount LeConte. Watch for a boulder on the left at 3.0 miles that you can stand on to see over the heath into the valley below, with English Mountain to the northeast and Sugarland Mountain to the southwest. The trail climbs through a tunnel of rhododendron and laurel, then passes through a stone gateway into a spruce-fir forest. Rounding a bend below the sandstone bulwark of Balsam Point, ascend to a level walk below the summit at 6.0 miles. The small peak of West Point stands on your right.

At 6.3 miles, the Bull Head Trail ends at a junction with the Rainbow Falls Trail (hike 4), where you have several choices. You can return as you came, for a 12.6-mile round trip. You can descend on the Rainbow Falls Trail to the left for 6.0 miles back to Cherokee Orchard Road where you began this hike, for a 12.3-mile round trip. Or, straight ahead, you still have a 0.5-mile climb to the summit of Mount LeConte, where you'll find LeConte Lodge, the backcountry shelter, and connections with the Trillium Gap (hike 6), Alum Cave (hike 54), and The Boulevard Trails (hike 56).

6 | TRILLIUM GAP TRAIL

Distance: 6.4 miles one way (8.7 miles one way in winter); to Grotto Falls, 1.2 miles one way (3.5 miles one way in winter)
Difficulty: Strenuous; to falls, moderate
Elevation gain: 3,350 feet; to Grotto Falls, 560 feet
Season: Year-round (access road closed in winter)
Cautions: Crowds going up to see Grotto Falls, small creek crossings, long ascent
Connections: Brushy Mountain Trail, The Boulevard Trail, Alum Cave Trail, Rainbow Falls Trail, Bull Head Trail

Attractions: One of several trails up Mount LeConte, this route takes you by Grotto Falls, and a short spur trail offers views from Brushy Mountain. Trillium Gap is a swag between the peaks of Mount LeConte and the smaller Brushy Mountain to the north. In spring, the gap is one of the prettiest places in the park, with spring beauty scattered everywhere. It seems as if gravity has drawn the wildflowers down into the gap, which actually may have happened as seeds rolled farther downhill with each succeeding generation of plants. Curiously, few trillium can be found in Trillium Gap itself. In addition to rooms at LeConte Lodge at the summit, camping is available at Mount LeConte Shelter; reservations required.

Trailhead: Follow Cherokee Orchard Road to the Roaring Fork Motor Nature Trail, turn onto it, and continue for 1.7 miles to the Trillium Gap trailhead. When the Roaring Fork Motor Nature Trail is closed in winter, you must walk in from the Rainbow Falls Trail parking area (see hike 4). From that parking area, walk up to a junction of trails, with the Rainbow Falls Trail to the left and the Old Sugarlands Trail down to the right. Turn left on the Rainbow Falls Trail and immediately turn left again on the Trillium Gap Trail connector, a faint path compared to the others at this junction. This connector trail parallels Cherokee Orchard Road to cross a small creek at an old house site, cross a tributary of LeConte Creek, and then

Grotto Falls

reach a junction with the Baskins Creek Trail (hike 7) to the left in 0.7 mile. Stay on the connector, which then parallels the Roaring Fork Motor Nature Trail, passing along the lower slope of Mount LeConte. Rockhop the western fork of the Rocky Spur Branch of Roaring Fork at 2.2 miles and ascend to a junction at 2.4 miles, with the parking area 0.1 mile to the left and the main stem of the Trillium Gap Trail to the right; turn right and follow the main hike description below.

Description: From the far end of the parking area, ascend from the road into a hemlock woods. In 0.1 mile, reach a junction with the Trillium Gap Trail connector to the right (it leads 2.4 miles west to the Rainbow Falls parking area, the winter access described above). Stay left to continue up the mountain on the Trillium Gap Trail, the only trail to the summit of Mount LeConte used to pack supplies to LeConte Lodge at the top of the mountain—rather than horses, the lodge managers use llamas.

In spring you'll find a multitude of wildflowers, including trillium, as the trail makes a gentle ascent. The trail moves in and out along the contour of the slope, crossing small streams that course down the mountainside. At 0.9 mile rockhop the eastern fork of Rocky Spur Branch, a tributary of the Roaring Fork. You'll then hear Roaring Fork below and soon after begin paralleling the creek upstream as it stair-steps down the mountain. The creek is the steepest stream in the park; from its spring high on Mount LeConte, it drops a vertical mile before joining the West Prong of the Little Pigeon River near Gatlinburg.

At 1.1 miles, the creek drops through a two-step falls into a deep pool. Then at 1.2 miles, enter a narrow, rock-walled defile where the Roaring Fork sails 30 feet over Grotto Falls. A depression has developed behind the falls, a recess shielded by the stream of falling water from which the falls gets its name. The trail actually passes behind the waterfall through this grotto. Take care walking on wet rocks. This passage may be very difficult at times of high water and in winter with ice everywhere.

Past Grotto Falls, the trail curves back left to ascend from the Roaring Fork and soon after swings right to continue east along the slope of the mountain. Rock outcrops of Thunderhead Sandstone protrude from the slope. At 2.4 miles, rockhop Surry Fork, another tributary of the Roaring Fork. The trail then ascends into Trillium Gap at 2.8 miles, and a trail junction with the Brushy Mountain Trail (hike 40), which leads both straight ahead into the Greenbrier area and to the left to the top of Brushy Mountain for fine views (reached in 0.4 mile, 200 feet elevation gain from the gap); turn right to continue on the Trillium Gap Trail.

Now make the long climb to the top of Mount LeConte. At 3.3 miles, the trail crosses back over Surry Fork and later curves left up the steep valley of the Roaring Fork. At 4.2 miles, after a slight descent, reach a switchback up to the left just before the Roaring Fork. Here the creek cascades down a steep slide, which you mostly just hear; you'll only catch a glimpse of the water.

The trail continues to climb, swinging to the right around a point of the ridge and then right again to make the final assault on the mountain. Ascend along high ridges through red spruce and Fraser fir to the summit of Mount LeConte, passing the spring that is the source of Roaring Fork. At the end of the trail and a junction at 6.4 miles, LeConte Lodge lies to the right. To the left, The Boulevard Trail (hike 56) leads past the Mount LeConte Shelter and over High Top. To the right, beyond the entrance to LeConte Lodge, lie connections with the Alum Cave (hike 54), Bull Head (hike 5), and Rainbow Falls (hike 4) Trails.

7 BASKINS CREEK TRAIL

Distance: 2.7 miles one way; to Baskins Creek Falls, 1.5 miles
one way; to Rainbow Falls trailhead, 3.4 miles one way
Difficulty: Moderate
Elevation change: 700 feet; to Baskins Creek Falls,
560 feet (loss)
Season: Year-round (access road closed in winter)
Cautions: Creek crossings
Connections: Grapeyard Ridge Trail, Trillium Gap Trail,
Rainbow Falls Trail, Bull Head Trail, Old Sugarlands Trail

Attractions: This seldom-traversed trail takes you by a significant waterfall in the land encompassed by the Roaring Fork Motor Nature Trail. Sights along the way include the Baskins Cemetery; among the natural-rock headstones, you'll find the grave of "Baby Grace Floyd, 1925–1926."

Trailhead: From Cherokee Orchard Road, take Roaring Fork Motor Nature Trail 3.1 miles past the Trillium Gap parking and down the mountain to a paved pullout on the left for the Baskins Creek Trail. (The Grapeyard Ridge Trail, hike 38, joins the road just beyond the nearby bridge over Roaring Fork Creek.) You can also park a shuttle vehicle at the Rainbow Falls trailhead (hike 4), to avoid the return hike.

Description: Walk up a graveled path to swing left around the Roaring Fork Cemetery and descend as the trail turns from gravel to a forest path following an old roadway. At 0.1 mile, Rocky Spur Branch passes under the trail in a culvert. Then ascend to top a ridge at 0.4 mile and descend toward Baskins Creek.

The trail passes downstream to reach a ford to the left at 1.1 miles. A side path continues straight along the creek, probably made by anglers looking for trout and by hikers looking for the waterfall, but the falls is not on this branch. Ford the creek here and begin a climb of the ridge

Baskins Creek Falls

separating two branches of Baskins Creek. To your right, notice an old farm site in the flat below. Once over the ridge, descend to a trail junction at 1.3 miles.

Turn right onto a spur trail that leads 0.2 mile to the falls on Falls Branch of Baskins Creek. Pass a former house site on the right and then reach the top of the falls. Continue on to curve left and descend into a hollow, where the trail turns back along a rock wall to reach the base of the waterfall, a 30-foot, two-step drop of water. Retrace your steps back to the main trail (here you can go left to return as you came for 3 miles round trip or go right to resume the hike; the remaining mileages do not include the 0.4-mile side trip to the falls on the spur trail).

On the main trail, head up along Falls Branch to a rockhop ford at 1.4 miles. A side trail at 1.5 miles leads 0.1 mile through a shallow creek and up a steep slope to the Baskins Cemetery on the shoulder of a ridge.

Back on the main trail, continue your ascent out of the watershed of Baskins Creek. The trail eventually crosses the Roaring Fork Motor Nature Trail and reaches a junction with the Trillium Gap Trail (hike 6) connector at 2.7 miles. From here, you can return as you came for 6.0 miles round trip (including side trips), or you can turn to the right to get to the trailhead parking for the Rainbow Falls Trail (hike 4) in another 0.7 mile and connections with the Old Sugarlands Trail (hike 2) and the Ball Head Trail (hike 5).

FIGHTING CREEK GAP

Providing an east-west passage through the mountains, Fighting Creek Gap divides the waters in this region of the park. To the east, streams flow into Fighting Creek, which passes behind the Sugarlands Visitor Center to join the West Prong of the Little Pigeon River. To the west, waters flow toward Little River.

Getting there: From Gatlinburg, drive west on US 441 (Newfound Gap Road) to the junction with Little River Road. Turn right and pass the Sugarlands Visitor Center, heading west on Little River Road. At 3.9 miles from Sugarlands Visitor Center, enter Fighting Creek Gap. Park on the north side of the road for the Laurel Falls Trail and on the south side for the Sugarland Mountain Trail.

8 LAUREL FALLS TRAIL

Distance: 4.1 miles one way; to Laurel Falls, 1.3 miles one way; to old-growth forest, 1.9 miles one way
Difficulty: Moderate; to falls, easy
Elevation gain: 1,800 feet; to falls, 320 feet; to old-growth forest, 700 feet
Season: Year-round
Cautions: Lots of people at Laurel Falls
Connections: Sugarland Mountain Trail, Little Greenbrier Trail, Cove Mountain Trail

Attractions: After passing between two-tiered Laurel Falls, this hike ascends through an old-growth forest of large oaks, basswoods, maples, and hemlocks, with interspersed silverbell, a tree that has white, bell-shaped flowers in spring. This forest also has yellow poplars. The yellow poplar is, in fact, a member of the magnolia family, as might be expected from the tree's large, greenish yellow flowers. Because the flowers resemble tulips, the yellow poplar is also called "tuliptree." Colloquially, it's often called "tulip poplar." The yellow poplar is found throughout the park except in the highest elevations and is one of the tallest of the eastern hardwood trees, usually growing straight up as it reaches for the sky.

From this peaceful forest, you ascend onto Chinquapin Ridge. The name of the ridge comes from either the chinquapin oak tree, which is actually scarce in the Great Smoky Mountains, or the Allegheny chinquapin, which

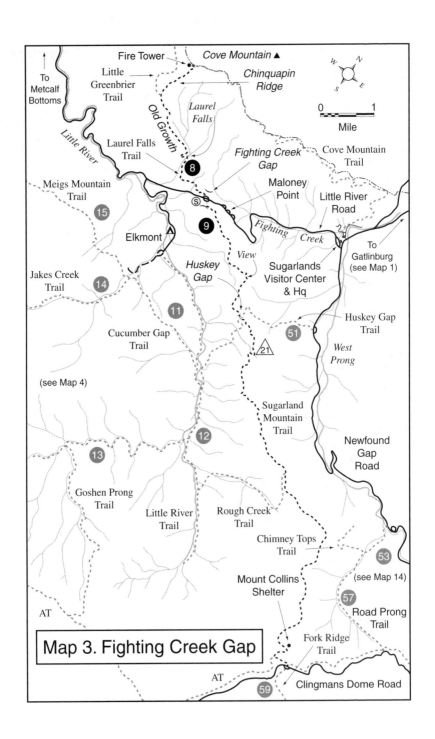

Map 3. Fighting Creek Gap

is related to the chestnut and so is gone from the Smokies because of the chestnut blight. The name is an Indian word meaning "large." The hike continues to the summit of Cove Mountain with a fire tower that is one of three that remain in the park, in addition to a historic stone and wood lookout on Mount Cammerer. (The other two are atop Mount Sterling and the Shuckstack on the North Carolina side of the mountains. Once there were also fire towers on Spruce Mountain, Greenbrier Pinnacle, High Rocks, Bunker Lead, Rich Mountain, and Blanket Mountain.) With a lower priority given to putting out small fires that start naturally, the close monitoring of the early years is not necessary, and staffed fire towers are no longer needed.

Laurel Falls

Trailhead: Park at Fighting Creek Gap.

Description: The first section of the Laurel Falls Trail has been paved to prevent erosion by the multitudes walking to see the falls. The trail bends to the right up Laurel Branch Valley, where a bench on the right at 0.9 mile affords a resting spot with a view through the trees to the left across Little River Valley. The trail then hugs the slope high above Laurel Branch, which flows down on your left to join Little River.

At 1.3 miles Laurel Branch spills down from the highlands to cross the trail. The 75-foot Laurel Falls is a two-step drop, with the trail crossing a ledge between the upper and lower falls. A concrete walkway takes you across a gap in the ledge. The water from the falls passes under you, spills down the second falls to your left, and continues down the narrow valley.

Beyond the falls the trail is not paved, and along this stretch you'll find more solitude. Ascend on a dry, south-facing slope thick with mountain laurel and rhododendron to a switchback to the right at a small spring at 1.6 miles. Then at 1.8 miles the trail curves left up the drainage of Jay Bird Branch and makes a steady climb up Chinquapin Ridge, which runs south from Cove Mountain.

At 1.9 miles enter a forest of giant yellow poplars and hemlocks standing guard along the trail. Watch for two massive yellow poplars standing together to the right of the trail. This old-growth stand is one of the most beautiful forests in the Smokies; the tall trees lend a quiet to your walk that makes you want to linger in the peace and solitude.

The trail gains the crest of Chinquapin Ridge and curves to the right up the ridge to a junction at 3.1 miles with the Little Greenbrier Trail to the left (which leads down to the Little Brier Gap Trail, hike 18, in 2.4 miles); keep straight to follow Chinquapin Ridge to the crest of Cove Mountain at 4.0 miles and a junction. (Here the Cove Mountain Trail heads east 8.6 miles to the Sugarlands Visitor Center.) Turn left for a 0.1-mile side trip to the summit to see the fire tower built by the CCC in the 1930s. Once you could climb the steps for a view into the park, but the way is now blocked by air-quality monitoring equipment installed just up from the base of the tower. Return as you came.

9 | SUGARLAND MOUNTAIN TRAIL

Distance: 12.3 miles one way; to Mount LeConte Overlook,
  2.3 miles one way
Difficulty: Moderate
Elevation gain: 3,500 feet; to overlook, 650 feet
Season: Year-round
Cautions: Long ascents
Connections: Laurel Falls Trail, Huskey Gap Trail, Rough
  Creek Trail, Appalachian Trail, Fork Ridge Trail

Attractions: This ascending trail links Little River Road with the Smokies crest at Clingmans Dome Road, passing a view of Mount LeConte. Sugarland Mountain runs up to Mount Collins, a peak on the crest of the Smokies named for Robert Collins, the guide who led Swiss geographer Arnold Guyot through the Smokies in the 1800s. Camping is available at Medicine Bluff Branch Campsite (21) and Mount Collins Shelter.

Trailhead: Park at Fighting Creek Gap. To run a shuttle, leave a car on the Smokies crest at the parking area for the Fork Ridge Trail (hike 59) on Clingmans Dome Road, but keep in mind this road is closed in winter.

Description: The Sugarland Mountain Trail ascends steeply from Little River Road and immediately turns left. Climb through a pine-hemlock woods and turn right at 0.1 mile into a cove hardwood forest to then curve left through a couple of steep drainages.

At 0.9 mile the trail turns to the right at a point of the ridge where you have a view to the east. The trail then levels off on a drier pine-laurel ridge. Many of the pines are dead from beetle infestation. Top a knoll at 1.1 miles

View from Sugarland Mountain Trail

and then descend on the left side of the ridge, reaching Mids Gap at 1.5 miles, thick with rhododendron.

The trail ascends, now on the right side of the ridge above the deep cove of Mids Branch. Back at the ridgeline at 2.1 miles, the trail crosses through a small gap to pass below the crest on the left side. At 2.3 miles you reach an open view. The Sugarlands valley sweeps up to Mount LeConte, with Bull Head in the foreground and the peaks of Cliff Top and High Top on the summit.

The trail climbs gradually, reaching Huskey Gap and an intersection at 3.1 miles. (To the left, the Huskey Gap Trail, hike 51, leads 2.0 miles down to Newfound Gap Road; to the right, it leads 2.1 miles to connect with the Little River Trail, hike 12, out of Elkmont. Either direction makes a good day hike if you have a shuttle vehicle waiting.)

Continue straight on the Sugarland Mountain Trail. At 4.1 miles, the Medicine Branch Bluff Campsite (21) lies beside Big Medicine Branch, which can be dry in summer. The trail crosses the stream and continues up Sugarland Mountain. At a trail junction at 7.3 miles (where the Rough Creek Trail to the right leads 2.8 miles down the southwest side of the ridge to connect with the Little River Trail, hike 12), continue straight.

At 9 miles, an arrow carved in a tree on the left marks a junction with an unmaintained path that connects with the Chimney Tops Trail. This is a difficult route; do not go this way.

The trail remains level and even descends for a time, but then climbs once more. At 11.8 miles, a side path leads left to the Mount Collins Shelter. At 12.1 miles the Sugarland Mountain Trail ends at a junction with the AT. Turn to the left. In 0.2 mile at a junction, the AT continues straight for 4.3 miles to Newfound Gap; turn right, and walk out to Clingmans Dome Road across from parking for the Fork Ridge Trail (hike 59).

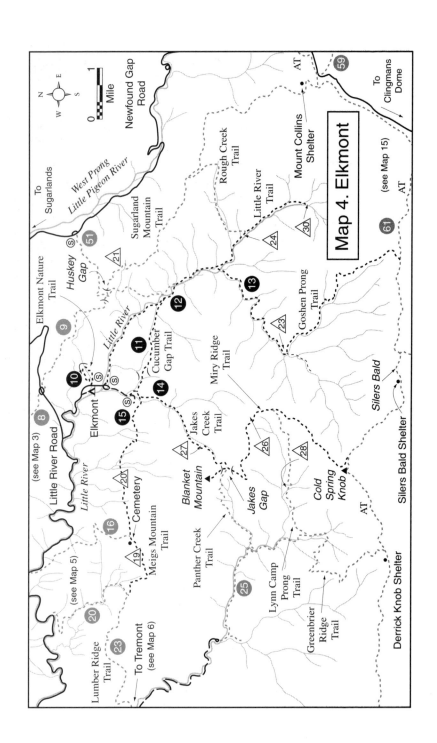

Map 4. Elkmont

ELKMONT

The Little River Road from the west and the road into Elkmont are the route of the Little River Railroad, part of the Little River Lumber Company, a major logging enterprise in the early 1900s. Logs were hauled to a mill at Townsend outside what is now the park boundaries. Elkmont was one of several lumbering camps. The rail lines were laid into Elkmont in 1908 and taken up seventeen years later when the timbering was finished. Logs were hauled to a mill at Townsend outside the park boundaries.

On the road into Elkmont, you'll pass a gravel road that leads up to the Old Elkmont Cemetery and then reach the Wonderland Hotel on the left. Built by C. M. McCarter for the Wonderland Park Company, which was formed to subdivide tracts of Little River land, the hotel opened in 1912. In 1919, a group of businessmen calling themselves the Wonderland Club purchased the

Wonderland Hotel

hotel and opened it to the public that rode the logging train into the mountains for weekend excursions. The Wonderland was sold to the state to become part of the park in the late 1920s, but the owners received a lifetime lease to operate it as a hotel. In 1952 this lease was traded in for a twenty-year lease that allowed electricity to be brought in to the river valley. In 1972 the lease was extended for another twenty years. By 1992, the hotel was abandoned. A long flight of stairs leads up to the old Wonderland, which is beginning to sag and crumble; do not enter the building.

Elkmont also contains a community of cabins built in the 1920s as part of the summer resort that included the Wonderland Hotel. Memberships were sold in the Wonderland Club, which provided a lot on which a cabin could be built. About eighty members built summer homes. When the park was established, the homes and lots were purchased and the owners received a lifetime lease. They were later involved in the lease trades and extensions of the Wonderland Hotel, which extended their time to 1992. The cabins now stand empty while the Park Service decides what to do with them.

Getting there: From Gatlinburg, drive west on US 441 (Newfound Gap Road) to the junction with Little River Road. Turn right and pass the Sugarlands Visitor Center, heading west on Little River Road. In 3.9 miles from Sugarlands Visitor Center, pass through Fighting Creek Gap, and at 5.1 miles, turn left into the Elkmont area. The road parallels the Little River; this main channel is sometimes called the "East Prong." Just before the Elkmont Campground at 1.6 miles from Little River Road, turn left to continue into the Elkmont area. At 1.9 miles the Elkmont Nature Trail (hike 10) lies on the left. Cross a bridge over the Little River and reach a fork at 2.3 miles; to the left the road is now closed, and is the Little River Trail (hike 12); to the right, a one-way road continues through some of the abandoned Elkmont cabins for another 0.2 mile to reach parking on the right for the Jakes Creek Trail (hike 14).

10 | ELKMONT NATURE TRAIL

Distance: 0.7-mile loop
Difficulty: Easy
Elevation change: 120 feet
Season: Year-round
Cautions: Footbridges, wet areas
Connections: None

Attractions: This short loop walk crosses an old railbed and passes house sites. Camping is available in nearby Elkmont Campground. You can walk to the east through the campground to cross the road and reach the nature trail.

Trailhead: In Elkmont, 1.9 miles from Little River Road, the Elkmont Nature Trail begins on the left.

Description: On the right side of the parking area, the trail drops to cross a footbridge over Mids Branch, a tributary of Little River that passes under the road to flow through the campground. Walk onto the flat of an old railbed that was a spur line leading up Mids Branch, where the first logging took place. Turn left on the old railbed and soon turn up the slope on a footpath to the right.

The trail drops to cross a flow of water from a bricked-in spring on the right. There is no sign of the homesite that once stood here, other than the spreading daffodils that bloom in spring.

Then descend into a lowland. The way is a bit confusing with paths in several directions. Take the path that heads north across the wet lowland. On the other side, turn upstream along Mids Branch to a footbridge crossing at 0.3 mile. The trail continues upstream to soon curve left onto a drier, south-facing slope that has more sun exposure and grows pine and laurel.

The trail descends with a switchback left; stone steps take you down to a mountainside patio where scattered flagstones have settled into the ground; perhaps a cabin once stood here. The trail descends through several switchbacks that return you to trailhead parking at 0.7 mile.

11 | LITTLE RIVER, CUCUMBER GAP, AND JAKES CREEK TRAILS

Distance: 5.1-mile loop
Difficulty: Easy
Elevation change: 600 feet
Season: Year-round
Cautions: Creek crossings
Connections: Meigs Mountain Trail

Attractions: This hike forms a loop combining the Cucumber Gap Trail with the Little River and Jakes Creek Trails. The Cucumber Gap Trail, which has many wildflowers that line the path in spring, gets its name from the cucumber magnolia, whose immature seed cones look like cucumbers. Camping is available in Elkmont Campground.

Trailhead: In Elkmont, at the road fork 2.3 miles from Little River Road, park along the road wherever you can find space. The road to the left, now closed, is the beginning of the hike.

Description: As you walk up the paved road on the Little River Trail, you pass by some of the abandoned Wonderland Club cabins. The road becomes gravel as it follows the old route of the Little River Railroad. Watch for a large patch of daylilies that mark an old house site. In spring you'll also see bishop's cap blooming tiny cream-colored flowers that resemble a mitered cap.

At 1.0 mile, a turnaround in the road marks an old trailhead from when the road was open to here. Continue up the railbed. In spring, also watch for white erect trillium, large-flowered trillium (also white but larger), spring beauty, and rue anemone. At 1.9 miles, a bench sits on the left at a drop in the river where the water splashes into a large pool.

At 2.1 miles cross a bridge that passes over Huskey Branch tumbling from the right down a rock chute. Then at a junction at 2.3 miles, turn right on the Cucumber Gap Trail (the Little River Trail continues straight). Ascend on an old spur rail line that led up Huskey Branch. The trail dips into a hollow where a small stream passes under the trail. At 2.6 miles, rock-hop Huskey Branch.

On the other side, turn left to continue upstream along a tributary. The trail alternates passing through trenches and across the tops of berms, signs of the old railbed. At 3.0 miles, cross over the stream and swing left to continue up the hollow.

In a more open wood, a slope on the left provides a show of wildflowers in spring, sweeps of spring beauty and rue anemone with sprinklings of trout lily and yellow violets. At 3.6 miles the trail swings through Cucumber Gap, a passageway between Burnt Mountain to the north and, to the south, Bent Arm, an appendage of Miry Ridge.

Elkmont cabin

As you descend, rockhop Tulip Branch, a tributary of Jakes Creek, and then reach another old railbed that's the Jakes Creek Trail at 4.6 miles (the Meigs Mountain Trail, hike 15, is 0.1 mile to the left); turn right. Heading down, cross Tulip Branch on a bridge and reach a junction with another road at a gate. (The road to the left leads to an old homesite.) Turn right to reenter the community of Elkmont cabins. Reach trailhead parking for the Jakes Creek Trail at 4.9 miles. Continue down the road to a junction with a one-way road through a cabin area that was called "Club Town," where the Appalachian Club had cabins. Turn right to close the loop at the fork at 5.1 miles.

12 | LITTLE RIVER TRAIL

Distance: 5.1 miles one way
Difficulty: Easy
Elevation gain: 1,000 feet
Season: Year-round
Cautions: Creek crossings
Connections: Cucumber Gap Trail, Huskey Gap Trail,
Goshen Prong Trail, Rough Creek Trail

Attractions: This walk on the old Little River railbed keeps company with the Little River. Occasional benches invite you to stop and enjoy the sunshine on violets, spring beauty, hepatica, and anemones in spring. You may also see people fly-fishing. The creeks and rivers harbor rainbow trout, brown trout, and bass. Fishing for the native brook trout, found in the cool streams at higher elevations, is prohibited. Logging in the early part of the century caused runoff that polluted the waters, driving the fish from many of its streams. The rainbow trout that were introduced, along with the brown trout that have invaded some streams, now dominate much of the brook trout habitat. Park researchers have determined the Smokies brook trout is a distinct strain and should be classified as a subspecies.

In the hollows along the trail in early spring, you can find ramps growing. The plant, a member of the lily family known as wild leek, is the only plant that can be legally picked and taken from the park, but only for your personal use. You can also gather berries, nuts, and mushrooms in small quantities. An annual spring festival held at Cosby in April celebrates the ramp, which is considered a delicacy with the taste of sweet spring onions. Camping is available at Elkmont Campground, plus Rough Creek Campsite (24) and Three Forks Campsite (30).

Trailhead: In Elkmont, at the road fork 2.3 miles from Little River Road, park along the road. The road to the left, now closed, is the beginning of the hike.

Description: Walk up the old railbed along the Little River, following the path of the Little River Railroad. Up the road 1.0 mile, pass through a turnaround at an old trailhead, then cross a bridge over Huskey Branch, and reach a junction at 2.3 miles with the Cucumber Gap Trail to the right; continue straight.

Pass a slide area and then cross the river on a road bridge at 2.6 miles to reach a junction at 2.7 miles with the Husky Gap Trail (hike 51) on the left (it travels over Sugarland Mountain to the Newfound Gap Road in 4.1 miles); continue straight.

Cross side streams on bridges at 3.1 and 3.6 miles, and walk up to a junction at 3.7 miles. The Little River Lumber Company's Fish Camp was located here. A commissary stood in the fork of the railbed. (To the right, the Goshen Prong Trail, hike 13, follows a branch of the old railbed. The Little River and Goshen Prong Trails can be combined to join with the AT heading west across Silers Bald, then the Miry Ridge Trail and Jakes Creek Trail, hike 14, for a tough 24.4-mile backpack loop out of Elkmont.) Stay left at this junction to continue on the Little River Trail.

The roadbed narrows. A bridge takes you across Rough Creek; then old railroad ties signal a boulder crossing where a bridge once crossed a smaller tributary of the Little River. The Rough Creek Campsite (24) lies just ahead on the right. At 4.4 miles, reach a junction with the Rough Creek Trail, which leads left to join the Sugarland Mountain Trail in 2.8 miles; continue straight.

At 4.6 miles ford Meigs Post Prong. Then at 5.1 miles the trail ends at Three Forks, where Grouse Creek and Spud Town Branch join the Little River. This was the location of another Little River logging camp. The Three Forks Campsite (30) is nestled in the forks.

13 | LITTLE RIVER AND GOSHEN PRONG TRAILS

Distance: 11.4 miles one way; to Camp Rock Campsite (23), 7.0 miles
Difficulty: Strenuous; to campsite, easy
Elevation gain: 3,000 feet; to campsite, 570 feet
Season: Year-round
Cautions: Relentless climb after campsite
Connections: Appalachian Trail

Attractions: The hike follows Fish Camp Prong, which tumbles down in numerous cascades and spillways, before reaching Camp Rock Campsite (23). From here, the hike turns up cascading Goshen Prong to make a long ascent to the AT. The route is also part of a loop backpack out of Elkmont. Elkmont Campground can be used as your staging area the night before.

Trailhead: In Elkmont, at the road fork 2.3 miles from Little River Road, park along the road. The road to the left, now closed, is the beginning of the hike.

Description: Follow the description in hike 12, Little River Trail, and walk up the trail 3.7 miles to the junction with the Goshen Prong Trail. At this junction, turn to the right off the Little River Trail onto the Goshen Prong Trail, again following an old railbed. A long metal bridge carries you high above Little River just above the confluence with the Fish Camp

Bridge over Little River

Prong. On the other side, the trail heads up Fish Camp Prong.

At 4.1 miles the old railbed is broken down, and so if it has not been repaired, you must drop down to the right and then climb back to regain the trail. Then pass through a rocky area thick with stinging nettle.

A drop in the creek at 4.8 miles marks the beginning of a series of cascades and spillways where the water splashes and skips down the valley. Pass a 20-foot slide of water, then a spillway where two chutes spout water onto a tilted rock ledge. More spillways and ledge falls dot the creek. The trail then crosses a rocky drainage at 5.1 miles where trees on the left are standing on stilt roots. A seed landing on a fallen tree will sprout and send roots into and around the rotting log. Eventually the log decomposes, leaving the new tree standing on its roots.

Travel along a bench hemmed between a rock wall on the left and the creek on the right. The trail follows the creek in two sweeping meanders to the right. At 6.6 miles, rockhop a branch of the creek to an island and then cross back to the left side of the creek. The trail then ascends to the Camp Rock Campsite (23) on the left at 7.0 miles. The camp rests in a broad clearing with several good tent sites.

Just beyond the campsite there is a junction. The trail continuing straight along Fish Camp Prong once led to a camp 0.9 mile up the creek, but the camp is no longer maintained. The Goshen Prong Trail turns left here to ascend along Goshen Prong, a tributary of Fish Camp Prong.

The trail climbs as it continues to follow an old railbed; cinders appear underfoot. At 8.3 miles, the creek pours down a series of drops and cascades as it tumbles down the mountain. After crossing a small secondary stream, cross a main tributary of Goshen Prong at 8.8 miles where the water spills down a large, slanted block of stone. Soon after, the trail skirts a rock wall where a small cave opens at the foot of the rock.

Along this relentless ascent toward the crest of the Smokies, Jenkins Ridge rises to your right, separating the main tributaries of Goshen Prong; the rounded peak of Silers Bald stands above the ridge. At 10.9 miles, ascend into red spruce near the crest. At 11.2 miles, the trail crosses some trickles that are the headwaters of Goshen Prong and then ascends to a junction with the AT at 11.4 miles.

From here you can go left to Clingmans Dome in 2.3 miles. Or you can turn to the right on the AT to Silers Bald, 2.3 miles, and on to Miry Ridge Trail (hike 14) to make a rugged backpacking loop of 24.4 miles (see hike 61, Silers Bald).

14 | JAKES CREEK AND MIRY RIDGE TRAILS

Distance: 8.2 miles one way; side trip to Blanket Mountain, 0.8 mile one way
Difficulty: Moderate
Elevation gain: 3,150 feet; side trip to Blanket Mountain, 550 feet
Season: Year-round
Cautions: Creek crossings
Connections: Cucumber Gap Trail, Meigs Mountain Trail, Panther Creek Trail, Lynn Camp Prong Trail, Appalachian Trail

Attractions: The Jakes Creek Trail climbs to Jakes Gap between Blanket Mountain to the north and Dripping Spring Mountain to the southeast.

From Jakes Gap, the old Blanket Mountain Trail leads to the summit of Blanket Mountain. There on the grassy knoll you'll find the base of a fire tower and the foundations and collapsed chimney of the watchman's cabin. Blanket Mountain received its name when Return Jonathan Meigs, Cherokee agent in the early 1800s, placed a bright blanket atop the mountain so the summit could be easily seen while he surveyed the boundary of Cherokee lands established by the Treaty of Tellico of 1798. Also from Jakes Gap, the Miry Ridge Trail climbs to the AT, a great mountain walk that can be part of a rugged backpacking loop. Camping is available at Lower Jakes Gap Campsite (27) and Dripping Spring Mountain Campsite (26). The Elkmont Campground can be your backpack staging area the night before.

Trailhead: At the fork in the Elkmont Road at 2.3 miles, turn to the right on a one-way road for another 0.2 mile and park on the right. Walk up the road a short distance to where the Jakes Creek Trail begins on the left.

Description: As you walk around the gate and up the Jakes Creek Trail, you are following an old railbed that ran up Jakes Creek. Near the beginning, Tulip Branch flows under the road. At 0.3 mile the Cucumber Gap Trail (hike 11) begins on the left; stay straight. Then at 0.4 mile at another junction, the Meigs Mountain Trail (hike 15) on the right heads west toward Tremont; continue straight.

The trail makes a gradual ascent while paralleling Jakes Creek on the right, which was named for one of various Jakes who lived in the area, most probably Jake Houser. At 1.0 mile, Waterdog Branch drips down the rock on your left. Soon after, a steep side path leads down to the creek where a large boulder overhangs a deep pool below a spillway. Then at 1.2 miles, the trail swings left to cross Newt Prong on a footbridge. Soon after, the trail bears left off the railbed, which continues straight ahead, now overgrown.

The trail follows a footpath on its ascent of Blanket Mountain. Jakes Creek, still on your right, spills down in minor drops. At 1.5 miles, you'll hear, more than see, a falls in the creek; above the falls, a side path to the right leads to the creek but does not afford a view. The trail ascends more steeply. At 1.7 miles, descend to rockhop Jakes Creek. The trail then switchbacks left and continues ascending while crossing small tributary streams.

At 2.0 miles, the trail passes beside the Lower Jakes Gap Campsite (27), separated by a small tributary stream, and then swings left across the stream to enter the camp. The campsite lies on the side of the mountain, but you can find small flat areas as you walk down the slope. If there is no water in the small stream that flows beside the camp, walk to the back of the camp, where Jakes Creek runs.

The ascent from the campsite is steeper as the trail climbs through rhododendron and mixed hardwoods. Watch for fringed phacelia, trout lily, and squirrel corn in spring. At 3.3 miles, the Jakes Creek Trail ends at a junction in Jakes Gap; the Miry Ridge Trail turns to the left. (Straight ahead, the Panther Creek Trail drops down the mountain to connect with the Middle Prong Trail, hike 25, out of Tremont.) To the right, the old Blanket Mountain Trail, which has now been abandoned, leads 0.8 mile to the summit of Blanket Mountain. Shrubs are quickly overgrowing the trail, but when I was last there, it was still possible to plow your way to the summit to see the site of the old fire tower. After this side trip, return to Jakes Gap.

Head up the Miry Ridge Trail, which ascends Dripping Spring Mountain, a ridge running northwest from Miry Ridge. At 3.6 miles, look back over your right shoulder to Blanket Mountain standing above Jakes Gap. At 3.8 miles, the trail swings left around the end of Dripping Spring Mountain and now traverses the southern slope.

The trail gradually curves south as Dripping Spring Mountain merges with Miry Ridge. Ascend through rhododendron in a cool hollow that is the headwaters of Lynn Camp Prong to the west. Then at 4.4 miles, the trail emerges onto a heath bald below a knoll on Dripping Spring Mountain. The area is covered in laurel and other heath plants. The open area affords views to the west. Some makeshift paths up the slope were worn by people in a mostly futile effort to get up high for better views.

Pass back into rhododendron and descend to the Dripping Spring Mountain Campsite (26) at 5.0 miles. A side path left leads 0.1 mile up to the campsite on a knoll at the junction of Dripping Spring Mountain and Miry Ridge; Bent Arm Ridge also leads out from this point to the northeast. There are several open areas on the nicely wooded knoll. Water is available from a spring that is part of the headwaters of the Newt Prong of Jakes Creek to the north. The spring lies to the left, down a drainage you crossed as you walked into the campsite. This is not a reliable source of water in late summer and early fall. When I stayed here in late September, my companion and I resorted to digging a hole in the creekbed to get water.

The trail descends gradually from Dripping Springs Mountain into a gap at 5.7 miles and a junction with the Lynn Camp Prong Trail to the right (which descends west to the Middle Prong Trail in 3.7 miles); stay straight on the Miry Ridge Trail and ascend Miry Ridge, which runs northeast down from Cold Spring Knob on the crest of the Smokies.

At 6.5 miles, the trail traverses a narrow ridgeline with exposed sandstone and views through trees to the west and an open view to the east. You'll see Silers Bald and the range of the Smokies with the watershed of the Little River below. This view is called "Ben Parton Overlook"; Parton, an employee with the Little River Lumber Company, watched for forest fires from this ridge. Large yellow birch trees stand along the path through thick grass. The trail moves to the east side of the ridgeline and ascends to a junction with the AT on the side of Cold Spring Knob at 8.2 miles.

To the right, the AT heads for the Greenbrier Ridge Trail in 1.6 miles and the Derrick Knob Shelter. To the left, the AT climbs over Silers Bald to pass the Goshen Prong Trail (hike 13) in 4.8 miles and continue on to Clingmans

Dome in another 2.3 miles. The Jakes Creek and Miry Ridge Trails can be combined with the AT and the Goshen Prong and Little River Trails (hike 13) to create a rugged backpack of 24.4 miles out of the Elkmont area.

15 | MEIGS MOUNTAIN TRAIL

Distance: 6.4 miles one way
Difficulty: Easy
Elevation gain: 500 feet
Season: Year-round
Cautions: Creek crossings
Connections: Cucumber Gap Trail, Curry Mountain Trail, Meigs Creek Trail, Lumber Ridge Trail

Attractions: Meigs Mountain was named for Return Jonathan Meigs, who was appointed U.S. agent to the Cherokees in 1801 and as part of his duties surveyed the line between white and Indian lands through the Smokies. His peculiar first name was given to him by his parents to commemorate his father's persistence in courting Return's mother; he returned again and again until she agreed to marry him. This trail joins the Elkmont area with trails leading to Metcalf Bottoms, The Sinks on Little River Road, and the Tremont Visitor Center. Camping is available at nearby Elkmont Campground, King Branch Campsite (20), and Upper Henderson Campsite (19).

Trailhead: At the fork in the Elkmont Road at 2.3 miles, turn to the right on a one-way road for another 0.2 mile and park on the right. Walk up the road a short distance to where the Jakes Creek Trail begins on the left.

Description: Follow Jakes Creek Trail (hike 14) 0.4 mile passing the Cucumber Gap Trail (hike 11) to the junction with the Meigs Mountain Trail, where Jakes Creek Trail continues straight. Turn right on the Meigs Mountain Trail to descend gently along an old road grade through mixed hardwoods and cross Jakes Creek on a footbridge at 0.6 mile. Then ascend from the creek, reaching a fork where a side trail to the right leads to a clearing that was the homesite of Lem Ownby. "Uncle Lem," as he was called, was the last lifetime lease holder in the park, living at this place until he died at the age of 100 in 1989.

On the main trail, continue along the flank of Meigs Mountain, crossing numerous small streams, about fifteen in all. These you can easily step across or rockhop. In spring, you'll walk through a lowland of moss and fern that at one time was occupied by about twenty families, so watch for stone fences, washtubs, pieces of metal, and other remnants of the former farming community. At 2.0 miles, soon after crossing Blanket Creek, which flows down from Blanket Mountain to the south, pass the King Branch Campsite (20).

At 4.5 miles, the trail reaches a junction with the Curry Mountain Trail (hike 16) to the right (which descends to the Little River Road at Metcalf Bottoms in 3.3 miles); continue straight, passing through an old farm site with a dried-up spring on the left; the house's rockwork foundations lie down the hill to the right. At 4.7 miles a side path on the right leads to an old community cemetery on a grassy knoll where Huskeys and Ownbys are buried. The main trail descends gently to the Upper Henderson Campsite (19) at 5.0 miles, in the vicinity of Henderson Prong. Ascend to Upper Buckhorn Gap below the ridge of Meigs Mountain at 6.2 miles. The trail then descends to Buckhorn Gap and ends there at an intersection of trails at 6.4 miles.

To the right, the Meigs Creek Trail (hike 20) drops 3.5 miles to The Sinks on the Little River Road. Straight ahead, the Lumber Ridge Trail (hike 23) passes over Lumber Ridge to the Tremont area in 4.0 miles.

METCALF BOTTOMS

The Metcalf family once lived here beside the Little River, where Metcalf Bottoms Picnic Area is now located. Also in the area are a cemetery and the Little Greenbrier School, which was used as a school and church by the community of Little Greenbrier until 1935. Farther up the mountain, the Walker sisters' log cabin still stands off the Little Brier Gap Trail.

Getting there: To approach Metcalf Bottoms from the east, take Little River Road west from Sugarlands Visitor Center, passing through Fighting Creek Gap in 3.9 miles and bypassing the Elkmont turnoff in 5.1 miles. Continue west on Little River Road to cross Little River, and then in 10 miles from Sugarlands turn right into the Metcalf Bottoms Picnic Area. To approach Metcalf Bottoms from the west, from Townsend take Hwy. 73 south into the park; from the Townsend Wye—the junction of Hwy. 73, Laurel Fork Road, and Little River Road—turn

Meigs Creek Falls

left (east) onto Little River Road and continue to Metcalf Bottoms (8 miles east from the Wye). To approach Metcalf Bottoms from US 321 east of Townsend, take Wear Cove Gap Road south 2.7 miles to Little River Road at the picnic area, passing the Roundtop trailhead (hike 19) just below Wear Cove Gap. To reach The Sinks parking area, on Little River Road drive 2.1 miles west from the Metcalf Bottoms Picnic Area or 5.9 miles east from the Townsend Wye.

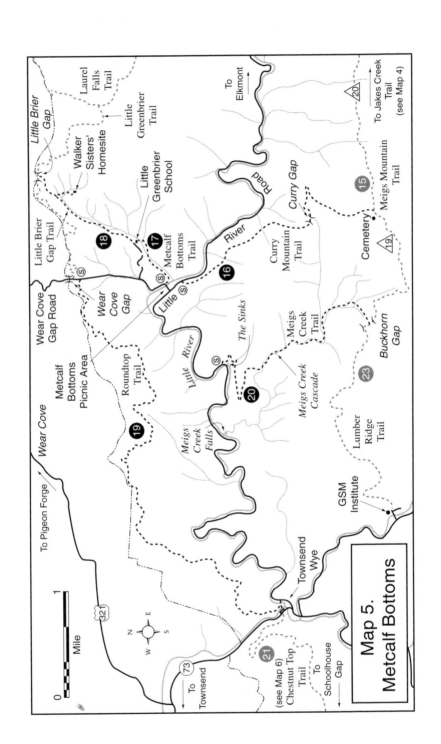

Map 5.
Metcalf Bottoms

16 | CURRY MOUNTAIN TRAIL

Distance: 3.3 miles one way; to view east, 2.5 miles one way
Difficulty: Easy
Elevation gain: 1,160 feet; to view east, 1,020 feet
Season: Year-round
Cautions: Steep ascents, rocky in places
Connections: Meigs Mountain Trail

Attractions: Often shrouded in rhododendron, the Curry Mountain Trail follows an old road along the northeast slope of Curry He Mountain. The odd name comes from a corruption of the Cherokee *gura-hi,* which simply indicated where a plant used as a salad green was located; the original settlers converted the strange-sounding word they thought was the name of the mountain into words they were familiar with, even though the words made no sense. This trail provides access from Metcalf Bottoms to Meigs Mountain, passing a view east of Sugarland Mountain and Mount LeConte.

Trailhead: At the Metcalf Bottoms Picnic Area, find a place to park, then walk back out to Little River Road and turn east, toward Elkmont. In 0.1 mile, you'll find the trailhead on the south side of the road. Take care crossing the road.

Description: At first the trail parallels Little River Road high above the roadway. At 0.6 mile pass through the steep drainage of Breakfast Branch, then curve to the right around an arm of the ridge at 0.7 mile, still paralleling Little River Road, which is now at a distance.

Cross shallow drainages and curve to the right over low ridges running down from Curry He. Through the trees, Cove Mountain stands to the north. Along a drier southeast slope covered in pine and laurel, watch for low-growing trailing arbutus, teaberry, and galax. At 1.8 miles, the trail passes through Curry Gap, a notch in the mountains between Curry He to the northwest and Curry She Mountain to the south; the locals gave women equal recognition.

Eventually make your way up to the spine of Long Arm Ridge, which runs northeast down from Curry She. At 2.5 miles, the trail makes a sharp right over the crest of this ridge at a point where fallen dead trees have opened up a grand view to the east of Sugarland Mountain and Mount LeConte in the distance.

The trail then passes along the dry southeast slope of Curry She Mountain; you'll see the long ridge of Meigs Mountain ahead. At 3.3 miles, the trail ends at a junction with the Meigs Mountain Trail on the side of Meigs Mountain.

This junction was once an intersection of roads; you can still see the old roadbeds leading off in several directions. From this junction, to the left

Meigs Mountain Trail (hike 15) heads toward Elkmont, and to the right it connects with Meigs Creek Trail (hike 20) in 1.9 miles.

17 | METCALF BOTTOMS TRAIL

Distance: 0.6 mile one way
Difficulty: Easy
Elevation gain: 100 feet
Season: Year-round
Cautions: Footbridges
Connections: Little Brier Gap Trail

Attractions: This pleasant woodlands walk leads up to the Little Greenbrier School, an old log structure built in 1882. A cemetery lies beside the building. You can enter the school and sit on the hard seats, and imagine what school was like at the turn of the century in these mountains.

Little Greenbrier School

Trailhead: At the Metcalf Bottoms Picnic Area, pass through the picnic area and cross a road bridge over Little River. The trail begins on the right after the bridge. (The schoolhouse is also accessible by driving up Wear Cove Gap Road from the picnic area for 0.5 mile to a right turn on a gravel road that leads to the school.)

Description: Walk up an old roadbed along Little River. At 0.1 mile, the road makes a sharp turn left uphill. Pass a water tank for the picnic area on the right and an old house site to the left through rock walls. At the end of the road, bear to the right down a footpath into a forest thick with rhododendron.

The trail parallels Little Brier Branch upstream and then crosses on a footbridge at 0.5 mile. Step over a wet-weather trickle of water and then cross a footbridge over the small tributary called Mossy Rock Branch. The trail recrosses Little Brier Branch on a third footbridge and ascends to the Little Greenbrier School at 0.6 mile. The Little Brier Gap Trail (hike 18) begins up the gated road above the school.

18 | LITTLE BRIER GAP TRAIL

Distance: 1.5 miles one way; side trip to Walker cabin, 0.2 mile one way
Difficulty: Easy
Elevation gain: 540 feet; to Walker cabin, 350 feet
Season: Year-round (access road closed in winter)
Cautions: None
Connections: Metcalf Bottoms Trail, Little Greenbrier Trail

Attractions: This hike visits the Walker sisters' homesite and in spring a field of pink lady's-slippers. John and Margaret King Walker raised eleven children at the homesite; seven were girls. One sister married and moved away; another died before the park was established. The remaining five stayed in their home with a lifetime lease, becoming quite famous as they continued a pioneer existence; the last died in 1964.

Trailhead: From the Metcalf Bottoms Picnic Area, continue up Wear Cove Gap Road past the Metcalf Bottoms Trail (hike 17) on the right. In 0.5 mile, turn right on a gravel road that leads to the Little Greenbrier School (the main road—Wear Cove Gap Road—continues on over the

Walker sisters' cabin

mountain ridge on the northern boundary of the park through Wear Cove Gap to connect with US 321 in Wear Cove). There is parking near the old log school building.

Description: Begin by walking up the gated gravel road above the school. The road fords Little Brier Branch and continues a gradual ascent, crossing back over the stream, which runs under the road in a culvert. At 1.0 mile, the road curves to the right and a dirt roadbed continues straight as Little Brier Gap Trail. For the 0.2-mile side trip to the Walker sisters' homesite, keep to the right on the gravel road.

As the gravel road curves to the right, it crosses back over Little Brier Branch just above the confluence of Straight Cove Branch. The road then follows this tributary upstream to cross it and lead up to the old log home where the five Walker sisters lived until the 1960s. The cabin and a shed sit in a cove beside a spring-fed trickle of water that runs from the springhouse. After exploring, return to the Little Brier Gap Trail.

Back on the trail, head up the dirt road that leads straight off the gravel road. Ascend toward Little Brier Gap, with Little Mountain to the left and Cove Mountain to the right. As you approach the gap, watch for one of the best collections of pink lady's slippers scattered across the slopes in spring; the flowers peek above downed timber, seemingly growing in improbable places.

At 1.5 miles, reach a junction with the Little Greenbrier Trail. To the right it leads to the Laurel Falls Trail (hike 8) in 2.4 miles, and to the left it reaches Wear Cove Gap Road in 1.9 miles, just north of the Roundtop trailhead (hike 19).

19 | ROUNDTOP TRAIL

Distance: 7.6 miles one way
Difficulty: Moderate
Elevation change: 1,480 feet
Season: Year-round
Cautions: Steep descent, river ford
Connections: Little Greenbrier Trail, Chestnut Top Trail

Attractions: This seldom-used trail offers solitude along the northern boundary of the park and displays of pink lady's slippers in spring. The ford of Little River at the end of the trail is a good excuse for splashing in the water on a hot summer day; people come to this spot on the river to swim and ride inner tubes downstream. In rainy seasons, when the water is high, this crossing is difficult and dangerous; at those times you should bushwhack downstream to a bridge over the river.

Trailhead: From Metcalf Bottoms Picnic Area, continue on Wear Cove Gap Road up the mountain, passing the Little Greenbrier Schoolhouse Road on the right and reaching the Roundtop Trail on the left at 1.1 miles. There's virtually no room to park, so continue up the road, passing the Little Greenbrier Trail on the right and crossing through Wear Cove Gap to a gravel parking space on the left at 1.3 miles. Walk back down the road 0.2 mile to the beginning of the Roundtop Trail. (You can run a shuttle by leaving a vehicle at the Townsend Wye, 8 miles to the west of Metcalf Bottoms Picnic Area on Little River Road.)

Description: Head straight into the woods and curve to the right uphill. The trail winds up a ridge. In spring watch for pink lady's slippers in bloom. At 0.2 mile, a view through the trees to the east reveals Cove Mountain, with Chinquapin Ridge running down to Chinquapin Knob. The trail then curves to the right up a deep hollow for a view to your left of Roundtop on the park boundary, although from this angle it does not appear very round. At a gap in the ridgeline at 0.5 mile, the trail brushes the park boundary for a view into Wear Cove and a few roads and buildings.

The trail then circles to the south of Roundtop. At 2.3 miles, the trail tops Joint Ridge, which runs down from Roundtop, and begins a gradual descent. At 2.7 miles, there's a view south through the trees with Roundtop to the left, which now appears round. At 3.0 miles, a break in the ridge allows you to see northwest to Townsend. Pine needles muffle the trail while you continue to descend. At 3.3 miles, turn left into a steep descent; watch your footing. The trail crosses a rocky drainage and swings left at 4.1 miles below Little Roundtop, another peak standing on the park boundary.

The trail begins a final descent at 6.5 miles. The deep drainage of Russell Hollow lies to the right. At 6.8 miles, the trail curves left with the Little River Valley now on the right; you can hear traffic below. Pass rock outcroppings on the left and traverse a shelf high above the river with a dropoff on your right. The trail turns to the right in a steep descent and winds down to the river's edge at 7.6 miles.

If the water level is up somewhat, you might want to bushwhack your way upstream, to the left, to get above the confluence of the West Prong that joins the Little River on the other side; above this confluence, there will be less water in the river. To make the crossing where the trail meets the river, first cross to an island, then go to the right around the edge to reach the main river channel. Select the best place to cross; you will get your feet wet even in late summer when there has been little rain. Do not attempt either crossing unless you are absolutely sure you can make it; the rocks are slippery and, even at low water, the force of the flow will push you downstream. If the water is high, do not enter the river under any circumstances; instead, bushwhack your way downstream out of the park to the first bridge crossing of the river, where you can cross and then walk back along the road to the parking area at the Townsend Wye; this adds 1.8 miles to the hike. At the parking area, you can pick up the Chestnut Top Trail (hike 21) on the west side of the road.

20 | MEIGS CREEK TRAIL

Distance: 3.5 miles one way; to Meigs Creek Cascades, 1.5 miles one way
Difficulty: Moderate
Elevation gain: 800 feet; to Meigs Creek Cascades, 230 feet
Season: Year-round
Cautions: Numerous creek crossings
Connections: Meigs Mountain Trail, Lumber Ridge Trail

Attractions: Numerous small waterfalls and cascades adorn Meigs Creek. The trail begins at The Sinks, where Little River spills over a ledge into a rock bowl and then makes a sharp right to pass easily downstream. The Sinks gets its name from the swirling of the water, as if a sink drain has been unstopped. A portion of the riverbed here was once dynamited to help break up a log jam; this created a new channel that cuts across a meander of the river to the left. From The Sinks, you can continue west on Little River Road for another mile to a pulloff where Meigs Creek flows into Little River. Just upstream, Meigs Creek Falls drops 30 feet. Here, the Little River Lumber Company had a swinging bridge that spanned the river for hauling timber out of the Meigs Creek drainage.

Trailhead: The parking area for The Sinks lies on the north side of Little River Road, 2.1 miles west of Metcalf Bottoms.

Description: Walk to the right from the parking area, following the trail that climbs above The Sinks, where you'll have a couple of good views. People sometimes dive from these rocks into the river—not a good idea. Pass over a ridge and swing left to cross the old meander of the riverbed. Watch for crested dwarf iris in spring and maidenhair fern. The trail climbs a couple of hundred feet to cross a higher ridge, then descends along a south-facing slope.

At 1.0 mile the trail reaches Meigs Creek, which flows down from Meigs Mountain. The trail fords the creek and its tributaries more than fifteen times; there are no footbridges. You might want to wear some older shoes and wade across, but do not cross in high water. Numerous small waterfalls and cascades dot the creek, tucked within banks of rhododendron as it drops down Meigs Mountain. After you've made four crossings, a

The Sinks

10-foot cascade at 1.5 miles scoots over a smooth rock face.

The trail enters a forest of large hemlocks; at 2.0 miles, watch for a large beech tree. Meigs Creek then remains on your right and you continue to cross tributaries from the left. At 3.5 miles the trail ends at a junction in Buckhorn Gap.

To the left, Meigs Mountain Trail (hike 15) leads to Elkmont in 6.0 miles; to the right, the Lumber Ridge Trail (hike 23) leads to Tremont in 4.0 miles.

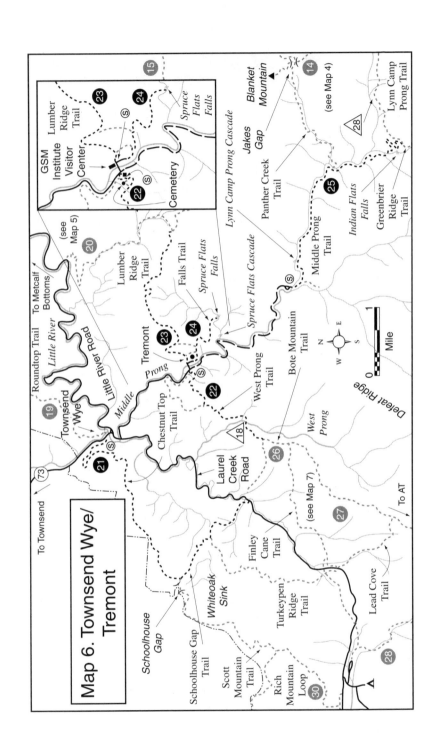

Map 6. Townsend Wye/ Tremont

To Townsend

73

To Metcalf Bottoms

Roundtop Trail

Little River

Townsend Wye

19

20 (see Map 5)

Little River Road

Middle Prong

Tremont

23

24

Falls Trail

Lumber Ridge Trail

Spruce Flats Falls

Chestnut Top Trail

22

West Prong Trail

Spruce Flats Cascade

Lynn Camp Prong Cascade

25

Middle Prong Trail

Panther Creek Trail

Jakes Gap

Blanket Mountain

14 (see Map 4)

28

Lynn Camp Prong Trail

Indian Flats Falls

Greenbrier Ridge Trail

West Prong

Bote Mountain Trail

18

Laurel Creek Road

26

(see Map 7)

27

To AT

Lead Cove Trail

28

Finley Cane Trail

Turkeypen Ridge Trail

30

Rich Mountain Loop

Scott Mountain Trail

Whiteoak Sink

Schoolhouse Gap Trail

Schoolhouse Gap

Defeat Ridge

N
W   E
S

0   1 Mile

GSM Institute Visitor Center inset

Lumber Ridge Trail

23

24

Spruce Flats Falls

S

22

Cemetery

S

15

On the Tennessee side of the park, you can reach the Tremont area via Townsend, "the peaceful side of the Smokies." Townsend was founded as part of the Little River Lumber Company operations, replacing a small community called "Tang." Logs were hauled out of the mountains on the Little River Railroad to a mill in Townsend. The community was named for W. B. Townsend, one of the founders and the manager of the company. In Townsend, you'll see the Little River Railroad Museum where Shay Engine No. 2147, which carried logs out of Elkmont, is on exhibit. The museum rests on the site of the Townsend mill.

As logging was finished in the Elkmont area around 1926, operations were shifted to Tremont, a company town that included shacks for housing, a post office/store, a hotel, and an all-purpose building that served as school, church, and theater. A railroad was built up the Middle Prong of the Little River, linking Tremont with the mill in Townsend. Logging of the Middle Prong watershed continued until 1939 after the national park was established; the company retained the right to harvest trees for fifteen years after the land was sold. By the time the company shut down in 1940, it had produced 560 million board feet of lumber at the Townsend mill.

The Great Smoky Mountains Institute at Tremont, operated by the Great Smoky Mountains Natural History Association, is an active educational facility that offers workshops on the natural and cultural resources of the Smokies.

Getting there: From the northwest along US 321, 17 miles from Maryville, enter Tuckaleechee Cove and the community of Townsend. After the Townsend Visitor Center on the right, US 321 turns left, heading northeast through Wear Cove to Pigeon Forge; continue straight on Hwy. 73, which enters the park in a few more miles. At 0.6 mile from the park boundary, you will reach the Townsend Wye, where Hwy. 73 meets Little River Road (which heads east/left) and Laurel Creek Road (which heads west/right); this is also where the West Prong joins Little River, also forming a wye. Trail parking for the Chestnut Top Trail (hike 21) and access to the Little River lie on the left just before the Townsend Wye.

You can also reach the Townsend Wye from the east via Little River Road, 18 miles west of Sugarlands Visitor Center; when you arrive at the Wye, turn right as if you were leaving the park, and you'll find the Chestnut Top Trail parking area immediately on the right.

To reach Tremont, head west from the Townsend Wye on Laurel Creek Road, paralleling the West Prong of the Little River on the right. In 0.2 mile, after crossing a highway bridge over the Middle Prong just above its confluence with the West Prong, turn left onto the Tremont Road. Cross bridges over the Middle Prong twice more, and at 2.2 miles a side road on the right leads up to a pumphouse for the Great Smoky Mountains Institute and the trailhead for the West Prong Trail (hike 22). Just past this side road turn left on a road leading across a bridge over the Middle Prong into the institute grounds at Tremont. Visitor parking is on the left.

You can also continue to the end of the Tremont Road, past the left turn into the Great Smoky Mountains Institute; watch for a pullout on the right where you can pick up a driving guide to the area. The road becomes gravel as it follows the old railbed up the Middle Prong. In 1.1 miles from the institute watch for a cascade across the river to your left, where Spruce Flats Branch spills down to join the creek. Soon the valley opens up at Spruce Flats where a logging camp was located. The road then crosses a side stream on a one-lane bridge at 2.0 miles and another one-lane bridge over the Middle Prong at 2.4 miles. At 3.2 miles, at the end of the road and the site of the old Tremont community, you reach a turnaround and the trailhead for the Middle Prong Trail (hike 25).

Shay Engine No. 2147, Little River Railroad

21 | CHESTNUT TOP AND SCHOOLHOUSE GAP TRAILS

Distance: 6.3 miles one way
Difficulty: Moderate
Elevation change: 1,100 feet
Season: Year-round
Cautions: None
Connections: Roundtop Trail, Scott Mountain Trail, Turkeypen Ridge Trail, Bote Mountain Trail

Attractions: The first half mile of the Chestnut Top Trail is an outstanding wildflower walk in spring. On a sunny mid-April day, my group counted more than 40 species of blooming plants, including Solomon's seal, purple phacelia, white erect trillium, rue anemone, chickweed, violets, toothwort, foamflower, spring beauty, cinquefoil, lousewort, and crested dwarf iris. Beyond the wildflowers, this hike heads up Chestnut Top Lead to Schoolhouse Gap. An old road, originally the Anderson Turnpike, later Schoolhouse Gap Road, and now the Schoolhouse Gap Trail, passes through the gap. Schoolhouse Gap received its name when children walked up the road through the gap to school in Townsend.

Trailhead: Parking for the Chestnut Top Trail lies on Hwy. 73 on the left just before the Townsend Wye; you must then cross the road to pick up the trail. From this parking area you can reach the Roundtop Trail (hike 19) by fording Little River to the east; enter the river only at low water. To run a shuttle, for this hike, turn right (west) on Laurel Creek Road and proceed 3.7 miles to parking for the Schoolhouse Gap Trail on the right.

Description: The Chestnut Top Trail begins an immediate climb from the road. On this excellent wildflower trail, watch for a large display of fire pink at 0.2 mile and large patches of bishop's cap at 0.3 mile. At 0.5 mile the trail enters a rhododendron thicket and rounds a point with a view of the valley of Rush Branch, a tributary of Little River. You'll also see Townsend through the trees. The trail now passes through a drier pine and laurel forest. At 1.2 miles, top Chestnut Top Lead, a ridge leading down from Chestnut Top to the west. The trail crosses over to stay on the south slope as the ridge hooks back to the west. The trail then gradually ascends to the highest point on the trail at 2.4 miles.

The trail descends to Bryant Gap at 3.1 miles, at the boundary of the park; you'll find a boundary marker set in the ground. The trail then ascends to a confrontation with Chestnut Top, a tall, steep-sided knoll standing atop the ridge. Fortunately the trail skirts to the left rather than climbing the knoll and descends to end at a junction with Schoolhouse Gap Trail at 4.3 miles. To the right, the old road leads 0.2 mile to Schoolhouse

Gap (beside a small house is a gravel road that leads up from Tuckaleechee Cove); straight ahead, the Scott Mountain Trail heads west to the Indian Grave Gap and Crooked Arm Ridge Trails in 3.6 miles (sections of the Rich Mountain Loop, hike 30). Turn to the left onto the Schoolhouse Gap Trail.

Follow the old roadway down the mountain through a mixed pine-hardwood forest. Originally the Anderson Turnpike dropped into White-oak Sink, a cove to your right where several families lived. At 5.2 miles on the right, you'll encounter an unmaintained trail that penetrates the hollow of Whiteoak Sink, which contains a small cave system. Beyond this trail is Dosey Gap and a junction with the Turkeypen Ridge Trail to the right (leading 3.6 miles southwest to an intersection of trails on Laurel Creek Road at Big Spring Cove); stay straight on Schoolhouse Gap Trail and, soon after, follow Spence Branch on the right.

At 6.2 miles watch for a small drop in the creek where the water slides down a slanted rock. Soon after, cross Spence Branch, which flows under the trail in a culvert. Beyond, the branch joins Laurel Creek. The trail bears right to parallel Laurel Creek and Laurel Creek Road. At 6.3 miles, emerge on Laurel Creek Road at a parking area. (From here, you can pick up the Bote Mountain Trail, hike 26, to the left in 0.1 mile and across the road.)

22 | WEST PRONG TRAIL

Distance: 2.7 miles one way
Difficulty: Easy
Elevation change: 650 feet
Season: Year-round
Cautions: Long footbridge
Connections: Bote Mountain Trail

Attractions: This pleasant walk takes you down to the West Prong of the Little River. The first logging for the Little River Lumber Company occurred along the West Prong; an old railroad bed ran along the creek. The company later shifted operations to Elkmont. Camping is available at West Prong Campsite (18).

Trailhead: At 2.2 miles on the Tremont Road, just before the Great Smoky Mountains Institute, turn to the right toward the pumphouse and bear to the right into a parking area. Ahead and left, a path leads up to a junction with the unmarked Dorsey Branch Trail to the right; take the path to the left up to the pumphouse, behind which the West Prong Trail begins.

Description: The trail bears left and uphill to a fork where a side trail to the right leads 0.1 mile past a cemetery bounded by a wooden fence; stay on the main trail to the left, and curve to the right in an ascent of Fodderstack Mountain. At 0.3 mile, reach a junction with the other end of the cemetery trail, which ascends steeply from the right.

The West Prong Trail ascends along the slope of Fodderstack, crossing drainages at the head of steep hollows. At 1.0 mile, reach a junction with the other end of the Dorsey Branch Trail to the right (it becomes faint in places as it circles back to the trailhead, making it difficult to find your way); stay straight on the West Prong Trail.

At 1.2 miles cross a steep, rocky drainage that is the upper reaches of Spicewood Branch. The trail then levels across Fodderstack Mountain without ever attaining the

West Prong

summit, up to your left. At 1.3 miles descend, swinging around a point at 1.6 miles where you have a view to the right of distant ridges.

Continue to descend through rhododendron, rockhopping a shallow stream with a small cascade to the left and dropping into the hollow of the West Prong. At creek level, the trail turns to the right to cross a small stream on rocks and pass through the West Prong Campsite (18) to a long footbridge over the cascading stream at 2.0 miles.

Across the footbridge stay straight, then turn to the right downstream and watch for the trail turning up to the left; it's easy to miss the trail among the paths made by campers and by anglers of rainbow trout; the West Prong is a popular fly-fishing stream. The trail ascends the slope of Bote Mountain, curving left through the head of a hollow and ending at a junction with the Bote Mountain Trail at 2.7 miles.

To the right the Bote Mountain Trail (hike 26) leads 1.2 miles to Laurel Creek Road. To the left, the Bote Mountain Trail connects with the AT in 5.7 miles.

23 | LUMBER RIDGE TRAIL

Distance: 4.0 miles one way
Difficulty: Easy
Elevation gain: 1,200 feet
Season: Year-round
Cautions: None
Connections: Falls Trail, Meigs Mountain Trail, Meigs Creek Trail

Attractions: This pleasant route up Mill Ridge provides access from Tremont to Elkmont and Metcalf Bottoms trails.

Trailhead: At 2.2 miles on the Tremont Road, turn left to cross a bridge over the Middle Prong into the Great Smoky Mountains Institute at Tremont. Turn left into the parking area in front of the visitor center. From here, walk up the road and, where the paved road curves right, take the gravel road straight ahead. It ascends to a dormitory, where you turn left across the grassy lawn just before the building; the trailhead lies at the edge of the woods.

Description: The Lumber Ridge Trail heads left to begin an ascent along the northwest slope of Mill Ridge. In just a few yards, a faint path to the right that's part of the complex of trails around the institute leads 0.2 mile to the Falls Trail (hike 24); stay straight. At 0.1 mile curve to the right to swing through a hemlock-filled hollow. Mountain laurel blooms in late May and early June. At 0.4 mile, the trail swings to the right across a shoulder of the ridge through exposed rock. Traverse a shelf with the valley below and a rock wall to the right. At 0.5 mile, the trail turns to the right up the valley of Pigpen Branch, which you may be able to hear below. At 0.7 mile at a junction, a side trail to the right descends Mill Ridge to a junction with the Falls Trail in 0.5 mile; stay straight.

As you continue to ascend Mill Ridge, the trail crosses over the ridgeline and turns in to cross the headwaters of Pigpen Branch. The trail continues along the side of the ridge, crossing small streams and drainages that angle down the slope. The point at which Mill Ridge joins Lumber Ridge is virtually indistinguishable, but you'll bear right and reach a gap on Lumber Ridge at 2.4 miles. The names "Mill" and "Lumber" reflect a time when the Little River Lumber Company had a company town at Tremont and cut timber all over the area. The trail now descends to cross a saddle ridge connecting Lumber Ridge with Meigs Mountain and ascends to end at a junction of trails at Buckhorn Gap on a shoulder of Meigs Mountain.

To the left, the Meigs Creek Trail (hike 20) descends along Meigs Creek to The Sinks on Little River Road in 3.5 miles. Straight ahead, the Meigs Mountain Trail (hike 15) passes the Curry Mountain Trail (hike 16) in 1.9

miles (it descends to Metcalf Bottoms on Little River Road) and continues east to the Jakes Creek Trail (hike 14) out of Elkmont in another 4.1 miles.

24 | FALLS TRAIL

Distance: 1.0 mile one way
Difficulty: Moderate
Elevation change: 250 feet
Season: Year-round
Cautions: Steep and rocky descent to falls
Connections: Lumber Ridge Trail

Attractions: This hike begins at the Great Smoky Mountains Institute at Tremont, which occupies a flat, open area called "Walker Fields," named for Will Walker, who lived here through the turn of the century. Until near the end of his life, Walker refused to sell any land to the Little River Lumber Company, which is probably why the Middle Prong was the last to be logged. This was also the site of a CCC camp after establishment of the park. This little-known trail out of the institute grounds is frequented by student groups at Tremont and leads to Spruce Flats Falls, which drops through a several-step cascade 60 feet into a plunge pool.

Spruce Flats Falls

Trailhead: At 2.2 miles on the Tremont Road, turn left to the Great Smoky Mountains Institute and then left again into the parking area in front of the visitor center. Walk up the paved road into the Tremont complex; a gravel road to the left gives access to the Lumber Ridge Trail (hike 23), but stay on the paved road. At the end of the pavement in 0.2 mile, the trail begins.

Description: Walk up steps into the woods and turn left uphill. At 0.1 mile at a junction with a path going straight that circles back above the institute buildings, turn up to the right on the Falls Trail. At a water tank that serves the institute, the trail switchbacks left to continue the climb. At 0.2 mile at another junction, the path going straight connects with the Lumber Ridge Trail (hike 23) in 0.5 mile; turn up to the right again.

The Falls Trail continues its ascent, passing a rock outcrop on the left and offering a view to the right up to Thunderhead Mountain on the crest of the Smokies. In early fall, the trees along the ridgelines turn color first, drawing red lines down the slope of the mountain.

The trail hugs the side of Mill Ridge with the Middle Prong far below. Cross two rocky drainages that are the headwaters of Bull Branch, a tributary of Middle Prong. At 0.8 mile, the trail curves left around the end of Mill Ridge, following the Middle Prong as it meanders through the mountains. The trail then bears right and descends through rocks and exposed tree roots to a last steep descent to Spruce Flats Falls. Spruce Flats Branch continues on down the mountain to join the Middle Prong in the valley below.

25 | MIDDLE PRONG TRAIL

Distance: 4.1 miles one way; to Lynn Camp Prong Cascades, 0.3 mile one way; to Indian Flats Falls, 3.7 miles one way
Difficulty: Moderate
Elevation gain: 2,700 feet; to Indian Flats Falls, 2,600 feet
Season: Year-round
Cautions: Rough unofficial paths to falls
Connections: Panther Creek Trail, Miry Ridge Trail, Jakes Creek Trail, Greenbrier Ridge Trail, Lynn Camp Prong Trail

Attractions: This hike passes through the site of Tremont, the last of the logging towns of the Little River Lumber Company. The Middle Prong, a beautiful stream with deep pools and spillways, is a popular trout fishing stream. The first half mile of the Middle Prong Trail follows the cascading Lynn Camp Prong; farther up the mountain the trail follows Indian Flats Prong to a significant waterfall.

Trailhead: Begin at the end of the Tremont Road, 5.4 miles from Laurel Creek Road.

Description: The Middle Prong Trail begins on a substantial metal bridge over Lynn Camp Prong, just above where the Lynn Camp and Thunderhead Prongs join to create the Middle Prong. To the right from the bridge, you can see the confluence of Thunderhead Prong. Look to your left over the bridge railing down to the creekbed to see the concrete foundations of the water-powered generator that supplied electric power to the Tremont community.

Just beyond the bridge the railbed forks, with the right fork headed up Thunderhead Prong; the Middle Prong Trail takes the left fork, following Lynn Camp Prong upstream. The Tremont store and post office stood in the fork of the two railbeds. Up the trail, you will pass the site of the doctor's office on the left and then, across the creek, the site of the Tremont hotel, a two-story building that had twenty-two rooms. No sign of the hotel remains other than the nonnative English ivy growing up trees that stand at the site.

The trail continues up the old railbed, now a gravel road. In spring watch for crested dwarf iris, rue anemone, trillium, and squirrel corn. A rock bluff lines the right side of the trail where the railbed was hewn out of the slope. A small avalanche has strewn boulders across the trail. Walk around a large block that separated from the slope and slipped down onto the railbed.

At 0.3 mile lies Lynn Camp Prong Cascade, where the creek slides into a pool. Up the trail, a more expansive view shows the upper part of the cascade, a long glide down bare rock, and the final plunge. On up the creek, at

Cadillac on Middle Prong Trail

Lynn Camp Prong

0.5 mile you'll see another series of cascades; a side path down to the base gives you a look upstream to an upper falls, from which the water stair-steps down to a final drop where the creek splits into three streams. Far-ther up the trail, the stream drops over ledges in the rocky creekbed. Soon after, look for an old abutment on both banks of the stream, the site of a bridge, or perhaps a splash dam where logs were held in a pond and then released downstream.

On up the road, watch for Marks Creek joining Lynn Camp Prong on the other side of the creek. At 1.6 miles, apples fall in the trail in late sum-mer from surrounding trees that inhabit a former orchard. A clearing to the right with a small stream was probably where the house stood. At 1.7 miles, a path on the right leads to the rusting hulk of an old car, a Cadillac aban-doned when the CCC worked this area. You cannot see the car from the trail because of an earthen berm. Blue-fringed phacelia blankets the area in spring, especially around the car skeleton.

At 2.3 miles, reach a junction with the Panther Creek Trail to the left (it fords Lynn Camp Prong and heads up to Jakes Gap, hike 14, in 2.2 miles); continue straight. Watch for a brick chimney in the woods on the left at 2.7 miles. Then walk up to a terraced open area that was a small camp along the rail line or perhaps a loading area.

The railbed curves to the right at 2.9 miles and soon after curves back left as the trail continues uphill. In both curves, the roadway continues straight ahead for a distance, which provided room for the engine and loaded cars to negotiate the turns. Encountering such a curve, the engineer would pull straight ahead into the turnaround area until the back of the train cleared the curve. He would then back the train downhill until the next curve, where he would continue backing into the turnaround until the front of the train cleared the curve. He could then continue downhill moving forward.

Lynn Camp Prong turns to the west, and now the railbed parallels the Indian Flats Prong tributary. At 3.1 miles watch for an old washtub on the right sitting beside a spring, now dried up. Then the trail drops off the railbed to the left to cross a wide bridge over Indian Flats Prong. Bear to the right upstream and rejoin the railbed, where it once crossed the creek on a wooden bridge that has collapsed and now molders under a covering of bright green moss.

Up the railbed, reach a turn to the left at 3.3 miles near the bottom of Indian Flats Falls, but here you can barely see the stream. Continue on the road away from the creek. At 3.5 miles, switchback right and continue up to a switchback left at 3.6 miles. At the turn, look for a footpath to the right that leaves the road to edge along the rock bluff and drop through rocks to the side of Indian Flats Prong in 0.1 mile. Here the stream makes four falls of water as it stair-steps down the mountain, a grand sight. The 20-foot upper falls stands to your left, the second and third falls are below to the right, and the fourth is out of sight on down the mountain. The Middle Prong Trail continues up, switching back to the right again and reaching its end at a junction at 4.1 miles.

To the left, the Lynn Camp Prong Trail turns up another switchback and connects with the Miry Ridge Trail (hike 14) in 3.7 miles. Straight ahead, the Greenbrier Ridge Trail continues out a spur of the railbed and eventually gains the crest of the Smokies at a junction with the AT in 4.2 miles. (You can make a good backpack loop by heading up the Greenbrier Ridge Trail to the AT, then turning northeast to the Miry Ridge Trail and going down that trail to the Lynn Camp Prong Trail, and then back to this junction, a loop of 12.0 miles, for a total trip of 20.2 miles from the Middle Prong trailhead.)

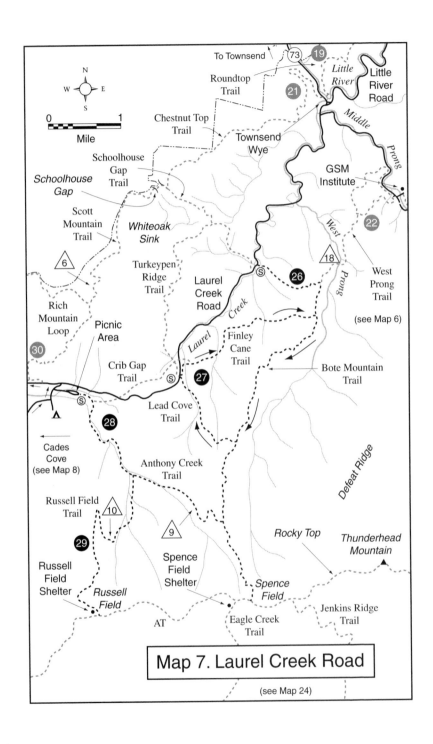

Map 7. Laurel Creek Road

(see Map 24)

From the Townsend Wye, Laurel Creek Road heads west to Cades Cove, providing the only road access to this popular area. Several trails lead off the road for hikes to the crest of the Smokies and for pleasant loop walks.

Getting there: From the Townsend Wye, head west onto Laurel Creek Road, which parallels the West Prong of the Little Pigeon River, crossing the Middle Prong just above its confluence with the West Prong. At 0.2 mile, you will pass the turn into Tremont. Laurel Creek Road soon passes through a tunnel and crosses a bridge over the West Prong. The road then follows Laurel Creek, a tributary. On the left at 3.6 miles from the Townsend Wye, there's parking for maybe two vehicles at the trailhead for the Bote Mountain Trail (hike 26). Just 0.1 mile farther up the road lies a parking area on the right for the Schoolhouse Gap Trail, from which you can then walk back down the road to the Bote Mountain Trail. At 5.8 miles from the Wye, there is shallow parking on both sides of the road for several trails.

Passing over a ridge, the road descends into Cades Cove. At 7.5 miles, the Laurel Creek Road ends at a junction with the Cades Cove Loop Road straight ahead; turn left toward the Cades Cove Campground and take an immediate left into the picnic area to access Anthony Creek and Russell Field Trails (hikes 28 and 29).

26 | BOTE MOUNTAIN AND APPALACHIAN TRAILS TO ROCKY TOP

Distance: 7.9 miles one way; to AT, 6.9 miles one way; to Spence Field, 7.2 miles one way
Difficulty: Moderate
Elevation gain 3,860 feet; to AT and Spence Field, 3,375 feet
Season: Year-round
Cautions: Steep ascent
Connections: Schoolhouse Gap Trail, West Prong Trail, Finley Cane Trail, Lead Cove Trail, Anthony Creek Trail

Attractions: The old Bote Mountain Road runs from Laurel Creek Road to the crest of the Smokies with views from Spence Field and Rocky Top. Spence Field, one of the largest balds in the park, is becoming overgrown as the forest reclaims the open area. James and Carolyn Spence, who cleared much of the bald area, grazed livestock here from early spring to

Bote Mountain Trail

late fall. Get here in May and June for mountain laurel blooming pink-white scattered along the ridge. The best views are farther along at Rocky Top, an outcropping of rock on the western edge of the summit of Thunderhead Mountain.

Bote Mountain Road is a continuation, from the Schoolhouse Gap Road, of the Anderson Turnpike, which was sponsored by Isaac Anderson, president of Maryville College, who in the 1830s saw the need for road access into the mountain communities for education and missionary work. When this section of the turnpike was built in the 1830s, Cherokee workers were asked which ridge the road should follow. They pointed to the mountain where an old Indian trail ascended and said something like "vote," as in "We vote for that one." But because they were unable to clearly speak English, the word came out more like "bote," which was taken to be the name of the mountain. The Anderson Turnpike was intended to cross the Smokies into North Carolina, but the road was never completed and the section up the Tennessee side of the mountains was eventually abandoned. Camping is available at the Spence Field Shelter.

Trailhead: The Bote Mountain Trail begins on the left side of Laurel Creek Road, 3.6 miles from the Townsend Wye. There's parking for maybe two vehicles. Just 0.1 mile farther up the road lies the larger Schoolhouse Gap Trail parking area on the right, from which you can walk back down the road to the trailhead.

Description: From Laurel Creek Road, head straight into the woods on the old roadbed to cross a small tributary of Laurel Creek and begin the long ascent to the crest of the Smokies. After a couple of broad curves to the right, reach a junction at 1.2 miles with the West Prong Trail to the left (hike 22, which leads to the Tremont area); continue to the right up the road, with views of the ridge of Bote Mountain ahead. At 1.5 miles reach a junction with the Finley Cane Trail (hike 27) on the right (which leads down to Laurel Creek Road in 2.7 miles); continue straight.

At 2.3 miles, the road swings through a gap in the ridge, and along a more open area, pale purple joe-pye weed and goldenrod bloom in late summer. You'll have a view through the trees to the left across the valley of the West Prong to Defeat Ridge. This mountain ridge running parallel with Bote Mountain was not selected in the vote taken by the workers constructing the road, and so the name.

At 4.0 miles reach a junction with the Lead Cove Trail to the right (hike 27, which drops off to Laurel Creek Road in 1.8 miles); stay straight. At 5.2 miles, reach a junction with the Anthony Creek Trail (hike 28) on the right (which descends to the Cades Cove picnic area in 3.4 miles); again, continue straight.

At 5.7 miles, you reach a turnaround; the road was once maintained to this point. Continue straight up the ridge along an old washed-out roadbed, and reach the mountain crest and the end of Bote Mountain Trail at its junction with the AT at 6.9 miles (to the right, in 0.1 mile the Eagle Creek Trail turns down the mountain to the Spence Field Shelter in 0.2 mile).

Turn left on the AT to get to the bald areas of Spence Field. A knoll at 7.2 miles offers views along the crest. From the knoll, the AT passes a junction with the Jenkins Ridge Trail to the right; stay straight to climb steeply up another knoll, drop through a swag, and then climb steeply to Rocky Top at 7.9 miles. You'll have panoramic views. To the east, you can see the AT winding up to the summit of Thunderhead Mountain, which is covered with heath, so you do not get a view from the peak.

27 FINLEY CANE, BOTE MOUNTAIN, AND LEAD COVE TRAILS

Distance: 7.0-mile loop
Difficulty: Moderate
Elevation change: 1,360 feet
Season: Year-round
Cautions: Creek crossings, rocky footing, steep ascent
Connections: Turkeypen Ridge Trail, Crib Gap Trail

Attractions: This loop hike offers a pleasant woodland walk with patches of yellow fringed orchid in August. To hike the loop clockwise, head up the Finley Cane Trail, named for a family that owned land in the region and for the cane that still grows in places along Laurel Creek. Then turn up a 2.5-mile section of the Bote Mountain Trail (hike 26), and complete the loop on Lead Cove Trail. The name comes from lead ore once mined in the area, and so the pronunciation should be "led" rather than "leed."

Trailhead: On the southeast side of Laurel Creek Road at 5.8 miles from the Townsend Wye lie the trailheads for Lead Cove Trail and Finley Cane Trail. (The Turkeypen Ridge trailhead stands on the northwest side of the road.)

Description: Head left down the Finley Cane Trail, which parallels the road, with Sugar Cove Prong flowing to your right. The trail soon crosses the creek and heads through a forest of many small hemlocks. At 0.1 mile reach a junction with the Crib Gap Trail to the left (it follows Sugar Cove Prong and passes under Laurel Creek Road through a short tunnel, intersecting with the Turkeypen Ridge Trail); continue straight on the Finley Cane Trail.

Soon after, pass a large sinkhole to the left that's part of Big Spring Cove; here the trail turns to the right to head away from the road. At 0.2 mile, make a muddy crossing of a small stream and ascend into a rhododendron thicket.

The trail descends to a rockhop crossing of the two streams of Laurel Cove Creek at 0.6 mile, then begins a gentle ascent of Bote Mountain. The trail traverses the slope, swinging into coves and hollows, crossing drainages, and passing over ridges running down from the main ridgeline. At 1.7 miles, the trail drops into Finley Cove to cross a drainage that flows down the hollow. After crossing another drainage, ascend to a junction with the Bote Mountain Trail at 2.7 miles (to the left, it descends to Laurel Creek Road in 1.5 miles); turn right and ascend the roadway lined with rhododendron.

Pass below a peak of the mountain and continue ascending. In mid-August watch for the yellow or orange blooms of yellow fringed orchid. At 5.2 miles reach a junction with the Lead Cove Trail (straight ahead, the Bote

Mountain Trail continues to the AT in 2.9 miles); turn right to head down the Lead Cove Trail.

The trail crosses several drainages that form the headwaters of Laurel Cove Creek as you descend the slope of Bote Mountain. At 5.9 miles, enter a rhododendron thicket that forms a long tunnel over the trail. Descending, approach Sugar Cove Prong on your left. At 6.6 miles, the trail passes a broken-down chimney where a cabin once stood. Then rockhop Sugar Cove Prong and pass through more rhododendron to descend into the forest of young hemlocks that you encountered at the beginning of this hike. The trail drops off to the right to reach a lower level, where you'll walk out to Laurel Creek Road to complete the loop at 7.0 miles.

28 | ANTHONY CREEK AND BOTE MOUNTAIN TRAILS

Distance: 5.1 miles one way
Difficulty: Moderate
Elevation gain: 2,920 feet
Season: Year-round
Cautions: Steep ascent
Connections: Crib Gap Trail, Russell Field Trail, Appalachian Trail

Attractions: This combination of the Anthony Creek and Bote Mountain Trails takes you to the AT for panoramic views from Spence Field. This route can be combined with the AT west to Russell Field and then the Russell Field Trail (hike 29) for a loop out of the Cades Cove Picnic Area. Camping is available at Cades Cove Campground, Anthony Creek Campsite (9), and the Spence Field Shelter.

Trailhead: Where Laurel Creek Road ends at a junction with the Cades Cove Loop Road (which goes straight ahead), turn left toward the Cades Cove Campground and take an immediate left into the picnic area. At the far end lies the trailhead. If you're backpacking, you must park at the campground store or the parking area at the beginning of the loop road; there is no overnight parking in the picnic area.

Description: The Anthony Creek Trail heads up a gravel road through a mixed forest of hemlock, hardwood, and rhododendron with Anthony Creek on your right. In 0.3 mile reach a junction with the Crib Gap Trail to the left (it heads toward Laurel Creek Road, reaching the Turkeypen Ridge Trail in 1.6 miles); stay straight.

Pass through a horse camp and, at 0.5 mile, cross Anthony Creek on a road bridge. On the other side, a road to the right leads to a water supply

Spence Field

station; stay straight. From here up, the road becomes more rocky. At 0.8 mile, cross the creek on a footbridge and again on a road bridge at 1.0 mile. The trail then ascends more steeply, crossing the Left Prong of Anthony Creek on a footbridge at 1.4 miles, just above its confluence with Anthony Creek. At 1.5 miles lies a junction with the Russell Field Trail (hike 29) to the right (which ascends to the AT in 3.5 miles); turn left to stay on the Anthony Creek Trail.

Ascend along a footpath that follows a less obvious old road. At 2.0 miles the trail crosses Anthony Creek on a footbridge. As you continue your ascent with Anthony Creek now on your right, notice a small waterfall at 2.1 miles. Rockhop a small stream and reach the Anthony Creek Campsite (9) at 2.8 miles on Anthony Creek. The trail turns left, away from the creek, in a steep climb up Bote Mountain to end at a junction at 3.4 miles with the Bote Mountain Trail (to the left, the trail follows the route of old Bote Mountain Road for 5.2 miles to Laurel Creek Road); turn right onto the Bote Mountain Trail (hike 26). Ascend to the mountain crest and reach a junction with the AT at 5.1 miles.

To the left, the AT reaches Spence Field in 0.3 mile and, for more views, continues on 0.7 mile to Rocky Top on the side of Thunderhead Mountain. To the right, the AT passes a junction with the Eagle Creek Trail in 0.1 mile (which leads to the Spence Field Shelter in 0.2 mile). The AT traverses an area along the mountain crest that was once also part of Spence Field, but has now become overgrown, and continues west over a knoll to connect with the Russell Field Trail in 2.6 miles for a good 12.7-mile loop hike or backpack out of the Cades Cove Picnic Area.

29 | ANTHONY CREEK AND RUSSELL FIELD TRAILS

Distance: 5.0 miles one way
Difficulty: Moderate
Elevation gain: 2,400 feet
Season: Year-round
Cautions: Muddy areas
Connections: Appalachian Trail

Attractions: This trail through Russell Field can form part of a loop hike. The field was probably named for Russell Gregory, as was Gregory Bald (see hike 35). While Gregory Bald is being maintained by the Park Service, Russell Field is becoming overgrown. There you'll see the encroaching vegetation that will one day reclaim the open area. Camping is available at Cades Cove Campground, Leadbetter Ridge Campsite (10), and Russell Field Shelter.

Trailhead: Where Laurel Creek Road ends at a junction with the Cades Cove Loop Road (which goes straight ahead), turn left toward the Cades Cove Campground and take an immediate left into the picnic area. At the far end lies the trailhead. If you're backpacking, you must park at the campground store or the parking area at the beginning of the loop road; there is no overnight parking in the picnic area.

Description: Walk 1.5 miles up the Anthony Creek Trail (see hike 28) to the start of the Russell Field Trail (to the left, the Anthony Creek Trail heads up to the Bote Mountain Trail in 1.9 miles); turn to the right onto the Russell Field Trail.

Cross a couple of trickles and then a wide, shallow stream that is a tributary of the Left Prong of Anthony Creek. At 2.1 miles, cross the Left Prong itself on a footbridge. The trail crosses another tributary on stepping stones as you begin an ascent of Leadbetter Ridge.

At 2.3 miles, pass the Leadbetter Ridge Campsite (10) on the right and continue the ascent. Along this section, you'll pass through a forest of large trees—buckeyes, poplars, magnolias, and, farther up, oaks, maples, and hemlocks. At 3.2 miles, at the top of Leadbetter Ridge, turn left to ascend less steeply along the ridgeline.

You'll have glimpses of Cades Cove through the trees to the right at 4.4 miles. At 4.7 miles, the trail passes Russell Field, a grassy area encircled by trees that are slowly invading and will eventually reclaim the bald. Pass a spring and at 5.0 miles reach the end of the trail at a junction with the AT at the Russell Field Shelter.

To the right, the AT leads to the Mollies Ridge Shelter in 2.5 miles. To the left, the AT reaches Spence Field and a junction with the Bote Mountain Trail in 2.6 miles. Using the Bote Mountain and Anthony Creek Trails (hike 28) to return to the Cades Cove Picnic Area makes a good 12.7-mile loop hike or backpack.

CADES COVE

Cades Cove

In the formation of the Smokies, folding and faulting caused older rock to be pushed over younger rock to the northwest. In places, erosion opened coves in the older rock above to reveal the younger rock below. These openings, such as Cades Cove, act as "windows" through which we can see the younger rock buried beneath the mountains. This younger rock is primarily limestone, which makes for rich, fertile valleys.

When white settlers arrived in Cades Cove around the time of Calhoun's Treaty of 1819, the Cherokees called the cove *Tsiyahi*, or at least had a settlement here by that name. The cove came to be called "Cades Cove" after Chief Kade, a Cherokee chief about whom little is known. The local Cherokees continued to frequent the area, but they were gradually pushed out by the whites who steadily arrived. Fields were cleared; houses and barns were built. By 1850 there were 671 people living in a hundred households.

There was postal service as early as 1833. A telephone line entered the cove in 1896. Goods were brought in from Maryville or Knoxville, first over old Indian trails, then roads, including the Indian Grave Gap and Rich Mountain Roads across Rich Mountain from Tuckaleechee Cove. Cooper Road to the west and Parson Branch Road to the southwest linked with roads outside the cove that led to Maryville. The first car, a Cadillac, arrived in 1915. The present Laurel Creek Road was completed in 1922.

When land purchases began to be made for the national park in 1928,

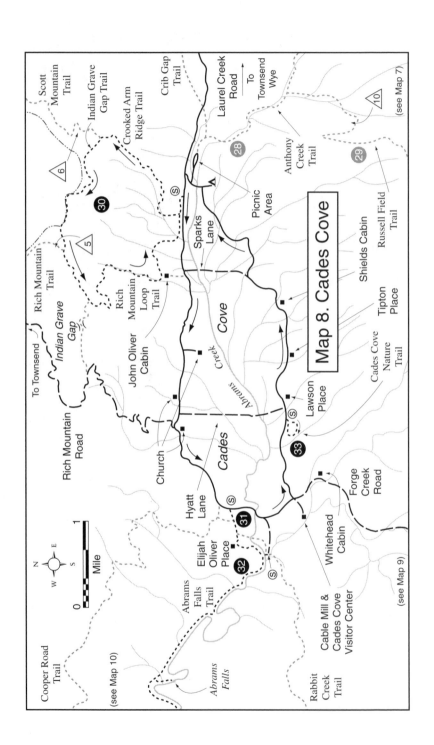

Map 8. Cades Cove

Cades Cove from Rich Mountain Road

most people sold immediately. Many of the homes were destroyed before a decision was made to preserve the human history of the cove. Today, twenty-eight structures remain that represent life during the period from 1825 to 1900.

Getting there: Follow Laurel Creek Road from the Townsend Wye west 7.5 miles to Cades Cove. At the beginning of the 11-mile one-way Cades Cove Loop Road, a left turn leads past the picnic area and into the campground. Continue straight past a sheltered exhibit and parking area, where you can pick up a booklet guide to the cove, and begin the one-way road through Cades Cove. The trailhead for the Rich Mountain Loop (hike 30) is immediately on the right. At 1.0 mile, the graveled Sparks Lane to the left crosses the cove to the other side of the Cades Cove Loop Road; continue straight. Parking for the John Oliver Cabin lies at 1.1 miles; later, a gravel road to the left leads to the Primitive Baptist Church. The Methodist Church is on the right at 2.6 miles. Hyatt Lane at 3.0 miles is another gravel road that cuts to the left across the cove; continue straight.

At 3.1 miles, the Missionary Baptist Church stands on the left, and the one-way Rich Mountain Road to the right ascends Cades Cove Mountain. (The road is closed in winter. A mile up is a grand view on the right of Cades Cove, with the Methodist Church nestled among trees; the road continues on to pass over Rich Mountain and descend into Tuckaleechee Cove.)

Continuing straight on the loop road, pass the Cooper Road Trail (hike 36) on the right at 4.4 miles, one of the principal routes out of the cove in the 1800s. The loop road then makes a steep descent and curves left to cross the lower end of the cove. At 4.6 miles lies parking on the left for the Elijah Oliver Place. At 5.1 miles, a gravel road to the right leads 0.5 mile to the Abrams Falls trailhead.

Continue on the Cades Cove Loop Road to a four-way junction at 5.6 miles. The loop road continues to the left. Straight ahead is the gravel Forge Creek Road, which leads to the Gregory Bald trailheads. A right turn leads into the Cable Mill area, where you'll find the Cades Cove Visitor Center. The John Cable Grist Mill, built in 1868, has an overshot waterwheel on Mill Creek. The Gregg-Cable House, built in 1879, was probably the first framed house in Cades Cove.

From the four-way junction, the Loop Road continues east, headed back toward the upper end of Cades Cove. Soon a gravel road on the right leads to the Cable Cemetery. Then at 6.0 miles along the Loop Road lies trailhead parking on the right for the Cades Cove Nature Trail.

From here, pass a large frame barn on the left and in a steep descent reach the other end of Hyatt Lane at 6.8 miles. Just beyond sits the Dan Lawson Place on the right; the house, built around 1856, is a mixed construction of log cabin with wood framed additions and a brick chimney. The newer house up to the left is occupied at this writing by a person who has a permit to graze cattle in the cove.

The Tipton Place lies at 7.5 miles. Built soon after the Civil War by Hamp Tipton, the house is also mixed construction. A blacksmith shop stands on the right before the house. The building below the house was the smokehouse. Across the road on the left is a double-pen corn crib and behind it a cantilever barn that is a 1968 reconstruction, using some old materials from several barns. Cantilever barns were used mainly in east Tennessee; the structure allowed a wagon to pull under the top floor so hay and feed could be easily loaded and unloaded, and animals could take shelter under the overhang.

At 8.0 miles, watch the field to the left for an old barn in a state of collapse. The Carter Shields Cabin stands on the right at 8.4 miles. Sparks Lane rejoins the road at 8.8 miles. A horse trail crosses the road where the stables sit in the woods to the left. At the end of the Loop Road at 11.0 miles, you reach a T junction. To the right lie the ranger station, a country store, and Cades Cove Campground. Turn left and shortly pass by the picnic area and return to Laurel Creek Road.

30 | RICH MOUNTAIN LOOP

Distance: 8.5-mile loop
Difficulty: Moderate
Elevation change: 1,900 feet
Season: Year-round
Cautions: Steep ascent, creek crossings, muddy spots in spring
Connections: Scott Mountain Trail, Rich Mountain Trail

Attractions: This loop combines the Crooked Arm Ridge, Indian Grave Gap, and Rich Mountain Loop Trails to take you high for views into Cades Cove and to skirt Cerulean Knob where the Rich Mountain fire tower once stood; only the foundation remains. Surrounding trees prevent the knob from having a good view. Rich Mountain got its name when John C. Post prospected for gold in 1846; he found only small amounts of copper and iron. From Rich Mountain, the trail descends to the John Oliver Cabin. John Oliver, along with his wife, Lucretia, and their baby daughter, Polly, are believed to be the first white settlers in Cades Cove. They came in the fall of 1818 while it was still Cherokee land and stayed first in an Indian hut, but soon built a crude shelter. They nearly starved that first winter, but the Indians brought them pumpkin to eat. In 1820 they built the cabin that can be seen on this hike. Camping is available at Cades Cove Campground, Turkeypen Ridge Campsite (6), and Rich Mountain Campsite (5).

Trailhead: Park at the sheltered exhibit at the beginning of Cades Cove Loop Road and walk down the road a few paces to the trailhead on the right.

Description: Ascend slightly and then parallel the road on a level trail through a pine and mixed-hardwood forest. Broad and worn, the trail swings away from the road, passing a field on the left where a mound stands, which has been determined not to be of Indian origin. Then rockhop Crooked Arm Branch, which is usually shallow, and reach a junction at 0.5 mile (the Rich Mountain Loop Trail straight ahead is your return route); turn to the right onto the Crooked Arm Ridge Trail, hiking this loop counterclockwise.

The trail ascends, swinging left away from the stream and then circling back to Crooked Arm Branch. Watch for a picturesque 30-foot cascade at 0.7 mile. At 0.8 mile ford the creek on stepping stones.

The trail continues to ascend through several switchbacks; in rainy seasons, horse traffic may churn the trail into a muddy mess. At 1.1 miles, emerge onto the ridgeline of Crooked Arm Ridge, which leads left up Rich Mountain. The trail follows the ridge, continuing to ascend with switchbacks. Turn left at an open strip in the forest that was once the path for powerlines that ran down to the campground; the lines are now underground. At a switchback to the right at 1.9 miles, you'll have a long view of Cades Cove; the rich farming valley is surrounded by mountains.

At 2.5 miles, a side trail to the right leads up a knoll to a good lunch spot and descends to rejoin the main trail, which then ascends to a junction at 2.6 miles with the Scott Mountain Trail on the right (the Turkeypen Ridge Campsite, 6, lies 0.3 mile down this trail); go straight ahead on the Indian Grave Gap Trail.

Climb and level off on the old Indian Grave Gap Trail, which swings left below the ridge of Rich Mountain. In spring, you'll see white serviceberry blooms, which were gathered to decorate the mountain churches for the spring revival service; the tree has red berries in late summer.

The trail passes a gap where you can see north to Tuckaleechee Cove and ascends to the top of Rich Mountain at 4.1 miles. (A steep side trail to the right leads to the top of Cerulean Knob.) Continue down the road, de-

Cades Cove from Crooked Arm Ridge

scending to a junction at 4.3 miles with the Rich Mountain Trail to the right (this trail follows the long ridge of Rich Mountain to the northwest and connects with the Rich Mountain Road out of Cades Cove; just down from the junction lies the Rich Mountain Campsite, 5, which has few level places since it rests in a hollow; water flows down the hollow from the campsite); stay straight on the Indian Grave Gap Trail.

Descend left to pass below the two peaks of Double Mountain, a ridge running down from Rich Mountain. At 5.3 miles reach a junction with the Indian Grave Gap Trail continuing to the right (it passes through Indian Grave Gap to the Rich Mountain Road; it's not known for sure if there are any graves actually in the gap); turn down to the left on what is now the Rich Mountain Loop Trail (although this section of trail does not form a loop but is only part of the loop).

You'll soon have a good view across Cades Cove to the Smokies crest, and then another view. The trail descends steeply with several switchbacks, crossing streams and eventually following Marthas Branch down to the John Oliver Cabin at 7.6 miles. You'll probably encounter a number of sightseers who have walked up from Cades Cove Loop Road. The present cabin was built by the Olivers in 1820. A pile of stones just to the north is thought to be the chimney of their first shelter.

When you've finished exploring, take the well-trod path behind the cabin. The trail crosses a couple of small streams on stepping stones and closes the loop at the junction with the Crooked Arm Ridge Trail at 8.0 miles. Continue going straight; it's 0.5 mile back to the parking area.

31 | ELIJAH OLIVER PLACE TRAIL

Distance: 1.0 mile one way; to Elijah Oliver Place, 0.5 mile one way
Difficulty: Easy
Elevation gain: 50 feet
Season: Year-round
Cautions: None
Connections: Abrams Falls Trail

Attractions: The Elijah Oliver Place has a collection of buildings representative of a pioneer homestead. Elijah Oliver was the son of the first settlers, John and Lucretia Oliver (see hike 30). Elijah bought the two-story log cabin here in 1865. The house, built by John Anthony, is a hewn-log structure on a stone foundation. The kitchen, which was once the Herron home, was brought here and attached to the living quarters in back. Nearby stands the smokehouse. The buildings of the homesite are located in typical fashion, with the springhouse higher than the other structures to ensure clean water and the barn the farthest down the slope. Here the Olivers lived close to the land, raising nearly everything they needed.

Elijah Oliver Cabin

Trailhead: Parking for the Elijah Oliver Place is on the left at 4.6 miles from the beginning of Cades Cove Loop Road; the trail is on the right side of the road. To run a shuttle, drive 0.5 mile farther along the loop road to the turnoff for the 0.5-mile side road to the Abrams Falls Trail (hike 32) parking area.

Description: A broad graveled path leads west through open areas that were once fields in the Cades Cove community. Pass over a rise and descend to cross a small, shallow stream that flows across the trail. A path to the right is the Wet Bottom Trail, which connects with the Cooper Road Trail (hike 36); continue straight. In an open area on the right at 0.2 mile stands a large barn made of wood siding, one of the more modern structures in the cove.

Beyond the barn and into the woods, the path to the left is the continuation of the Wet Bottoms Trail (it fords Abrams Creek and ends at the Abrams Falls trailhead); stay straight to reach the Elijah Oliver Place at 0.5 mile.

In the hollow behind the cabin, the springhouse uphill from other structures protected the water souce and provided a cool place for storing food. The barn, a three-pen structure, is farthest down the slope. Also downhill stands a smaller structure, probably a pig barn. At the bottom of the clearing, look for the continuation of the trail. At 1.0 mile you will reach Abrams Creek on your left and a junction with the Abrams Falls Trail. To the left, a long bridge crosses Abrams Creek to the parking area for Abrams Falls. You can either return as you came, or return via a shuttle vehicle.

32 | ABRAMS FALLS TRAIL

Distance: 4.2 miles one way; to Abrams Falls, 2.5 miles one way
Difficulty: Easy
Elevation change: 200 feet
Season: Year-round
Cautions: Creek crossings, slippery rocks at base of falls
Connections: Rabbit Creek Trail, Wet Bottoms Trail, Elijah Oliver Place Trail, Hannah Mountain Trail, Hatcher Mountain Trail

Attractions: One of the most popular hikes in the park, this easy trail follows Abrams Creek, the primary drainage for Cades Cove. Just downstream from the trailhead, Mill Creek joins Abrams. This trail passes Abrams Falls on the way to its junction with Hannah Mountain Trail (hike 37). Abrams Creek, one of the best trout streams in the park, is named for

Cherokee Chief Oskuah of the Chilhowee Village that was once on the Little Tennessee River to the southwest. "Abraham," or just "Abram," was a name the chief adopted in later life. Cades Cove was part of the land that was claimed by Abram and the Cherokees under him. Some say Cades Cove was named for Chief Abram's wife, whose name was Kate.

Trailhead: At 5.1 miles from the beginning of the Cades Cove Loop Road, after passing the path up to the Elijah Oliver Place, turn to the right on a gravel road that leads 0.5 mile to the Abrams Falls trailhead.

Description: From the parking area, the trail passes through trees to a junction with the Rabbit

Abrams Falls

Creek Trail to the left, which fords Mill Creek, and the unmarked Wet Bottom Trail to the far right, which heads toward the Cooper Road Trail; bear right to cross the bridge over Abrams Creek. On the far side of the bridge, the Elijah Oliver Place Trail turns to the right toward the Elijah Oliver Place; turn left on the Abrams Falls Trail.

Walk through rhododendron and at 0.2 mile cross a side stream on a footbridge. The trail begins a gradual ascent to top Arbutus Ridge at 1.0 mile in a gap 200 feet above the creek. At this point the creek has taken a wide meander around the end of the ridge, nearly doubling back on itself.

The trail descends, crossing side streams and reaching creek level again at 1.7 miles. Climb a small ridge at another creek meander and descend to cross Wilson Creek on a footbridge. At 2.5 miles, a side trail leads left to Abrams Falls, recrossing Wilson Creek on another footbridge. Abrams Falls spills 20 feet over a rock ledge. The waterfall kicks up a spray that keeps the rocks at the base of the falls wet and slippery. The pool below the falls is one of the largest in the park and is often used for wading. At times of high water, it is dangerous to enter the stream; at no time should children be allowed in the creek without an adult.

The more isolated remainder of the Abrams Falls Trail continues along Abrams Creek, climbing a couple of ridges and crossing Kreider Branch and Oak Flats Branch. At 4.2 miles the trail ends at a junction.

The Hannah Mountain Trail (hike 37) to the left fords Abrams Creek, a difficult crossing at high water. The Hatcher Mountain Trail (hike 36) continues straight 0.2 mile to the Little Bottoms Trail, which leads 3.1 miles to the Abrams Creek Campground.

33 | CADES COVE NATURE TRAIL

Distance: 0.5-mile loop
Difficulty: Moderate
Elevation change: 170 feet
Season: Year-round
Cautions: Steep ascent and descent
Connections: None

Attractions: This short nature loop introduces the tree species of Cades Cove. You'll see trees that the pioneer settlers in Cades Cove used to construct a home and make a living: white pine for furniture, yellow poplar for logs to build a cabin, sugar maple for syrup, dogwood for wooden tools, chestnut oak for tannin to cure hides into leather, white oak for baskets.

Trailhead: Parking for the nature trail is on the right at 6.0 miles along the Cades Cove Loop Road.

Description: Begin by walking to the right, headed up an old roadbed. Soon, turn left up steps to walk a path that loops across the side of the mountain. Along the way stand white pine, yellow poplar, sugar maple, dogwood, chestnut oak, and white oak. A steep climb reaches the top of the loop at 0.25 mile; then it's downhill past other useful forest species: sourwood for honeybee habitat and sled runners, lichens for yellow dye, and a berry patch for eating. The trail drops back to the old roadbed. Turn right to close the loop and return to the parking area.

PARSON BRANCH ROAD

Near the lower end of Cades Cove from the Cable Mill area, Forge Creek and Parson Branch Roads connect Cade Cove to the roads outside the west end of the park. They also provides access to trails to Gregory Bald. The highland meadow of Gregory Bald is the largest grassy bald in the park and is famous for its late-June display of hybridized azaleas. The tall shrubs bloom red-orange, pink, peach, yellow, and white.

Balds, which are not bare rock but, rather, openings in the forest, are of two types in the national park—heath balds, such as the summit of Brushy Mountain (see hike 40), and grassy balds, such as Gregory. The grassy balds are covered by a thick grass with interspersed shrubs and small trees, while heath balds are covered with an impenetrable thicket of shrubs. Heath balds occur mostly in the northeast quadrant of the park; grassy balds are found mostly in the western half.

The origin of the balds remains a mystery; fire, landslides, grazing, insect infestation, and exposure to the winds and cold temperatures have probably all played a part. Grazing maintained the grassy balds once they

Gregory Bald

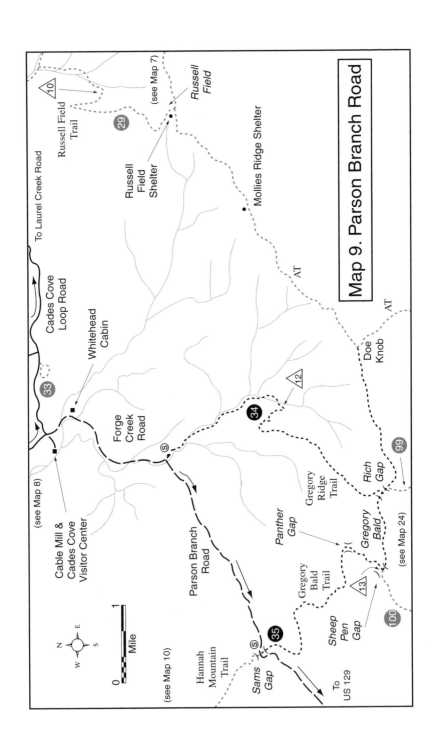

Map 9. Parson Branch Road

Hybrid azalea

were created. In historic times, cattle and sheep were pastured on the balds in summer. Before that, bison and elk may have kept the balds open. And thousands of years before that, megaherbivores may have grazed these mountaintops—mastodons, mammoths, musk oxen, ground sloths. During past ice ages, these peaks may have stood above tree line, and then succeeding generations of grazing animals kept them open until the time when the park was established.

The grassy balds are rapidly being invaded by trees now. Gregory Bald, though, has been designated an experimental research subzone within the park, where the Park Service is using various techniques, including manual clearing, to prevent the forest from claiming the open area. The only other maintained bald is Andrews on the North Carolina side of the park (see hike 62). Gregory Bald is the most diverse of the grassy balds, having more rare plant species.

The bald is named for Russell Gregory. Although he was active in the Cades Cove community and had a house there, Gregory loved the wilderness and built a stone cabin atop the bald that came to bear his name. Each summer he tended his own and others' cattle; he was known for his skill in summoning the herds to the top of the bald by blowing a horn.

During the Civil War, Gregory was loyal to the Union, though his son Charles had joined the Confederacy. With the young men gone to war, Gregory organized and led the women, children, and old men to confront a band of Confederate raiders who had been pillaging the area during 1864. Unknown to Gregory, Charles was part of the raiding party. No one was killed in the confrontation in which the raiders were turned back, but some of them returned in the night and murdered Russell Gregory in retaliation. Gregory is buried in the cemetery of the Primitive Baptist Church.

Getting there: From the four-way junction near the Cable Mill area 5.6 miles from the beginning of the Cades Cove Loop Road, drive straight ahead down the gravel Forge Creek Road. Cross bridges over small creeks and pass the Henry Whitehead Cabin, built in 1898 of sawn logs with a brick chimney, now reconstructed. The road crosses four bridges over Forge Creek, named for the Cades Cove Bloomery Forge built by Daniel D. Foote in 1827 in this lower end of the cove; the forge was used for smelting iron. At 2.2 miles from the Cades Cove Loop Road is the turnoff on the right for the Parson Branch Road. Past the Parson Branch Road turnoff, you will reach the end of Forge Creek Road at 2.3 miles at a turnaround and trailhead parking for the Gregory Ridge Trail (hike 34).

The Parson Branch Road leads to Sams Gap at the beginning of the Gregory Bald Trail (hike 35). Once you are on this 8-mile one-way gravel road, you must continue to its end where it emerges from the park onto US 129. Along the way you'll ford creeks over concrete spillways, which are usually not a problem, but after a recent rain can be daunting. In a downpour, you should not drive the road at all. Parson Branch Road is closed in winter.

34 | GREGORY RIDGE TRAIL

Distance: 4.9 miles one way
Difficulty: Moderate
Elevation gain: 2,700 feet
Season: Year-round
Cautions: Steady ascent, footbridges
Connections: Gregory Bald Trail, Long Hungry Ridge Trail

Attractions: This hike passes through old-growth woods up Gregory Ridge to Rich Gap. Each fall here, the region's farmers corralled stock that had been left to graze on the mountain balds during the summer. One account says there were as many as 1,600 cattle along this crest during the season. Gregory Bald lies a half mile to the right from Rich Gap on the Gregory Bald Trail (hike 35). Camping is available at Forge Creek Campsite (12) and nearby at Sheep Pen Gap Campsite (13).

Trailhead: Parking is at the end of Forge Creek Road, 2.3 miles from Cades Cove Loop Road.

Description: From the trailhead, bear to the right uphill as the Gregory

Ridge Trail leads around the base of a ridge and heads upstream along Forge Creek. Bower Creek flows down to join Forge Creek on the other side at 0.3 mile. Then cross Forge Creek on a footbridge.

At 0.7 mile the trail enters an old-growth forest that stretches for a mile, hosting massive oaks, eastern hemlocks, yellow poplars, and basswoods. This forest was once dominated by the American chestnut. Decaying, moss-covered stumps and chestnut logs, remnants of the chestnut blight, lie along the trail. The trail steepens and at 1.7 miles turns left over Forge Creek on a footbridge, then climbs the slope passing between two colossal poplars before crossing the creek on a footbridge again at 1.8 miles. At 1.9 miles the Forge Creek Campsite (12) lies beside the creek.

Above the camp, the trail curves right and ascends Gregory Ridge. At 2.2 miles walk around large, smooth boulders offering a resting place before you continue your climb through a drier forest of pine, laurel, and maple along with sourwood, which signals the coming of fall with its dark red foliage. The remainder of the trail is a steady climb up Gregory Ridge. At 4.9 miles the trail ends at Rich Gap on the crest of the Smokies.

To the left the Gregory Bald Trail leads past the Long Hungry Ridge Trail (hike 99) in 0.1 mile and reaches the AT at Doe Knob in 2 miles. To the right the Gregory Bald Trail leads 0.5 mile to Gregory Bald (elevation gain from the gap is 320 feet), famous for flowering azalea in late spring. Descending from the bald another 0.5 mile, you reach the Sheep Pen Gap Campsite (13). Straight ahead in Rich Gap, an unmaintained path leads to Moore Springs, where there was once a backcountry shelter.

35 | GREGORY BALD TRAIL

Distance: 7.1 miles one way; to Gregory Bald, 4.5 miles one way
Difficulty: Moderate
Elevation gain: 2,170 feet
Season: Year-round (access road closed in winter)
Cautions: Steep in places
Connections: Hannah Mountain Trail, Wolf Ridge Trail, Gregory Ridge Trail, Long Hungry Ridge Trail, Appalachian Trail

Attractions: This is the shortest route and one of the most frequently used trails to Gregory Bald. If you're headed up to see the azalea, first check with the park visitor centers to learn if they've had reports of the azalea blooming, so you won't be disappointed. Camping is available at Sheep Pen Gap Campsite (13).

Trailhead: On Forge Creek Road at 2.2 miles from the Cades Cove Loop Road, turn to the right on the Parson Branch Road. In 3.2 miles, reach parking in Sams Gap on Hannah Mountain for the Gregory Bald Trail and the Hannah Mountain Trail (which leads northwest to Scott Gap, where it intersects the Rabbit Creek Trail in 7.6 miles). The Gregory Bald Trail begins on the other side of the road from the Hannah Mountain Trail and heads southeast up Hannah Mountain.

Description: The trail climbs moderately through a forest of mixed hardwood, hemlock, and pine. At 1.6 miles, pass through a gap and ascend into a more mature forest with a few large oaks and yellow poplars. At 1.8 miles, the trail crosses a ravine, and just after, a huge poplar stands on the right.

At 3.2 miles in Panther Gap, the trail turns south to climb more steeply and reach the crest at Sheep Pen Gap at 4.0 miles. There was a pen here for gathering sheep after a summer of grazing on the balds. The Sheep Pen Gap Campsite (13) rests in the gap. Straight ahead is the Wolf Ridge Trail (hike 100), which leads to Parson Bald, much smaller than Gregory Bald; turn left.

At 4.5 miles top the mountain and walk out into the open grassy area of Gregory Bald. The field of blooming azalea is something to behold at the end of June. The Gregory Bald Trail then continues west over the bald to a junction at 5.0 miles with the Gregory Ridge Trail (hike 34) to the left; continue straight.

Just 0.1 mile beyond is another junction, with the Long Hungry Ridge Trail (hike 99) to the right (it drops off the crest into North Carolina); continue straight. Along the Smokies crest, the Gregory Bald Trail ends at the AT near Doe Knob at 7.1 miles.

To the left, the AT goes past Mollies Ridge Shelter to Russell Field in 4.9 miles. To the right, the AT goes through Sassafras Gap to Fontana Dam in 6.8 miles.

ABRAMS CREEK

Abrams Creek Campground rests beneath towering pines and hemlocks beside Abrams Creek. This remote area near the western boundary of the park offers solitude, a respite from the bustle you may encounter at other trailheads and campgrounds. Two loops can be hiked by combining trails out of the Abrams Creek access.

Getting there: From Maryville, take US 411/129 southwest 4.0 miles and turn left on US 129 where it separates from US 411. In 18 miles pass the western end of the Foothills Parkway and reach the turn for the Abrams Creek Ranger Station on Happy Valley Road. Or from Fontana Village, head northwest on Hwy. 28 to US 129 and turn right to continue northwest to the Abrams Creek turnoff. From either direction, when you have gone 6.0 miles along Happy Valley Road, turn right to enter the Abrams Creek access.

36 | COOPER ROAD, HATCHER MOUNTAIN, AND LITTLE BOTTOMS TRAILS

Distance: 10.9-mile loop
Difficulty: Moderate; strenuous on Little Bottoms Trail
Elevation change: 880 feet
Season: Year-round
Cautions: Stream crossings, boggy areas, rough footing, several ascents and descents
Connections: Gold Mine Trail, Cane Creek Trail, Beard Cane Trail, Abrams Falls Trail

Attractions: This trail combination provides a loop day hike. The Cooper Road Trail also leads to Cades Cove. The trail traces the old Cooper Road, which was the main road providing access for the Cades Cove settlers to this western end of what is now the park and roads that could be traveled to Maryville. The road was laid out by Daniel Foote, an early entrepreneur on the western end of Cades Cove, and was constructed in the 1830s by Joe Cooper. Near the park boundary, the Cooper Road Trail passes the Gold Mine Trail; gold, although of low quality, was actually found in this area. Camping is available at Abrams Creek Campground, Cooper Road Campsite (1), and Little Bottoms Campsite (17).

Trailhead: From the turnoff at Happy Valley Road, drive 1 mile to the Abrams Creek Ranger Station, and continue into the campground to the

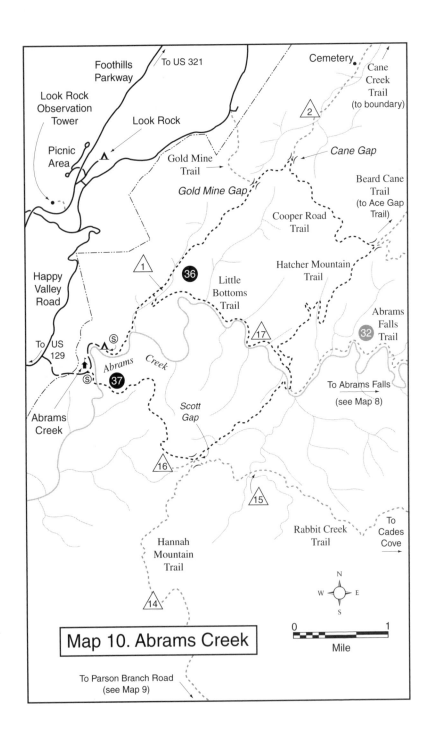

Foothills Parkway

To US 321

Look Rock Observation Tower

Look Rock

Picnic Area

Cemetery

Cane Creek Trail (to boundary)

⚠2

Cane Gap

Gold Mine Trail

Gold Mine Gap

Cooper Road Trail

Beard Cane Trail (to Ace Gap Trail)

Hatcher Mountain Trail

Happy Valley Road

⚠1

●36

Little Bottoms Trail

⚠17

●32 Abrams Falls Trail

To US 129

Ⓢ

▲

Abrams Creek

Ⓢ ●37

To Abrams Falls (see Map 8)

Abrams Creek

Scott Gap

⚠16

⚠15

Rabbit Creek Trail

To Cades Cove

Hannah Mountain Trail

N
W ✦ E
S

⚠14

Map 10. Abrams Creek

0 ▬▬▬▬▬ 1
Mile

To Parson Branch Road (see Map 9)

end of the road at the trailhead. If you are not camping, or during winter when the road beyond the ranger station is closed, you must park just past the ranger station and walk 0.4 mile to the trailhead in the campground.

Description: The Cooper Road Trail follows Abrams Creek upstream on your right through a beautiful hemlock and pine woods. At 0.5 mile, the trail curves left away from Abrams Creek. Rockhop Kingfisher Creek. In another 20 yards the trail crosses this tributary again and then crosses a small stream. At 0.9 mile reach a junction with the Little Bottoms Trail to the right (this is your return route); continue straight.

The Cooper Road Trail continues to the Cooper Road Campsite (1) at 1.2 miles. At 1.6 miles cross Kingfisher Creek again. Then climb to Gold Mine Gap and a junction at 2.6 miles with the Gold Mine Trail to the left (it follows an old road 0.8 mile to the park boundary, connecting with roads outside the park); stay straight.

The Cooper Road Trail descends steeply through a pine woods; watch for the stand-up leaves of galax and trailing arbutus growing close to the ground. At 3.2 miles reach a junction in Cane Gap with the Cane Creek Trail to the left (it follows an old road 2.1 miles to the park boundary, where it dead-ends; along the way you ford Cane Creek to reach the Cane Creek Campsite, 2, in 0.6 mile, and ford twice more to access the Buchanan Cemetery at 1.3 miles); stay to the right.

The Cooper Road Trail swings through Cane Gap and climbs steeply. At 3.4 miles reach the ridgeline and continue ascending to an intersection on Hatcher Mountain at 4.9 miles. To the left, the Beard Cane Trail heads north (passing the Beard Cane Campsite, 11, in 1.0 mile and the Hesse Creek Campsite, 3, in another 2.5 miles to connect with the Ace Gap Trail, which heads east to the Rich Mountain Road). Straight ahead, the Cooper Road Trail continues toward Cades Cove (emerging on the Cades Cove Loop Road in 5.6 miles). Turn to the right (southeast) on the Hatcher Mountain Trail.

Ascend through a pine woods and then descend along the ridge of Hatcher Mountain. At 6.5 miles along this loop hike, the trail swings to the right off the ridge and drops into a rhododendron cove to cross Oak Flats Branch. Ascend across a drier slope of pine and laurel, and descend to a junction at 7.7 miles with the Hatcher Mountain Trail to the left (it continues 0.2 mile to connect with the Abrams Falls and Hannah Mountain Trails); turn to the right on the Little Bottoms Trail

This rugged, narrow path hugs the slope above Abrams Creek. The exposed roots and jagged rocks make the footing difficult. At 7.8 miles descend to cross a small stream and then make a steep ascent. At 8.0 miles, the trail crosses a rough slide area. Then descend to creek level and the Little Bottoms Campsite (17) at 8.4 miles.

The trail now passes through a bottomland, crossing Mill Branch, a tributary of Abrams Creek. Where the trail once again becomes a narrow, rocky footpath beside Abrams Creek, cross Buck Shank Branch. At 9.5 miles, the trail ascends over a ridge and down the other side to cross Kingfisher Creek and reconnect with the Cooper Road Trail at 10.0 miles. Turn left to walk back to the Abrams Creek Campground at 10.9 miles (and the additional 0.4 mile to get back to the parking area near the ranger station, if necessary).

37 | RABBIT CREEK, HANNAH MOUNTAIN, AND LITTLE BOTTOMS TRAILS

Distance: 8.1-mile loop
Difficulty: Moderate; strenuous on Little Bottoms Trail
Elevation change: 1,000 feet
Season: Year-round
Cautions: An initial steady climb, difficult stream ford
Connections: Abrams Falls Trail, Hatcher Mountain Trail

Attractions: This combination of trails provides another loop day hike. There is no bridge over the wide Abrams Creek at the junction of the Abrams Creek and Hannah Mountain Trails, so you will get your feet wet at this crossing. If the water level is high, this is a dangerous crossing and should not be attempted; you can always come back another day. Camping is available at Abrams Creek Campground, Scott Gap Campsite (16), and Little Bottoms Campsite (17).

Trailhead: From the turnoff at Happy Valley Road, drive 1.0 mile to the Abrams Creek Ranger Station. Just before the ranger station, the Rabbit Creek trailhead is on the right. There's a little parking here, but the main parking is past the ranger station.

Description: From the trailhead, walk down a dirt lane to its end, and turn right. Hop across a small stream and parallel Abrams Creek downstream to a long footbridge over the creek. This footbridge is occasionally washed away by high water; if it is gone when you get here, you must ford the creek, but attempt the ford only at low water. Across the creek, bear left to stay on the trail.

The Rabbit Creek Trail gently ascends to an old homesite with a tumble-down chimney and, in spring, blooming daffodils. At 0.3 mile, begin a steeper climb that takes you above Abrams Creek on your right. The trail follows an old roadway that once led over Pine Mountain toward Cades trail finally tops the ridge, curves left, and descends to Scott Gap at 2.5 miles. Straight ahead, the Rabbit Creek Trail continues east 5.1 miles to Cades Cove. To the right, the Hannah Mountain Trail leads 7.6 miles southwest to Parson Branch Road across from the beginning of the Gregory Bald Trail (hike 35). A sharp right takes you 0.1 mile to the Scott Gap Campsite (16). To complete the loop walk, at Scott Gap turn left on the Hannah Mountain Trail.

You are now on a footpath, having left the old roadbed at Scott Gap. At

Abrams Creek crossing

3.6 miles, the trail begins a descent into the Abrams Creek watershed. Cross a small stream lined with galax at 3.8 miles. Where a watercourse flows down the mountain on your left, watch for a small waterfall at 4.0 miles; the water slides over a large boulder and drops a few feet. Round a point and descend steeply to Abrams Creek at 4.2 miles. There is no bridge over the creek, which is wide here, so you will get your feet wet on this ford. Do not attempt this crossing if the water level is high. Once you are across the creek, you will reach a junction with the Abrams Falls Trail to the right (it leads to Abrams Falls in 1.7 miles); turn left onto the Hatcher Mountain Trail.

Ascend steeply and at 4.5 miles reach a junction with the Hatcher Mountain Trail to the right (it leads to Beard Cane Trail and Cooper Road Trail, hike 36); bear left on the Little Bottoms Trail.

Follow the description for hike 36 to complete the remaining 3.6 miles back to the Abrams Creek Ranger Station.

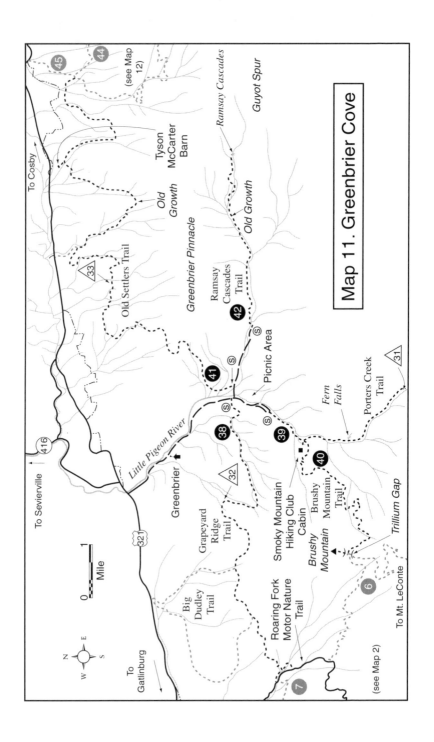

Map 11. Greenbrier Cove

GREENBRIER COVE

Settlers arrived in Greenbrier Cove in the early 1800s. Eventually a community formed, one of the largest in the Smokies, with post office, school, and country store. Remnants of the settlements can still be found—rock walls, gravestones, barns, and cabins. Trails out of the area lead to some of the best attractions the park has to offer: the finest collection of old settlement remains, the tallest waterfall accessible by trail, and perhaps the best wildflower walk.

Getting there: From Gatlinburg drive east on US 321; at 5.9 miles turn south into Greenbrier. The road follows the Little Pigeon River and becomes gravel in 1 mile. Shortly, pass the Greenbrier Ranger Station on the right, and at 3.2 miles, a left-hand road leads to trailheads for Old Settlers and Ramsay Cascades Trails. The road straight ahead passes a picnic area on the left that was the site of a CCC camp and reaches a loop turnaround at 4.0 miles. (The road continues on for another mile but is blocked by a gate and is now the Porters Creek Trail.)

38 | GRAPEYARD RIDGE TRAIL

Distance: 7.6 miles one way
Difficulty: Moderate
Elevation change: 1,000 feet
Season: Year-round
Cautions: Numerous stream crossings
Connections: Big Dudley Trail, Baskins Creek Trail

Attractions: Wildflowers are abundant on this trail that leads past old homesites and along Injun Creek, where you'll find the remains of an old steam engine that was used to run a sawmill and for log skidding during lumbering operations in the area. Using a cable, a skidder dragged logs down the mountain slope. As the engine was being relocated, it accidentally rolled over into the creek and was just left where it lay. Interestingly, the creek is spelled "Injun," as in "Indian," rather than "Engine," apparently a misinterpretation upon hearing the word "engine" spoken.

Trailhead: Just before the left turn to Ramsay Cascades, the Grapeyard Ridge Trail begins on the right side of the road. You'll find parking for a couple of vehicles on the left. You can run a shuttle vehicle to the old Jim Bales Place on the Roaring Fork Motor Nature Trail (see Getting There

Wrecked engine on Injun Creek

for Cherokee Orchard/Roaring Fork Motor Nature Trail). Keep in mind the Roaring Fork Motor Nature Trail is closed in winter.

Description: The Grapeyard Ridge Trail ascends on an old roadbed through old homesites and rock walls and past other roadways; stay with the well-traveled path. Top a ridge at 0.5 mile and descend into a hollow, crossing a couple of small streams and then Rhododendron Creek to follow it upstream, intertwining with the creek and its tributaries. In spring, wildflowers carpet this bottomland—spring beauty, mayapple, trillium, toothwort, chickweed, rue anemone.

The trail ascends over James Ridge through James Gap at 2.7 miles, then descends to cross Injun Creek. Just below the crossing, in the creek lies the old steam engine, turned over and left to the elements. The trail descends with Injun Creek stair-stepping down on your right. At 3.2 miles, a side trail on the right leads 100 yards to the Injun Creek Campsite (32; this path follows an old roadway back toward the Greenbrier Ranger Station); continue straight.

Cross a small stream and begin a climb up Grapeyard Ridge, named for the wild grapes that grew in the area. With switchbacks, the trail reaches a pass at 3.8 miles and winds along the slope of the ridge to then climb more gradually, finally topping the ridge at 4.2 miles. In spring, the slopes are clothed in bloodroot, rue anemone, spring beauty, trout lily, wood anemone, and toothwort.

Over the ridge, descend and soon switchback left. At 4.8 miles, the trail crosses Dudley Creek amid old stone walls and wildflowers. To the left, a bridge once spanned the stream; the stone footings remain. Follow the old roadbed covered in periwinkle to the right. At 4.9 miles reach a junction with the Big Dudley Trail to the right (it leads to the Smoky Mountain Riding Stables on US 321); turn left to stay on the Grapeyard Ridge Trail.

Top a ridge running north from Mount Winnesoka and descend to a fork in the trail. The right fork circles around to the stables on US 321; take the left fork.

At 6.3 miles the trail crosses Indian Camp Branch, a tributary of Roaring Fork; watch for large patches of wild geranium. At 6.5 miles the trail crosses a small stream where the slope above is covered in trout lily. The trail then passes over a small ridge to cross a tributary of Roaring Fork that pours through a bowl of boulders. Continue descending; white erect trillium stands on the slopes. Reach a junction at 7.5 miles where you can turn left and descend to a fording of two branches of Roaring Fork Creek and emerge on the Roaring Fork Motor Nature Trail in 0.1 mile; to complete the Grapeyard Ridge Trail, turn right at the junction.

The trail descends with the Roaring Fork to your left. Piles of stone up the slope to the right mark a former field. Then pass through a break in a line of rock and emerge into the old Jim Bales Place with a barn and a smaller corn crib. Farther along and to the right stands a cabin of thick hewn slabs that was the Alex Cole House, which was moved to this location. The trail reaches the Roaring Fork Motor Nature Trail at 7.6 miles. From here, return as you came, take a shuttle vehicle back to the trailhead, or just up the road to the left, across the bridge over Roaring Fork, connect with the Baskins Creek Trail (hike 7).

39 | PORTERS CREEK TRAIL

Distance: 3.7 miles one way; to Smoky Mountain Hiking Club Cabin and Messer Barn, 1.0 mile one way; to Fern Falls, 2.0 miles one way
Difficulty: Easy
Elevation gain: 1,550 feet
Season: Year-round
Cautions: Footbridge crossings
Connections: Brushy Mountain Trail

Attractions: This trail is arguably the best in the Smokies for spring wild-flowers. It also passes the Smoky Mountain Hiking Club Cabin. The hiking club began as a Knoxville YMCA group in the early 1920s. The hikers separated from the YMCA and formally became the SMHC in 1924. In the 1930s, the club constructed this cabin on the site of the Whaley homestead. The nearby Messer Barn was originally the Whaley Barn. The original Whaley frame house had been torn down, so the club used timbers from two Whaley log cabins to build the hiking club cabin. When the club's special use permit expired in 1975, the park took over the cabin and now maintains it as an historic structure. The hiking club currently maintains 100 miles of the Appalachian Trail through the park and into the Nantahala National Forest in North Carolina. Camping is available at Porters Flat Campsite (31).

Trailhead: On the Greenbrier Road, continue straight past the left turn for Ramsay Cascades to the end of the road at the loop turnaround at 4.0 miles from US 321.

Description: The first mile of this hike is on the gravel road that parallels Porters Creek, one of the tributaries of the Little Pigeon River. In March and April look for the blooms of bloodroot, trillium, mayapple, trout lily, chickweed, phlox, spring beauty, toothwort, showy orchis, and crested dwarf iris.

At 0.6 mile, moss-covered piles of stone mark the small farming community that once existed here; this cove on up the mountain was called "Porters Flat" after some early settlers. Through a break in a rock wall on the right, stone steps lead up to a house site with foundation stones and a fireplace. At 0.8 mile, the trail crosses Long Branch on a bridge. Another set of steps on the right leads to a cemetery nestled under hemlocks. The trail soon crosses a footbridge over a side creek. At 1.0 mile, the road ends in a loop turnaround. At the upper end, the Brushy Mountain Trail (hike 40) heads toward Trillium Gap, and, to the right, a side trail passes the Messer Barn and a springhouse to reach the Smoky Mountain Hiking Club Cabin; go straight ahead from the road turnaround to continue on the Porters Creek Trail.

Smoky Mountain Hiking Club cabin

Ascend through a mature woods of hemlock and hardwoods. At 1.5 miles a long footbridge carries you across Porters Creek. Beyond this crossing, step into a spring garden of white fringed phacelia with sprinklings of trillium, geranium, Dutchman's-breeches, squirrel corn, foamflower, and bishop's cap.

At 2.0 miles, the trail crosses a small stream with Fern Branch Falls to the left, a delicate waterfall sliding down rocks for most of its 45-foot length. Beyond, look for displays of white trillium, geranium, and plantain-leaf sedge among big trees. The trail enters the Porters Flat Campsite (31) at 3.7 miles, passing beyond to soon meet the creek. At one time, the trail crossed the creek and continued in a steep, difficult ascent to join the AT at the Smokies crest, but the route is no longer maintained.

40 | PORTERS CREEK AND BRUSHY MOUNTAIN TRAILS

Distance: 5.9 miles one way
Difficulty: Moderate
Elevation gain: 2,500 feet
Season: Year-round
Cautions: Stream crossings, steady climb
Connections: Trillium Gap Trail

Attractions: With displays of spring wildflowers, this trail reaches the summit of Brushy Mountain. On this mountain bald, the plant ensemble includes rhododendron, laurel, sand myrtle, blueberry, huckleberry, and, closer to the ground, wintergreen (also called teaberry), galax, and trailing arbutus. The plant oils of wintergreen are used for flavoring. The dense growth of this heath family crowds out trees, and so the summit is covered in brush, for which the mountain is named. When I was last there, two peregrine falcons wheeled and cavorted in the air—perhaps those that were reintroduced and now nest on Mount LeConte; in 1997 they produced the first hatchlings in fifty years within the national park.

Trailhead: On the Greenbrier Road, continue straight past the left turn for Ramsay Cascades to the end of the road at the loop turnaround at 4.0 miles from US 321.

Description: Walk 1.0 mile up the Porters Creek Trail to the end of the old road near the Smoky Mountain Hiking Club Cabin (hike 39). At the top of the road turnaround, the Brushy Mountain Trail begins toward the right. The trail ascends, crossing a small stream and passing a stone wall on the left, a reminder that people once lived here in Porters Flat. Patches of wildflowers in spring include violets, cinquefoil, toothwort, buttercup, trillium, chickweed, wood and rue anemones, and golden ragwort. At 1.4 miles, an old homesite has a collapsed chimney and a washtub, if it is still there. The trail follows a creek on the right, crossing at 1.9 miles.

At 2.0 miles, watch for large patches of wild geranium and then on the left a pile of stones that could be another collapsed chimney or just rocks picked up and piled in one place to get them out of a cornfield. The trail moves into a drier forest with rhododendron, laurel, and galax. A rock at 3.2 miles offers a step up to view the summit of Brushy Mountain ahead and the long northeast ridge of Mount LeConte. Amid the showy white flowers of hobblebush, or viburnum, at 3.7 miles cross Trillium Branch, which flows down through moss-covered boulders to join Cannon Creek below, a tributary of Porters Creek.

Partridgeberry lines the trail through a quiet hemlock woods. Brushy Mountain stands behind you. At 4.1 miles the trail switches right and then the mountain looms ahead through the trees. At 4.3 miles watch for huge hemlocks growing to the right of the trail. At 4.7 miles, fields of spring beauty, scattered trout lily, and squirrel corn decorate the remainder of the trail in early spring. At 5.1 miles, cross Trillium Branch again. At 5.5 miles reach Trillium Gap and a four-way intersection, with the Trillium Gap Trail (hike 6) going straight to descend to the Roaring Fork Motor Nature Trail—closed in winter—or left to the summit of Mount LeConte; turn right.

To reach the summit of Brushy Mountain in another 0.4 mile, ascend on an eroded and rocky trail, entering the heath community of evergreen shrubs on this mountain bald. Mount LeConte looms over your shoulder as you trudge up the mountain. To the right lies Porters Creek Valley.

41 | OLD SETTLERS TRAIL

Distance: 15.9 miles one way; to Noisy Creek spur trail, 8.9 miles
Difficulty: Moderate
Elevation change: 1,200 feet
Season: Year-round
Cautions: Numerous creek crossings, poison ivy in summer
Connections: Grapeyard Ridge Trail, Maddron Bald Trail, Gabes Mountain Trail

Attractions: This fairly moderate lowland path has displays of wildflowers in spring, old-growth forest, and the largest collection of old stone rows, foundations, and chimneys left from former settlements. Camping is available at Settlers Camp Campsite (33).

Trailhead: On the Greenbrier Road, at 3.2 miles from US 321, turn left on the road to Ramsay Cascades. In 0.1 mile, after crossing the second bridge over the Little Pigeon River, find parking and the Old Settlers trailhead on the left. To run a shuttle vehicle to a little past the hike's half-way point, go 11.7 miles east from Gatlinburg on US 321 (5.8 miles east from the Greenbrier turnoff), to the Noisy Falls Way road on the left and the highway bridge crossing of Noisy Creek. A spur trail comes out to the highway just before this point; you can park beside the highway in a grassy area. To run a shuttle vehicle to the end of this hike, see Maddron Bald Trail (hike 45), which adds 1.2 miles to this hike.

Description: The trail begins in a bottomland of hemlock and hardwood, paralleling a small stream on the right. You can still hear the Little Pigeon River on your left. Watch for patches of crested dwarf iris in spring. At 0.3 mile, cross Bird Branch and ascend, passing a rock overhang on the right and crossing a small creek. Topping the rise, the trail descends into a bottomland to cross several small streams amid large patches of wild geranium, crested dwarf iris, foamflower, and phlox in spring. The trail also passes old rock walls, your first sign of the settlements along these lowlands before the park was created.

At 1.2 miles cross Little Bird Branch. The trail then ascends, eventually affording views to the east of Greenbrier Pinnacle with its bare rock walls towering over the valley. Topping the ridge at 1.9 miles, curve right and descend the other side.

The trail crosses Snakefeeder Branch at 2.5 miles; watch for a 6-foot waterfall upstream. Ascend from the branch over another ridge at 2.9 miles to cross a small branch of Soak Ash Creek at 3.5 miles, then the main stem of the creek twice and then a third time at an old homesite on the left, with half a chimney still standing amid scattered rock. Down Soak Ash Creek, reach an open lowland where the trail crosses several small streams and then ascends along an old road to a junction at 4.7 miles with an unmaintained path continuing straight on the old roadbed; turn right to stay on the Old Settlers Trail.

Ascend along another old roadway. Cross Timothy Creek at 5.7 miles and ascend to pass an old homesite at the top of a knoll with a chimney and on the right a small outbuilding, probably a hog pen. The Settlers Camp Campsite (33) at 6.7 miles has an old chimney standing in its midst. Just beyond, the trail crosses Redwine Creek and ascends steeply. Go over a ridge, then descend, joining Ramsay Creek and crossing it five times. Watch for wild geranium at the creek's edge. At 8.3 miles, the trail turns away from the creek on an old roadbed. Pass several rock walls and reach a junction at 8.9 miles with an unmaintained path to the left (it joins Noisy Creek and follows it out to US 321 in 0.3 mile, where you can return to the trailhead with a shuttle vehicle); bear right on another old roadbed to stay on the Old Settlers Trail, paralleling Noisy Creek upstream.

At 9.2 miles, the trail turns left to reach Noisy Creek. A rock-walled bank on the right once held up a house site; on top stands a toppled chimney with an intact fireplace that has a lintel made of two slabs of rock forming an arch over the opening. Fording the creek, the trail continues upstream along the old roadbed; a long rock wall stands on the left. At a homesite at 9.4 miles where a collapsed chimney stands off to the left through the weeds, the trail crosses Noisy Creek and then back again.

Soon the trail ascends steeply into a wooded area to pass over a ridge and drops to cross Tumbling Branch at 9.8 miles. The trail switchbacks up from the creek to enter an old-growth forest of large hemlocks, oaks, and yellow poplars. Watch for a massive thick-bodied poplar on the right at 10.1 miles; others stand up the slope. As you near the top of the ridge, you'll

Chimney on Old Settlers Trail

see the prone hulks of old chestnut trees that long ago succumbed to the chestnut blight.

The trail tops the ridge at 10.4 miles and descends, passing a rock wall where tall phlox blooms in summer, to a crossing of Texas Creek at 10.6 miles. Join an old roadbed descending along the creek. At 11.2 miles notice on your left a long rock wall and a perfectly formed rectangular stack of rocks, not a chimney because there is no opening.

At 11.5 miles, after descending more steeply, encounter an old homesite on the right that had a chimney still standing until the mid-1990s, when a tree fell on it. This is still an interesting place because the home's two fireplaces remain intact. Past the homesite, the trail descends, following an old roadbed to a right turn on another old road at 11.7 miles.

The trail then descends to a bottomland where you cross small streams and ascend to encounter a large rock wall, about 5 feet high and 2 feet thick, at 12.4 miles. The trail bears left along the wall following an old country lane with rock walls on both sides eventually. Watch for more walls beyond the two that parallel the road; this must have been a sizable community at one time. The trail runs right into Webb Creek at 12.7 miles, where you must ford. Just before the ford, you reach a corner in the rock wall on the right where it turns upstream and continues on out of sight.

Across the creek, a 0.1-mile side trail leads left to the Tyson McCarter Barn, built around 1876. (Along an old lane you'll come to a dirt road in 50 yards; turn left and then right to reach the barn sitting at the top of the cove, with the old house site and springhouse below.)

Returning to the main trail, continue upstream. At 12.9 miles, the trail passes over a break in a rock wall and joins another old road bearing right. At 13.6 miles the trail turns left away from Webb Creek, leaving the old road. At the turn you'll see a few logs remaining from a cabin and leftover daylilies. Then descend to a crossing of a small creek you crossed earlier.

The trail climbs to the ridgeline of Snag Mountain at 13.8 miles. Around a point, a view opens to the southeast—Maddron Bald to the left, in the distance the crest of Pinnacle Lead that runs east from Greenbrier Pinnacle, and the main peak of Snag Mountain to the right. The trail descends with switchbacks and stream crossings. At 14.9 miles watch for a 3-foot-high rock wall on the right.

The trail curves right and drops to a rockhop of Dunn Creek at 15.0 miles and then a long footbridge crossing of Indian Camp Creek at 15.4 miles. Turn right to switchback up from the creek. Pass another old homesite and drop to a crossing of Maddron Creek at 15.5 miles. From this crossing, follow an old road until, at 15.7 miles, the trail turns off the road and ascends to end at a junction with the Maddron Bald Trail at 15.9 miles.

Straight ahead lies the Gabes Mountain Trail (hike 44) into Cosby. To the left, the Maddron Bald Trail (hike 45) leads 1.2 miles out to Laurel Spring Road off US 321. To the right, the Maddron Bald Trail continues on to Maddron Bald.

42 | RAMSAY CASCADES TRAIL

Distance: 4.0 miles one way
Difficulty: Moderate
Elevation gain: 2,200 feet
Season: Year-round
Cautions: Creek crossings, boulder passages
Connections: None

Attractions: This popular trail ascends through one of the largest pockets of old-growth forest in the Smokies. The trees include hemlock, yellow

poplar, black cherry, silverbell, yellow and sweet birch, and cucumber magnolia. Ramsay Cascades is a popular destination, so you might have to take your turn standing at the base of the falls to get a good view. At 100 feet, Ramsay Cascades is the tallest waterfall in the park that can be reached by trail; Mill Creek Falls, off-trail in the western part of the park, is reported to be the tallest. Ramsay Cascades and Ramsay Prong get their name from the Ramsays, who in the mid-1800s had a hunting camp of lean-tos in the area.

Trailhead: On the Greenbrier Road at 3.2 miles from US 321, turn left to cross a bridge over the Little Pigeon River and then a bridge over the Middle Prong; pass the trailhead for the Old Settlers Trail. The road crosses the Middle Prong again and in 1.5 miles reaches the trailhead at the end of vehicle access.

Description: Walk up the old road, which swings left to cross the Middle Prong on a wide bridge and turns right to continue upstream. Ascend through large boulders and a forest of hemlock and mixed hardwood. Watch for crested dwarf iris in late spring. At 1.2 miles, the trail crosses a bridge over Ramsay Branch and ascends to a junction at 1.4 miles with the old Greenbrier Pinnacle Trail, which is no longer maintained. Just beyond, the road ends in a turnaround.

The trail continues as a somewhat rocky footpath, soon turning up Ramsay Prong, one of the main tributaries of the Middle Prong. In spring, watch for blooming Dutchman's-breeches and white erect trillium.

Hop a side stream at 2.3 miles and wind down into a small gorge with the creek flowing over boulders and swirling below. A log footbridge takes you across the rushing stream. The trail then ascends through old-growth forest. At 2.5 miles pass between massive yellow poplars, and a third stands to the left, some of the largest trees in the park. At 2.8 miles an opening beside the stream provides a view of an upcoming footbridge across the Ramsay Prong.

Rockhop a branch of Ramsay Prong at 3.0 miles to a virtual island between this branch and the main channel of the creek, and then cross back over the branch. The trail swings away from Ramsay Prong for a time but returns.

The trail narrows and ascends more steeply through boulder passages that in wet weather have a stream running through them. At 3.9 miles, you must rockhop a tributary of Ramsay Prong that in wet weather is the most difficult crossing of the hike. Emerge at Ramsay Cascades, where Ramsay Prong descends Mount Guyot to spill over a ledge and fall as double streams that converge halfway down and cascade into the pool below. There are no trail connections, so you must return as you came.

Crossing Ramsay Prong

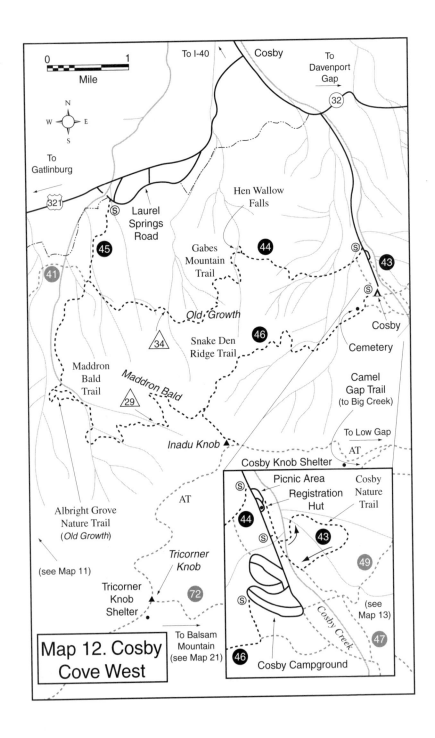

Map 12. Cosby Cove West

COSBY COVE WEST

A large campground nestles in the forest of Cosby Cove. When other campgrounds in the park are full and people are everywhere, remote Cosby is the place to be. Campsites are almost always available, and hikes in the area provide mountain vistas and old-growth forest. A nature trail mingles with Cosby Creek, and a major waterfall is just a moderate walk from the picnic area.

Getting there: From Cosby, which can be reached on US 321 east from Gatlinburg or by taking the Foothills Parkway west from I-40, take Hwy. 32 southeast. At 1.2 miles from Cosby, turn to the right into Cosby Cove. Pass the Gunter Cemetery on the right and reach the picnic area on the left in 2.0 miles. Just beyond the picnic parking is the hikers' parking area. A registration hut stands on the main road just uphill from the hikers' parking. Past the registration hut, the road enters Cosby Campground, which is closed in winter.

43 | COSBY NATURE TRAIL

Distance: 1.0-mile loop
Difficulty: Easy
Elevation change: 120 feet
Season: Year-round
Cautions: Numerous footbridges
Connections: Low Gap Trail

Attractions: This cool, shaded walk crosses nine footbridges. At a house site at about the halfway point, a rock wall to the left once surrounded a garden. You'll see a long rock fence row to the right and then a rock-walled spring in the ground where the family got their water.

Trailhead: Past the Cosby Cove picnic area and registration hut, look for parking for the nature trail on the left, across from a ranger's residence. You can also walk from the picnic area into the hikers' parking area to the Low Gap Trail and walk up to its junction with the nature trail.

Directions: The short path into the woods meets the Low Gap Trail; to the left the trail leads up from the hikers' parking area; turn to the right. With Cosby Creek on your left, the trail passes behind the campground amphitheater and crosses the first footbridge over a branch of Cosby Creek. Where the nature trail leaves the Low Gap Trail, turn left.

Cross another footbridge, and at 0.1 mile cross a long footbridge over the main stem of Cosby Creek. The nature trail turns left down the strip of land lying between two branches of the creek, passing between a large yellow poplar and a huge hemlock. Step over small streams and cross other footbridges as the trail curves right, upstream. Cross another footbridge and reach the house site on the right at 0.5 mile, marked by a collapsed stone chimney. The trail then enters a hemlock wood and reconnects with the Low Gap Trail at 0.7 mile; turn right.

Cosby Nature Trail

Cross a footbridge back over Cosby Creek and then a footbridge over a smaller branch. A path leads left out to the road to provide access from the campground. Continue straight to close the loop and turn left back to the trailhead at 1.0 mile.

44 | GABES MOUNTAIN TRAIL

Distance: 6.6 miles one way; to Hen Wallow Falls, 2.2 miles one way
Difficulty: Moderate
Elevation change: 1,300 feet
Season: Year-round
Cautions: Creek crossings
Connections: Maddron Bald Trail, Old Settlers Trail

Attractions: This trail that passes by Hen Wallow Falls and through old-growth forest is the first leg of one of the best backpacking loops in the park. The falls and Hen Wallow Creek likely got their name from a ruffed grouse wallowing in dust, a common practice of this "wood hen." Camping is available at Cosby Cove Campground and Sugar Cove Campsite (34).

Trailhead: Park in the Cosby Cove Picnic Area, or, if you are backpacking, proceed through the picnic parking to the hikers' parking area just beyond. Walk 100 yards back along the road in the direction from which you entered to find the trailhead on the left. To leave a shuttle vehicle at the beginning of the Maddron Bald Trail, see hike 45; this adds 1.2 miles to this hike.

Description: The Gabes Mountain Trail ascends on a wide rocky path with Rock Creek, a tributary of Cosby Creek, to the right. In 0.25 mile, a side trail to the left leads to the campground; stay right.

Cross Rock Creek on a footbridge at 0.3 mile and pass through a small old-growth forest of large hemlocks and oaks and crowds of rhododendron. The path is lined with partridgeberry, a ground-hugging vine that has double white flowers in spring that develop into a single red berry in late summer and fall. At 0.6 mile, the trail crosses two footbridges over headwater streams of Crying Creek, another tributary of Cosby Creek. At 1.0 mile cross a third stream on a rock bridge and walk up to a junction in Bearneck Cove with an old roadbed to the right that once provided access into this area.

Turn left to ascend along the flank of Snake Den Mountain to the south. Notice the smaller hemlocks; this area was obviously logged at one time, presumably for a field; rocks were stacked into piles to get them out of the way. At 1.7 miles, the trail enters a rhododendron tunnel where the branches reach overhead. When you emerge from the tunnel, bear left. At 1.9 miles, the trail passes a rock outcropping where water splashes down and runs across and under the trail. Later, a long rock wall leans toward the trail. At 2.1 miles, a side path on the right descends steeply to the base of Hen Wallow Falls, a long spill of 60 feet or more that fans out as it cascades down.

Hen Wallow Falls

From the waterfall, the main trail continues straight ahead, passing a huge rock sitting beside the trail on the left and descending to a crossing of Lower Falling Branch of Hen Wallow Creek just above the waterfall. The trail then switchbacks and climbs gradually, recrossing the creek twice more and passing through a gap on Gabes Mountain, a ridge running down from Snake Den Mountain.

The trail continues through an old-growth forest of hemlocks and poplars on the side of the ridge, crossing Gabes Creek. At 4.3 miles, top a ridge in a stand of massive hemlocks and then drop into Sugar Cove. At 4.8 miles, the trail crosses Greenbrier Creek to the Sugar Cove Campsite (34) on the other side.

The trail ascends to a small pass at 5.0 miles on Buckeye Lead, a ridge running from Maddron Bald. Pass through the gathering waters of Buckeye Creek and descend along Cole Creek. The trail eventually emerges to end at a junction at 6.6 miles with the Maddron Bald Trail (hike 45), which at this point is an old gravel road.

Straight across the road is the east end of the Old Settlers Trail (hike 41). To the right the Maddron Bald Trail takes you 1.2 miles to the Laurel Springs Road off US 321. To the left the Maddron Bald Trail leads to the Snake Den Ridge Trail (hike 46); together with this hike, these trails create a 17.2-mile loop that is one of the best backpacking trips in the park.

45 | MADDRON BALD TRAIL AND ALBRIGHT GROVE NATURE TRAIL

Distance: 7.0 miles one way; to Albright Grove, 3.0 miles one way
Difficulty: Strenuous; to Albright Grove, moderate
Elevation gain: 3,500 feet; to Albert Grove, 1,300 feet
Season: Year-round
Cautions: Creek crossings, steep ascent
Connections: Gabes Mountain Trail, Old Settlers Trail, Snake Den Ridge Trail

Attractions: Albright Grove—named for Horace M. Albright, director of the National Park Service from 1929 to 1933 and a proponent for establishing this national park—has one of the park's best stands of old-growth forest. It contains the largest known specimen in the park of the Tennessee state tree, the yellow poplar, or tuliptree. At 135 feet high and 25 feet, 3 inches in circumference, this giant forms a massive column in the forest. Yellow poplars are the largest living organisms in the park. You'll also find large hemlocks and several other tree species in the grove. After passing Albright Grove, you'll ascend into a heath bald. Sometimes called "laurel slicks" because of the wet appearance of the shiny evergreen leaves, heath

Albright Grove

balds were also called "hells" by the early settlers because the thickets were so difficult to walk through. Camping is available at Otter Creek Campsite (29).

Trailhead: On US 321, 15.7 miles east of Gatlinburg, pass the Yogi Bear Jellystone Park Camp Resort. The Laurel Springs Road at the edge of the campground once led to the trailhead, but the road has been washed out by flooding. Until it's repaired, continue past the campground another mile and turn to the right on Baxter Road. In 0.5 mile, at a junction with Laurel Springs Road, turn to the right to a gravel road on the left blocked by a gate; this is the trailhead.

Description: The old road ascends gradually and then more steeply. In spring watch for showy orchis in bloom, a relatively rare orchid that frequents old roadsides in the Smokies. At 0.6 mile, the Willis Baxter Cabin stands on the right, built in 1889. At 1.0 mile reach a junction with the Gabes Mountain Trail (hike 44) to the left toward Cosby Cove and the Old Settlers Trail (hike 41) to the right toward Greenbrier; the Maddron Bald Trail continues straight.

Ascend to the end of the road at a turnaround at 2.3 miles. The trail then enters the forest and ascends steadily, crossing Indian Camp Creek on a footbridge at 2.8 miles. At 3.0 miles, the Albright Grove Nature Trail turns off to the right. The 0.7-mile nature trail loops south and then east to rejoin the Maddron Bald Trail, passing through the stand of old-growth forest.

Willis Baxter Cabin

From the nature trail, the main trail climbs continuously. You'll have several rockhop crossings of streams—Indian Camp Creek, then its tributary, Copperhead Branch, back and forth across Indian Camp Creek, then across Copperhead Branch again. At 4.8 miles, as the trail crosses a ridge, a short path leads to a rock outcrop on the left with a view of Maddron Bald to the east and the Indian Camp Creek Valley below. At 5.5 miles, the trail crosses Otter Creek to the Otter Creek Campsite (29), a rocky, sloped site.

The trail climbs steeply, finally emerging on Maddron Bald at 6.0 miles, one of the park's heath balds. The trail ascends through the heath into a high-elevation spruce forest and ends at a junction with the Snake Den Ridge Trail at 7.0 miles.

To the right, the Snake Den Ridge Trail (hike 46) leads to the AT in 0.7 mile at Inadu Knob; to the left, it reaches the Cosby Campground in 4.6 miles. The Maddron Bald, Gabes Mountain, and Snake Den Ridge Trails form an excellent 17.2-mile backpacking loop out of Cosby Cove.

46 | SNAKE DEN RIDGE TRAIL

Distance: 5.3 miles one way
Difficulty: Moderate
Elevation gain: 3,500 feet
Season: Year-round
Cautions: Creek crossings, continuous ascent
Connections: Low Gap Trail, Maddron Bald Trail,
     Appalachian Trail

Attractions: This mountain walk forms part of a good backpacking loop.
The trail passes a cemetery that contains the grave of Ella V. Costner, who

Crossing at Inadu Creek

grew up in a cabin above Cosby Campground. She left home in the 1930s to become a nurse and wrote three books of poetry about the mountains and the pioneering people she had known. The Tennessee State Legislature bestowed on her the title "Poet Laureate of the Smokies" in 1971. The trail follows Inadu Creek, which flows down between Inadu Mountain to the southeast and Snake Den Mountain to the northwest. Inadu means "snake" in Cherokee; there are probably no more snakes here than elsewhere. Camping is available at Cosby Campground.

Trailhead: Proceed into the Cosby Campground to its southwest corner and a gated gravel road across from campsite B54. Because the campground is closed in winter, you may need to park at the hikers' parking area near the picnic area and walk into the campground.

Description: Walk up the gravel road. At 0.2 mile, a trail on the left connects with the Low Gap Trail in 0.4 mile; continue straight up the road.

Walk through second-growth deciduous forest that in the fall shines with brilliant reds and yellows. At 0.5 mile, the Cosby Cemetery lies on the right. The road ends at a turnaround at 0.6 mile. The trail passes through boulders to continue up a path, ascending to cross a footbridge over Rock Creek at 0.7 mile. Enter a beautiful mixed hardwood and hemlock forest along Inadu Creek. At 1.6 miles, ford Inadu Creek, which spills over a small waterfall below the trail and then flows down to join Crying Creek.

The trail heads up the slope of Snake Den Mountain, making several turns to gain the ridge at 2.2 miles. After rounding a dry, rocky point, look behind for a view of Mount Cammerer in the distance. The trail then heads up Snake Den Mountain. The trail alternately passes through hemlock forests and curves around dry, rocky points. At 2.8 miles, after rounding one of these points, again look back for a good view of Mount Cammerer. The trail becomes very rocky before reaching a junction at 4.6 miles with the Maddron Bald Trail (hike 45) to the right (the Snake Den Ridge, Maddron Bald, and Gabes Mountain Trails make one of the park's finest overnight loops, 17.2 miles); continue straight ahead.

The Snake Den Ridge Trail enters spruce-fir forest as it ascends to the crest of the Smokies and ends at a junction with the AT at Inadu Knob at 5.3 miles. You'll have a view to the left of the Cosby Creek Valley.

Along the AT to the left, you'll find Cosby Knob Shelter in 3.9 miles, and to the right, Tricorner Knob Shelter in 3.7 miles.

COSBY COVE EAST/ DAVENPORT GAP

When the national park was being established, fire towers were needed to keep watch for fires that could devastate the area. In addition to towers constructed on peaks scattered throughout the park, a lookout was constructed on Mount Cammerer above Cosby Cove.

Built in 1939 by the CCC, the stone and wood structure is referred to as a "lookout" because it is a low structure sitting on the ground, as opposed to a "fire tower" that stands above the trees. With the advantage of rock outcrops, the shorter lookout was all that was necessary for a person to see in all directions. The promontory where the lookout is located was called "White Rocks" before the mountain was renamed for Arno B. Cammerer, director of the National Park Service from 1933 to 1940 and supporter of the establishment of the park. The lookout was used until the 1960s.

Over the intervening years, the Mount Cammerer Lookout

Mount Cammerer Lookout

fell into disrepair. But in 1993 the Friends of the Great Smoky Mountains National Park was formed to raise funds for restoration, which took place in 1994. The Friends group has continued to successfully raise money for park projects. As a result of their efforts, you can now get up on the circular walkway around the outside of the structure for some of the best views in the park. Because of its unique character, the lookout has been listed on the National Register of Historic Places.

Mount Cammerer is reached by trails east out of the Cosby Campground

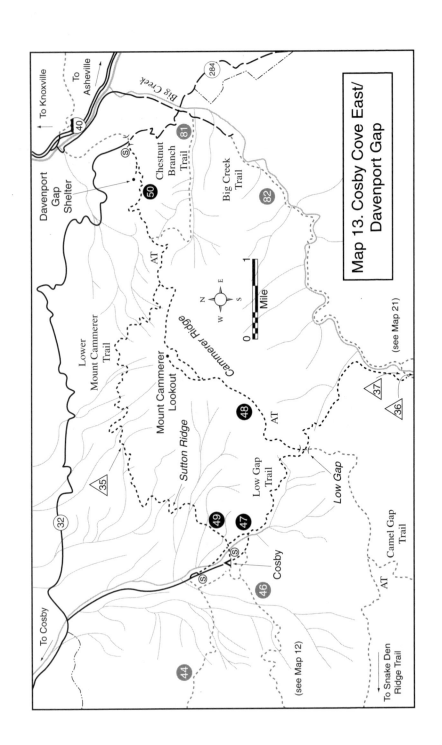

Map 13. Cosby Cove East/ Davenport Gap

To Knoxville
To Asheville
To Shelter
284
Big Creek
40
Davenport Gap Shelter
Chestnut Branch Trail
81
50
Big Creek Trail
82
AT
Lower Mount Cammerer Trail
N
E
W
S
0 Mile 1
Cammerer Ridge
Mount Cammerer Lookout
(see Map 21)
Sutton Ridge
48
AT
37
36
35
Low Gap Trail
Low Gap
32
49 47
Camel Gap Trail
Cosby
AT
46
To Cosby
44
(see Map 12)
To Snake Den Ridge Trail

and also along the Appalachian Trail from the east boundary of the park at Davenport Gap, named for William Davenport, who led a group that surveyed the state boundary through the mountains in 1821.

Getting there: To reach Cosby Cove, take Hwy. 32 southeast from Cosby. In 1.2 miles, turn to the right into Cosby Cove. You will reach the picnic area on the left in 2.0 miles. Just beyond is the hikers' parking area. A registration hut stands on the main road just uphill from the hikers' parking. Past the registration hut the road enters Cosby Campground, which is closed in winter.

To reach Davenport Gap, continue east from the Cosby Cove turnoff on Hwy. 32. The road winds up the mountain another 10.2 miles to reach the mountain crest at Davenport Gap. The AT emerges from the park in the gap. Parking is on the right near the trail.

47 | LOW GAP TRAIL

Distance: 5.4 miles one way
Difficulty: Moderate
Elevation change: 2,100 feet
Season: Year-round
Cautions: Steep ascent and descent
Connections: Cosby Nature Trail, Lower Mount Cammerer Trail, Appalachian Trail, Big Creek Trail

Attractions: The Low Gap Trail follows an old Indian trail over Low Gap to Walnut Bottom on Big Creek on the North Carolina side of the park. Walnut Bottom is known for bear activity, so if you're camping, be sure to hang your packs and food using the cable system strung between trees at Lower Walnut Bottom Campsite (37) and Upper Walnut Bottom Campsite (36). At the trailhead, camping is also available at Cosby Cove Campground.

Trailhead: In Cosby Cove, park at the hikers' parking area below the registration hut. The Low Gap Trail begins to the right.

Description: Enter the woods and bear to the right on a path that once led up from the picnic area. The trail passes connections with the Cosby Nature Trail (hike 43) and crosses footbridges over branches of Cosby Creek to emerge into an open area at a junction at 0.4 mile with the Lower Mount Cammerer Trail (hike 49) to the left and the campground 0.1 mile to the right; turn left and then turn off to the right to continue on the Low Gap Trail.

Parallel Cosby Creek and reach a junction at 0.8 mile with a branch of the Low Gap Trail to the right (it descends 0.4 mile to emerge in the campground across from campsite B98; along the way, the trail crosses Cosby Creek on a footbridge and passes a connector that leads west to the Snake Den Ridge Trail, hike 46); turn left.

Ascend beside Cosby Creek on a broad, rocky path through large hemlocks and poplars. At 2.2 miles, cross Cosby Creek, which at this elevation is a shallow stream, and ascend steeply to reach Low Gap at 2.9 miles and an intersection with the Appalachian Trail. To the left, the AT leads up Mount Cammerer (hike 48), and to the right, the AT leads to a junction with the Snake Den Ridge Trail at Inadu Knob; continue straight on the Low Gap Trail.

The trail descends to cross Low Gap Branch at 3.6 miles and follow the branch downstream. At 4.6 miles, cross a tributary drainage and curve to the right to parallel Big Creek upstream, eventually passing above Walnut Bottom and descending to end at a junction with the Big Creek Trail at 5.4 miles. The Lower Walnut Bottom Campsite (37) lies to the left for hikers; horseback riders turn to the right to the Upper Walnut Bottom Campsite (36).

On the Big Creek Trail (hike 82), to the left it's 5.1 miles to the Big Creek trailhead, and to the right, it's 0.5 mile to the Camel Gap Trail and another 0.5 mile to the Gunter Fork Trail (hike 83), which is the continuation of the old Indian trail that crossed the mountains. The Low Gap Trail combined with the Gunter Fork Trail up to the Balsam Mountain Trail (hike 72), then west to the AT and north to Snake Den Ridge Trail (hike 46) and back down into Cosby Cove makes a fine backpack loop of 24.4 miles.

48 | LOW GAP, APPALACHIAN, AND MOUNT CAMMERER TRAILS TO LOOKOUT

Distance: 5.6 miles one way
Difficulty: Moderate
Elevation gain: 2,780 feet
Season: Year-round
Cautions: Creek crossings, steep ascent
Connections: Cosby Nature Trail

Attractions: This trail provides the shortest route to the Mount Cammerer Lookout.

Trailhead: In Cosby Cove, park at the hikers' parking area below the registration hut. The Low Gap Trail begins to the right.

Description: Follow the Low Gap Trail (hike 47) 2.9 miles to Low Gap and a junction with the AT. Straight ahead, the Low Gap Trail descends to Walnut Bottom on Big Creek. To the right, the AT passes Cosby Knob

View from Mount Cammerer (Sondra Jamieson)

Shelter, dips through Camel Gap, and intersects with the Snake Den Ridge Trail (hike 46) at Inadu Knob in 4.7 miles. Turn left on the AT to head for the Mount Cammerer Lookout.

Ascend from Low Gap into the spruce-fir zone, rounding Sunup Knob, and reach a gap atop Mount Cammerer at a junction at 5.0 miles with the AT to the right and the Mount Cammerer Trail straight ahead. Take the Mount Cammerer Trail to get to the lookout. The trail out the ridgeline is rocky and rugged, so any horses should be left at this junction.

Pass through a maple woods along the ridgeline to emerge into a heath thicket. Curve to the right back into trees as the trail descends a little, and then continue up through rocks, eventually reaching hitching rails at 5.5 miles where horses must be left. The trail continues up through rocks 0.1 mile on a heath-covered ridge to arrive at the lookout perched atop the White Rocks outcrop. Here you'll have some of the best views in the park.

You can return to Low Gap the way you came, or you can continue east on the AT down to the Lower Mount Cammerer Trail (hike 49) and return to Cosby Campground on a 16.3-mile loop.

49 | LOWER MOUNT CAMMERER TRAIL

Distance: 7.4 miles one way
Difficulty: Moderate
Elevation gain: 1,180 feet
Season: Year-round
Cautions: Overgrown in summer
Connections: Low Gap Trail, Appalachian Trail

Attractions: This trail can be part of a long loop hike that passes the Mount Cammerer Lookout (see hike 48). Camping is available at Cosby Campground and Gilliland Creek Campsite (35).

Trailhead: Proceed to Cosby Campground, where the parking is limited, and begin this trail near campsite B100. The campground is closed in winter, so you may need to park at the hikers' parking near the picnic area and hike up the Low Gap Trail (hike 47) to its junction with the Lower Mount Cammerer Trail.

Description: From the trailhead in the campground, walk up the gravel road, which soon fords Cosby Creek, but you can cross on the footbridge to the right. Then enter an open area at 0.1 mile, where the Low Gap Trail (hike 47) merges from the left and, just beyond, turns to the right to make its ascent to Low Gap. On the left, a horse trail leads back down the mountain to connect with the road into Cosby. Continue straight up the road.

Cross small streams and pass over low ridges to the end of the road in a turnaround at 0.7 mile. The trail turns to the right on a footpath to ascend along the slope of Mount Cammerer. Rockhop a creek at 0.9 mile that flows down to Toms Creek on your left. The trail descends to cross that creek on a footbridge at 1.0 mile and then crosses another tributary.

Top Sutton Ridge at 1.4 miles. Here a side trail to the right climbs 200 yards to a view over Cosby Valley. The main trail descends the other side of Sutton Ridge to a long, slender stream cascading down innumerable steps to pass under the trail at 1.9 miles; this is the Riding Fork of Caney Creek, which exits the park to the northeast. Rockhop another branch of Riding Fork at 2.2 miles. As the trail ascends around Gilliland Ridge, parts of the trail can get overgrown with stinging nettle that hurries you along. At 2.9 miles a large yellow poplar stands on the right. At 3.5 miles, rockhop Gilliland Fork and ascend steeply to the Gilliland Creek Campsite (35) at 3.6 miles.

The trail continues straight to rockhop another branch of Gilliland Fork at 3.9 miles. As you continue up Mount Cammerer Ridge, cross several small streams, moving in and out along the slope contour. At 7.4 miles, the Lower Mount Cammerer Trail ends at a junction with the Appalachian Trail at the crest of the Smokies.

To the left, the AT leads 2.9 miles to the park boundary at Davenport Gap (hike 50). To the right, the AT ascends 2.3 miles to the summit of Mount Cammerer and a junction with the 0.6-mile Mount Cammerer Trail out to the Mount Cammerer Lookout (hike 48). You can continue west to the Low Gap Trail (hike 47) to make a loop back to the Cosby Campground, a total of 16.3 miles, including the walk out to the lookout.

50 Appalachian Trail from Davenport Gap to Mount Cammerer

Distance: 5.8 miles one way
Difficulty: Moderate
Elevation gain: 2,900 feet
Season: Year-round
Cautions: Long ascent
Connections: Chestnut Branch Trail, Lower Mount Cammerer Trail

Attractions: This section of the AT provides alternative access to the Mount Cammerer Lookout. This hike begins not from Cosby Cove but from Davenport Gap on the east boundary of the park. The AT crosses Hwy. 32 here to emerge from the park and continue its journey north. Camping is available at Davenport Gap Shelter, newly renovated by the Smoky Mountain Hiking Club, in cooperation with the Appalachian Trail Conference and the Park Service, and dubbed the "Smokies Sheraton." A spring below the shelter provides water.

Trailhead: From the Cosby Campground turnoff on Hwy. 32, continue east 10.2 miles to Davenport Gap. You'll find a few places to park vehicles beside the road, which continues down the mountain as a gravel road into the community of Mount Sterling at Big Creek.

Description: Take the AT southwest into the park. The trail ascends Mount Cammerer Ridge, with a tributary of Big Creek to the left and a tributary of Tobes Creek to the right, both of which flow into the Pigeon River to the east. At 0.8 mile, a path to the right leads to the Davenport Gap Shelter.

As you ascend, the trail curves left over the end of a finger ridge and stays level along the north slope of the mountain, passing rock outcrops on the left and traveling through a long rhododendron passage until it reaches a junction at 1.9 miles in a small gap. Here the Chestnut Branch Trail (hike 81) to the left descends 2 miles southeast to the Big Creek Road; stay straight on the AT.

Mount Cammerer

The trail once more ascends Mount Cammerer Ridge. Continue up to a second junction at 2.9 miles with the Lower Mount Cammerer Trail (hike 49) to the right (it leads 7.4 miles to the Cosby Campground); continue straight ahead.

The trail becomes more rocky in the higher elevations. At 3.9 miles, the trail curves right and then switchbacks left over a point of a ridge facing north. Pass rock outcrops on the right; watch for a large yellow birch on the left. The outcrop becomes a wall on the right side of the trail; cribbing supports the path against this wall as it leads up to a rock outcrop at 4.4 miles that affords an expansive view to the southeast. The trail curves back to the right and ascends into the spruce zone of the high mountains, still with scattered large hemlocks and yellow birches. At 5.2 miles, ascend into a gap on the summit of Mount Cammerer and a junction. Here the AT turns left to connect with the Low Gap Trail in 2.1 miles; turn to the right on the Mount Cammerer Trail to reach the Mount Cammerer Lookout at 5.8 miles. Here you'll have some of the best views in the park.

NEWFOUND GAP ROAD/ NEWFOUND GAP

Completed in 1932, Newfound Gap Road passes 30 miles through the park, crossing the crest of the Smokies northwest to southeast, and is the main route to the North Carolina side from Tennessee. Campbell Overlook, which offers views of Bullhead and Balsam Point on Mount LeConte, was named for Carlos Campbell, a strong advocate for a national park who later chronicled the efforts to establish the park in his book *Birth of a National Park*. Newfound Gap Road crosses the crest of the Smokies at Newfound Gap, 13.2 miles from the Sugarlands Visitor Center on the Tennessee side and 16 miles from the Oconaluftee Visitor Center on the North Carolina side. It was not until sometime in the 1850s that Arnold Guyot, who was mapping the Smokies, determined that, at 5,046 feet, this was the lowest gap across the mountains, and so it was called "new found." The stone Rockefeller Memorial stands to the left of the gap, built to commemorate the donation of $5 million from the

Mount LeConte from Campbell Overlook

Laura Spelman Rockefeller Memorial Fund for purchasing parkland. President Franklin D. Roosevelt dedicated the national park in 1940 while standing on the stone terrace here.

Getting there: From the Sugarlands Visitor Center, head south up the Newfound Gap Road. At 0.4 mile on the left you will pass the Sugarlands Valley Nature Trail, a universally accessible paved walkway along the West Prong of the Little Pigeon River. At 1.7 miles, there is a parking area on the left for the Huskey Gap Trail on the right. At 2.2 miles, there are two pull-outs for Campbell Overlook on the left. At 4.6 miles the Chimneys Picnic Area is on the right. At 5.4 miles, overlooks along the road offer views of the twin peaks of the Chimney Tops, or simply "The Chimneys," which tower over the valley of the West Prong of the Little Pigeon River. Just past

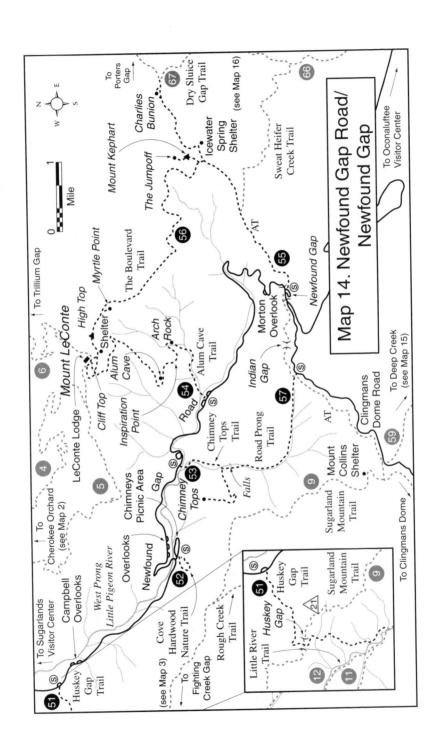

Map 14. Newfound Gap Road/
Newfound Gap

a tunnel at 7.1 miles there is parking along the road for the Chimney Tops Trail. At 7.3 miles Newfound Gap Road loops over itself in a spiral that was constructed to lessen the steepness of the road. At 8.8 miles parking on the road's east side is for Alum Cave. Watch for Morton Overlook at 12.5 miles for a grand view of the valley of the West Prong of the Little Pigeon River, wedged between Sugarland Mountain on the left and Anakeesta Ridge to the right; the overlook is named for Ben A. Morton, a supporter of the creation of the park. Newfound Gap, 13.2 miles from the Sugarlands Visitor Center, has access to the AT. Clingmans Dome Road, which is closed in winter, heads west from Newfound Gap.

From the Oconaluftee Visitor Center on the North Carolina side of the park, Newfound Gap is 16 miles, Alum Cave parking on the road's east side is 20.4 miles, the Chimney Tops trailhead is 22.1 miles, the Chimneys Picnic Area is 24.6 miles, and the Huskey Gap Trail parking area is 27.5 miles.

51 | HUSKEY GAP TRAIL

Distance: 4.1 miles one way; to Husky Gap, 2.0 miles one way
Difficulty: Easy
Elevation change: 1,300 feet
Season: Year-round
Cautions: None
Connections: Sugarland Mountain Trail, Little River Trail

Attractions: This pleasant walk over Huskey Gap in the ridge of Sugarland Mountain passes through a forest of hemlock and mixed hardwood and wildflowers in spring. This area was heavily logged before the park was established, but the forest has recovered well and offers a quiet walk through the woods.

Trailhead: At 1.7 miles from Sugarlands, turn into the parking area on the left, with the Huskey Gap trailhead on the right. From the North Carolina side of the park, find the parking area 11.5 miles down the mountain from Newfound Gap. Take care walking across the road to the trail.

Description: As you ascend the flank of Sugarland Mountain, pass through second-growth forest. At 1.0 mile, the trail follows an old road to skirt a ravine through limestone boulders. Flint Rock Branch falls from the hillside and passes through boulders under the trail to emerge downhill to your right.

At 1.5 miles, look behind to your right to see English Mountain in the distance, which is outside the park. Mount LeConte also comes into view, looming behind you. The trail reaches the ridgeline at 2.0 miles in Huskey Gap, a nondescript east-west passage across Sugarland Mountain. Here, you intersect with the Sugarland Mountain Trail (hike 9); to the right it leads 3.7 miles down to Little River Road, and to the left it leads to the AT near Clingmans Dome Road. Continue straight on the Huskey Gap Trail.

Descend the other side of the mountain, along the way crossing Big Medicine Branch and Phoebe Branch. The last part of the trail parallels Little River upstream, crossing small tributary streams and eventually ending at the Little River Trail (hike 12) at 4.1 miles.

To the right it's 2.7 miles to Little River trailhead at Elkmont; to the left the Little River Trail connects with the Goshen Prong and Rough Creek Trails.

52 | COVE HARDWOOD NATURE TRAIL

Distance: 0.8-mile loop
Difficulty: Moderate
Elevation change: 300 feet
Season: Year-round
Cautions: None
Connections: None

Attractions: This trail has the most easily accessible stand of old-growth forest and in spring provides a display of wildflowers.

Trailhead: From the Sugarlands Visitor Center continue up Newfound Gap Road and turn into the Chimneys Picnic Area on the right at 4.6 miles; from the North Carolina side of the park, it's 8.6 miles down from Newfound Gap. In the picnic area, stay to the right at a loop intersection, and park on the right.

Description: The trail heads up the slope to the right, crossing an old road to a picnic table and passing behind an amphitheater with a circular stone bench. Turn to the right across a short bridge over a drainage and ascend to a junction at 0.1 mile that is the loop part of the trail. Stay to the right.

Pass through an old field that has grown up in tall yellow poplars. Also watch for black locust with furrowed bark. At 0.2 mile, a large maple stands on the right; on the left a yellow birch grows out of the stump of a massive tuliptree that was cut long ago. The trail bears left up the slope of the mountain, ascending into an old-growth cove hardwood forest. At another large maple, the trail turns left and right, passing over a small stream running downhill. In spring, you'll find spring beauty, bishop's cap, wood anemone, Dutchman's-breeches, squirrel corn, trillium, and hepatica. In summer watch for the yellow blossoms of jewelweed.

The trail curves left back over the stream, ascends to a large black locust, and curves to the right to cross the stream again. The trail turns up left to pass between two large white basswood trees that send up sprouts from their bases; notice the broad, heart-shaped leaves.

At 0.5 mile stands a large yellow buckeye with palmate leaves, five leaflets resembling the fingers of a hand. The trail now descends, passing large maples and buckeyes. At 0.6 mile, the trail crosses an obvious line between the old-growth forest and an area that has been logged; walk among smaller trees growing more closely together. Close the loop at 0.7 mile. Turn to the right to return to the parking area.

53 | CHIMNEY TOPS TRAIL

Distance: 2.0 miles one way
Difficulty: Strenuous
Elevation gain: 1,650 feet
Season: Year-round
Cautions: Steep ascent, rocky tread with exposed roots,
    vertical drops at summit
Connections: Road Prong Trail

Attractions: This very popular trail ascends to the twin rock peaks of the Chimney Tops that tower over the valley of the West Prong of the Little Pigeon River. The Cherokees called the bare rock summits *Duniskwalguni,* meaning "forked antlers." To the early settlers, the pinnacles resembled chimneys standing above the treetops. The rock is of the Anakeesta Formation, a slate that weathers to the steep ridges and pinnacles in the park; since the tops of the mountains are where the Fraser fir grow, the Cherokees called the peaks *Anakeesta* for "place of the balsams."

Trailhead: At 5.4 miles from the Sugarlands Visitor Center, overlooks along Newfound Gap Road offer views of the twin peaks of the Chimney Tops, or simply "The Chimneys." As you continue up the road, pass through a tunnel and at 7.1 miles watch for parking along the road for the Chimney Tops Trail. From the North Carolina side, the trailhead is 6.1 miles down the mountain from Newfound Gap.

Description: Walk through a low stone wall and down a few stone steps to turn to the right into the woods. Then bear left to cross a bridge over Walker Camp Prong just above where the Walker Camp and Road Prongs join to create the West Prong.

Around to the right and then left, cross a bridge over the Road Prong as it drops over ledges and spillways to join Walker Camp Prong below. The

Lower pinnacle of The Chimneys

trail turns left and quickly ascends high above the creek on a wide, rocky path. Along much of this trail you'll see thickets of rhododendron that bloom in early summer.

At 0.3 mile, cross the Road Prong again on a bridge. The trail then ascends past large oaks. At 0.8 mile, cross the Road Prong again on a bridge, with the stream falling over rock shelves in veils above and below the crossing. Then at 0.9 mile, reach a junction with the Road Prong Trail (hike 57), which continues straight, ascending to the crest of the Smokies in 2.4 miles; turn right to continue on the Chimney Tops Trail.

The trail steeply ascends the slope of Sugarland Mountain. In summer jewelweed, sporting yellow and orange blossoms, stands in profusion along a drainage on your right. You'll encounter large yellow buckeye trees, so tall you must squint into the high branches to make out the leaves of five leaflets. The tree produces a smooth brown nut with a white spot that gives the buckeye its name; you'll find the shiny nuts along the trail in early fall.

At 1.3 miles, turn left across a drainage that runs under the trail in a culvert. Soon after, switchback right and ascend into a forest of red spruce. At 1.7 miles, the trail rounds a point and descends along the side of the ridge that runs out to The Chimneys, which stand through the trees to your right.

The ridgeline on your left descends to meet the trail at 1.9 miles. An unofficial and unmaintained path up the ridge connects with the Sugarland Mountain Trail in 0.4 mile; it's rough and confusing, so do not go this way. Straight along the ridgeline, the path becomes entangled in tree roots. At 2.0 miles reach the base of The Chimneys.

The climb to the top of The Chimneys does not require technical skill. But use extreme caution; there are vertical dropoffs to the sides. Do not attempt the climb if the rocks are wet and slippery. An easier route follows a path to the right where the shrubs and thin soil are peeling away from the rock face; you'll come to a shorter scramble to the top. At the top, you have a 360-degree view of the surrounding mountains, including Mount LeConte to the northeast, Mount Mingus to the southeast, and Sugarland Mountain to the west. Newfound Gap Road below winds up the mountain. The lower pinnacle of The Chimneys lies directly north at the end of a narrow ridge connecting the two peaks; do not attempt this route—people have died here. You'll find an opening down through the rock, like a chimney flue, which reinforces the name of the pinnacles. Under no circumstances should you climb down into the rock opening.

If you don't feel up to the climb, be content with having lunch at the base of The Chimneys and return the way you came.

54 | ALUM CAVE TRAIL

Distance: 4.9 miles one way; to Arch Rock, 1.3 miles one way; to Alum Cave, 2.2 miles one way
Difficulty: Strenuous
Elevation gain: 2,580 feet; to Alum Cave, 1,420 feet
Season: Year-round
Cautions: Steep ascent, precipitous steps, narrow rock ledges
Connections: Rainbow Falls Trail

Attractions: This shortest but very strenuous route to the top of Mount LeConte may be the most scenic trail in the park, with mountain vistas and geologic formations. The steepness of the mountain makes it susceptible to landslides; heavy rain loosens the soil that then slips away from the bedrock, surrendering to gravity as entire hillsides come crashing down. Many of the larger slide scars visible on Mount LeConte date from a 1951 thunderstorm that dropped several inches of rain in less than an hour. The trail visits Arch Rock, an arm of Anakeesta stone that arches overhead; the opening was formed by water that settled into cracks and broke the rock when it froze. Also on this hike is Alum Cave, actually a 100-foot overhang of Anakeesta rock with a high sulfur content. A sulfate form of sulfur is called

Alum Cave

alum, hence the formation's name. The alum here is potassium aluminum sulfate. Epsom salt, a magnesium sulfate, is also found in the bluff; there was a small and unsuccessful Epsom salts manufacturing operation here around 1841. Recently three previously unknown sulfates have been discovered. Rooms are available at LeConte Lodge and camping is available at Mount LeConte Shelter.

Trailhead: At 8.8 miles from the Sugarlands Visitor Center, or at 4.4 miles from Newfound Gap, find Alum Cave parking on the road's east side. Two parking areas are connected by a gravel path along Walker Camp Prong, a major tributary of the West Prong of the Little Pigeon River. The Alum Cave trailhead lies along this path.

Description: Cross a bridge over Walker Camp Prong to enter a mature forest of eastern hemlock and yellow birch with an understory of thick Rosebay rhododendron decorated with large white flower clusters in early July. At 0.1 mile cross a bridge spanning Alum Cave Creek, a tributary of Walker Camp Prong, and head upstream.

At 1.0 mile, the trail passes a drainage choked with debris beside a sandstone outcrop, evidence of the landslides that have scarred the slope of the mountain. Cross two footbridges over Alum Cave Creek and bear left up the tributary of Styx Branch. Just before a third footbridge at 1.3 miles, you'll see the scouring effects of a landslide: churned-up rocks and forest debris.

The footbridge crosses Styx Branch into a rock grotto where you turn left and enter Arch Rock. Climb stone steps up through the hole and emerge above the rock. The trail then ascends to a last footbridge crossing of Styx Branch, appropriately named since it drains Huggins Hell; the river Styx in Greek mythology was the principal river separating the underworld from the world above.

The trail passes through the woods to emerge into the open of a landslide scar at 1.5 miles. This landslide occurred when a 1993 thunderstorm sent an estimated 20-foot wall of water down the slope; fortunately, no one was in the way. The trail turns up the scar and then crosses to the left to reenter the woods. Notice the first red spruce on the left as you climb into the higher elevations. Ascend more steeply up another landslide channel and cross it to the left. The trail passes outcroppings of Anakeesta rock. Then look to your left at 1.8 miles to see Anakeesta Ridge to the southeast across the valley of Alum Cave Creek.

The trail ascends into a heath bald at 1.9 miles and out to Inspiration Point, an outcropping of Anakeesta rock providing a resting place and an open view of Sugarland Mountain to the west. In June the sand myrtle, dainty with its tiny evergreen leaves, has pale pink blossoms, and the Catawba rhododendron displays rose-purple flower clusters. The trail turns up to the right at the point to continue to the northeast, ascending the side of Peregrine Peak, a knoll on the side of Mount LeConte. Ascend through a heath tunnel and reach an opening at 2.0 miles with a view to the left of Little Duck Hawk Ridge; "duck hawk" was another name for the peregrine falcons that once nested in the area and have returned in recent years. Notice the round hole through the ridge near the top, caused by the prying of freezing water; to the left near the end of the ridge is a second hole.

You can steady yourself on a cable strung along the rock wall as the path steepens at the bluff's edge. Climb steps and ascend steeply up to Alum Cave at 2.2 miles. You can actually smell the sulfur here. From Alum Cave, continue uphill along the bluff in the loose sand and watch for a sign sending you left along the trail carved into the bluff's edge. The trail now circles to the north around Peregrine Peak, which stands above Alum Cave Bluffs. Bare rock ledges offer views down onto Little Duck Hawk Ridge.

The trail then traverses a saddle between Peregrine Peak and the main mass of Mount LeConte ahead. Then it's up again with the way steep, narrow, and rocky. To the right through the trees, across Huggins Hell, stands The Boulevard, a long ridge spanning the gap between Mount LeConte and the

View from Cliff Top

main crest of the Smokies to the southeast.

At 3.7 miles, the trail switchbacks left up some stairs where you can hear and just glimpse the upper reaches of Styx Branch splashing down the mountain slope. After making the turn and ascending, look back over your shoulder for a view of a landslide that begins at the crest and makes a long scar down the face of the mountain. The trail continues as a rocky, narrow path, sometimes wedged into cracks in the rock where cables offer a handhold. Springs wet the rocks after recent rains.

At 3.9 miles, ascend to a point and turn right, climbing now through spruce forest intermingled with Fraser firs that are mostly dead, standing trees killed by an insect, the balsam woolly adelgid. Young firs are still thick and green, as yet unaffected. Cross the top of an old landslide where thick grass now spills down the slope. Watch for mountain ash, a high-elevation tree that adds a splash of red berries in late summer, and dwarf rhododendron, with smaller leaves than either the Catawba or Rosebay.

The trail swings to the right to an expansive view of Cliff Top, a rock outcrop on the west side of Mount LeConte and the perch from which overnighters at the lodge traditionally witness sunset. The trail heads in to the side of the mountain and curves left across the top of another old slide to pass beneath Cliff Top. You then circle to the right, passing over the ridgeline that leads west from the summit of Mount LeConte to West Peak. The trail circles the summit, passing along a wet trail lined with young Fraser fir, to end at a junction with the Rainbow Falls Trail (hike 4) at 4.9 miles.

To the left the Rainbow Falls Trail leads to the Bull Head Trail (hike 5); to the right it reaches LeConte Lodge in 0.1 mile. Just before the lodge, on the right, is a spur trail that climbs 0.1 mile to Cliff Tops. Just beyond the lodge, the Trillium Gap Trail (hike 6) drops off to the left and The Boulevard Trail (hike 56) continues straight past the Mount LeConte backcountry shelter.

55 | APPALACHIAN TRAIL TO CHARLIES BUNION

Distance: 4.0 miles one way
Difficulty: Moderate
Elevation change: 1,000 feet
Season: Year-round
Cautions: High bluffs
Connections: Sweat Heifer Creek Trail, The Boulevard Trail, Dry Sluice Gap Trail

Attractions: This section of the AT leads along the main crest of the Smokies. The trail passes Mount Kephart, named for Horace Kephart, who

Charlies Bunion

came to the Smoky Mountains from the Midwest in 1904. He was an advocate of the establishment of the Great Smoky Mountains National Park during the formative years and assisted in the development of the Appalachian Trail through the park. Kephart's study of the Appalachian mountain people, *Our Southern Highlanders*, has long been considered one of the best regional studies of the mountain culture, although later scholars say he neglected to take note of communities such as Cades Cove and Cataloochee. Until his death in an auto accident in 1931, Kephart lived among the mountain people in the area of Bryson City, North Carolina.

This hike takes you to the rock promontory of Charlies Bunion; the origin of this name provides an interesting story. In the early 1920s, timbering operations on the south side of the ridge had left tree branches and brush scattered down the slope. This debris fueled a fire in 1925 that swept up the mountain and over the crest of the Smokies. Visitors to Paul Adams's camp atop Mount LeConte watched the great fire for a week. The fire destroyed the forest cover, exposing the soil. Then a storm in 1929 washed soil and logs down the mountain. A group of hikers that included Horace Kephart and Charlie Conner, who was raised in the Smokemont area of the park, set out to have a look at the damage and found the exposed rock along the crest that had been beneath the mountain soil. When the group

View from Appalachian Trail on way to Charlies Bunion

stopped to take a rest at the newly bared rock, Conner took his shoe off to rest a sore foot. Kephart said he would put Charlie's name on the map; in later interviews, Conner said he did not recall having a bunion. Camping is available at Icewater Spring Shelter.

Trailhead: The Appalachian Trail crosses the Newfound Gap Road at Newfound Gap, where there is a large parking area.

Description: From the far northeast end of the parking area, take the AT headed east. Ascend along a rocky trail in yellow birch, spruce, and scattered mountain ash. Some views to the right through trees reveal Oconaluftee Valley to the south. Climb along the rocky crest, crossing a knoll and descending to a junction at 1.7 miles with the Sweat Heifer Creek Trail to the right (it turns off in a gap carpeted with spring beauty and trout lily in spring; the name probably originated with the practice of driving cattle to the crest of the Smokies during the summer months to graze on the grassy balds); continue straight on the AT.

Porters Creek Valley from Charlies Bunion

Ascend from this gap and pass a grand view to the south at 2.0 miles. The trail continues up to the crest of Mount Ambler. Watch for views to the north of Mount LeConte, recognizable by the scars of landslides along its flank. The trail soon descends to a junction at 2.7 miles with The Boulevard Trail (hike 56) to the left (it leads to the summit of Mount LeConte in 5.3 miles; a path leading to the sheer cliff of The Jumpoff, with its view to the east, is just 0.1 mile up this trail); continue straight on the AT.

The trail then swings southeast around Mount Kephart. Pass Icewater Spring Shelter at 3.0 miles, to your right off the trail. Icewater Spring flows in the middle of the trail 0.1 mile beyond the shelter. The trail descends from the spring to emerge onto a narrow, open ridge that offers views to the north. At 3.6 miles, you can see the bare rock promontory of Charlies Bunion ahead. At 4.0 you miles reach a junction where the AT swings to the right around Charlies Bunion; use this route if there is ice on the trail in winter. The path to the left takes you onto Charlies Bunion, where you scramble over rock to pass between the upper and lower peaks.

Charlies Bunion is Anakeesta rock, like The Chimneys (see hike 53). The outcrop provides spectacular views into the Tennessee side of the park. The Porters Creek Valley and Greenbrier Cove lie to the northeast. Mount Kephart looms to the west. Mount LeConte stands to the northwest, and on its right side, you can see the heath bald on top of Brushy Mountain. Around the rocks, there are 1,000-foot dropoffs, so use caution.

From Charlies Bunion, the AT continues to the northeast, crossing a rock shelf to a junction with the bypass around the back side of Charlies Bunion. The AT passes an open area of grass and brambles at Dry Sluice Gap and ascends past a junction with the Dry Sluice Gap Trail.

56 | APPALACHIAN AND THE BOULEVARD TRAILS TO MOUNT LECONTE

Distance: 8.0 miles one way
Difficulty: Moderate
Elevation gain: 1,600 feet
Season: Year-round
Cautions: Slide areas, high bluffs, rough footing
Connections: Trillium Gap Trail, Alum Cave Trail, Rainbow Falls Trail

Attractions: The Boulevard Trail follows the high mountain ridge connecting the main crest of the Smokies with Mount LeConte, including some of

View from The Jumpoff

the most famous overlooks in the park. This is perhaps the easiest route to the summit of Mount LeConte because of the relatively small gain in elevation, although it is the longest walk. Myrtle Point is a favorite spot to watch the sunrise if you have spent the night at LeConte Lodge or the Mount LeConte Shelter. Any time of day, the platform of stone adorned with sand myrtle, which sports pink blossoms in May, offers a panoramic vista of the eastern half of the park. No view is offered from High Top, the mountain's highest peak, but pause a moment there to toss a stone on the rockpile to the trail's left. It was a custom of the Cherokees to throw a stone on such a pile that had been started as an offering to an evil spirit. Rooms are available at LeConte Lodge and camping is available at Mount LeConte Shelter.

Trailhead: The parking area at Newfound Gap provides access to the AT.

Description: Follow the AT toward Charlies Bunion 2.7 miles to its junction with The Boulevard Trail (see hike 55) and turn left on The Boulevard Trail, which ascends the west flank of Mount Kephart. At 2.8 miles (just 0.1 mile from the AT), a rugged 0.4-mile spur trail to the right passes over the summit of Mount Kephart and drops to The Jumpoff, a promontory affording spectacular views of Porters Creek Valley to the east and Charlies Bunion to the right; the name derives from the 1,000-foot sheer drop from the overlook.

The main trail soon descends, skirting the headwaters of Walker Camp Prong, a primary tributary of the West Prong of the Little Pigeon River. Then at 3.7 miles begin a gentle ascent to the summit of Mount LeConte.

At 5.2 miles, the trail swings to the right past Anakeesta Knob and soon after dips through Alum Gap to continue up the ridge of The Boulevard, passing through beech gaps and following ridgelines lined in spring by the blooms of spring beauty, trillium, trout and bead lilies, and mountain laurel. Fraser fir and mountain ash stand along the trail.

Swing around the eastern end of Mount LeConte and ascend toward the summit from the east. Switchback left at 7.5 miles to a 0.25-mile side trail to the overlook of Myrtle Point with its view to the east.

The main trail continues up, topping High Top at 7.7 miles, the highest peak of Mount LeConte at 6,593 feet. From High Top, descend past a grand view to the south and the Mount LeConte Shelter on the left at 7.9 miles; water is available at the lodge or from the spring down the Trillium Gap Trail (hike 6) that is the source of the Roaring Fork. The Trillium Gap Trail is on the right just before LeConte Lodge at 8.0 miles. Past the lodge entrance, a side trail leads left up to Cliff Top, the place for sunset views of the western half of the park. Straight from the Cliff Top turnoff are connections to the Alum Cave (hike 54), Rainbow Falls (hike 4), and Bull Head (hike 5) Trails.

57 | ROAD PRONG TRAIL

Distance: 2.4 miles one way
Difficulty: Strenuous
Elevation loss: 1,500 feet
Season: Year-round (access road closed in winter)
Cautions: Creek crossings, steep descent
Connections: Appalachian Trail, Chimney Tops Trail

Attractions: This steep trail follows the Road Prong as it gathers waters for its many spills and cascades. The Road Prong of the West Prong of the Little Pigeon River is named for the original road over the mountain. An Indian trail once crossed near this location through Indian Gap, which is just to the east. In 1839, the trail was widened to make a rough road over the mountain and for a time was called the "Oconaluftee Turnpike." When a transmountain road was proposed in the 1900s, the old Indian Gap Road was suggested as the route, but Newfound Gap provided a better grade and so the road over the Smokies crossed there.

Trailhead: From Newfound Gap, turn west on Clingmans Dome Road (closed in winter). In 1.3 miles, trailhead parking lies on the right. To run a shuttle vehicle, park a second car at the Chimney Tops trailhead (see hike 53).

Description: Head straight down the mountain from the parking area. Cross the Appalachian Trail (which leads left toward Clingmans Dome and right to Newfound Gap). Somewhere near here you join the route of the original road.

Descend on a rocky path through a spruce-fir forest. The Road Prong gathers waters to your left. At 0.7 mile, the trail moves in and out of the creek, until at 1.0 mile the trail climbs away from the creek over a rise and descends, paralleling the creek on your left. At 1.6 miles, the creek plunges over a slanted boulder to form a 5-foot waterfall and from here on makes a delightful series of spills and cascades that hold your attention.

Descending steeply and crossing a small tributary, pass a slab of rock standing on its side just on the left of the trail. Most such rocks were fractured and brought down the mountainsides by the freezing and thawing that occurred during the last ice age around 20,000 years ago. Just below

Road Prong Falls

the standing stone, rockhop the Road Prong at 2.0 miles. If the water is high, this can be a difficult crossing.

Descending now on the west side of the creek, pass a 20-foot waterfall that you glimpse over the bushes. The trail continues down, passing through a gully at times, worn down by erosion and centuries of human passage. At 2.4 miles, the trail ends at a junction with the Chimney Tops Trail (hike 53).

The Chimney Tops Trail to the left leads 1.1 miles to The Chimneys or to the right leads 0.9 mile out to the Chimney Tops trailhead. The old road over the mountain essentially coincided with this lower part of the Chimney Tops Trail, joining what is now Newfound Gap Road at the Chimney Tops trailhead and continuing on down the mountain. Return as you came, or continue down the Chimney Tops Trail to a shuttle vehicle.

Midnight Hole on Big Creek

NORTH CAROLINA DISTRICT

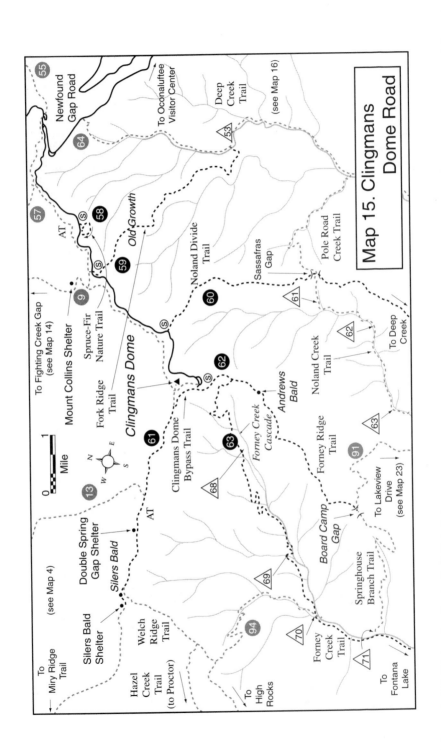

Map 15. Clingmans
Dome Road

CLINGMANS DOME ROAD

Crowds of people come to walk the 0.5-mile paved Clingmans Dome Trail to the top of Clingmans Dome, at 6,643 feet the highest peak in the park. A tower built here in 1959 to replace an earlier tower built by the CCC lifts you above the treetops for a 360-degree view of the Smokies range. The mountain peak was originally called "Smoky Dome" but was later renamed for Thomas Lanier Clingman, a promoter of this region, which he explored in the 1850s when he was a U.S. Congressman. Several trails lead off Clingmans Dome Road, which runs from Newfound Gap to Clingmans Dome.

Getting there: Take the Clingmans Dome Road west from Newfound Gap Road at Newfound Gap, 13.2 miles from the Sugarlands Visitor Center on the Tennessee side of the park and 16 miles from the Oconaluftee Visitor Center on the North Carolina side of the park. Trailheads are located along the road and at the end of the road at 7 miles, at the Forney Ridge Parking Area below Clingmans Dome. Note that Clingmans Dome Road is closed in winter.

View from Clingmans Dome

58 | SPRUCE-FIR NATURE TRAIL

Distance: 0.5-mile loop
Difficulty: Easy
Elevation change: None
Season: Year-round (access road closed in winter)
Cautions: Falling trees in high wind or heavy rain
Connections: None

Attractions: This walk through a spruce-fir forest illustrates the changes occurring at high elevations. This boreal forest exists in the eastern part of the park westward to a couple of miles beyond Clingmans Dome. Farther west the spruce-fir forest is absent. The peaks are not as high in the western half of the park, but are high enough for red spruce. One explanation for the absence of spruce trees theorizes a warming that occurred after the last glaciation, which confined the spruce and fir to the highest peaks. During the subsequent cooling, the spruce repopulated down to 4,000 feet, spreading westward, but was slowed by the beech forests that had spread across Double Spring Gap east of Silers Bald. On this short hike in addition to red spruce, you'll see fir trees that bear the name of a Scotsman, John Fraser, who explored the region, sending plants back to his nursery in England, and on one trip in 1800 was a commissioned botanist for the Czar of Russia. Fraser was the first to recognize that this tree was different from the balsam fir of the north; the Fraser fir is found only in the southern Appalachians, primarily in the Smokies. The fir has flat needles while the red spruce has four-sided needles.

Trailhead: Parking for the nature trail lies on the left of Clingmans Dome Road at 2.7 miles from Newfound Gap Road.

Description: Drop into the woods and bear right to enter a grove of giant red spruce at 0.1 mile, where you encounter the loop part of the trail. The standing dead trees you see are the mature Fraser fir, killed by an insect, the balsam woolly adelgid. Young fir trees are still healthy and green, as yet unaffected by the insect. Turn left on the loop to walk clockwise. Blackberry thickets have grown up now that the sun can penetrate the forest canopy.

Notice the compound leaf of the mountain ash, which sports brilliant red berries in late summer and early fall. Yellow birch forms part of the canopy. The leaves of both trees add yellow to the colors of fall. If the spruce trees also die back from the effects of air pollution, this forest will likely become a birch-ash forest. The understory includes hobblebush, which has heart-shaped leaves, white blossom clusters in spring, and bright red berries in summer. Past some benches, complete the loop at 0.4 mile and turn back to the trailhead at 0.5 mile.

59 | FORK RIDGE TRAIL

Distance: 5.1 miles one way; to old-growth forest, 2.0 miles one way
Difficulty: Moderate
Elevation loss: 2,800 feet; to old-growth, 500 feet
Season: Year-round (access road closed in winter)
Cautions: Steep descent near end of trail
Connections: Appalachian Trail, Sugarland Mountain Trail, Deep Creek Trail

Attractions: This trail descends Fork Ridge through old-growth forest. Big spruce and big hemlock intermingle in this forest that has some of the largest trees in the park. Camping is available at Poke Patch Campsite (53).

Trailhead: Parking for the Fork Ridge Trail is on the left at 3.7 miles from Newfound Gap Road. (Across the road, you can access the Appalachian Trail and to the west the nearby Sugarland Mountain Trail, hike 9.) To run a shuttle vehicle to the Deep Creek trailhead on Newfound Gap Road, see hike 64.

Description: Drop from the road and turn to the right to pass through a spruce-fir forest with scattered mountain maple and mountain ash. Dark green patches of shining club moss grow on the forest floor. The trail runs almost level along the side of the mountain before making a broad curve to the left and beginning a gradual descent.

At 1.8 miles, curve back right and head out Fork Ridge, which leads southeast from the Smokies crest. Watch for a huge eastern hemlock tree at 2.0 miles as you enter the old-growth forest. A huge spruce on the right is one of the largest in the Smokies. A massive hemlock on the left at 2.5 miles is virtually the last of the old growth on this trail.

Fork Ridge narrows as the trail passes through thickets of rhododendron. At 2.9 miles, descend through an oak forest where in late summer and fall acorns scatter across the trail. Their falling sets up a clatter throughout the woods.

As the crest of Fork Ridge passes into a drier environment, mountain laurel intermingles with the rhododendron. The trail swings left around a shoulder of the ridge and passes through a laurel tunnel with the ground covered in galax and trailing arbutus. Curve left over the end of a finger ridge and continue descending to pass a clump of Fraser magnolia that forms an awning over the trail. Scotsman John Fraser discovered both the Fraser fir and this magnolia. Curve to the right through a drainage to pass through another laurel tunnel at 3.6 miles and head out the narrow ridge crest; the Left Fork of Deep Creek lies in the valley between Fork Ridge and Noland Divide on the right, and the main stem of Deep Creek flows between Fork Ridge and Thomas Divide to the left.

At 4.2 miles, descend into Deep Creek Gap, where the path turns left to drop off the ridge in a steep descent; watch for large oaks, basswoods, and yellow poplars. At 5.0 miles, near the bottom of the descent, the trail bears to the right into a hollow and switchbacks right and left to reach the edge of Deep Creek at 5.1 miles. Notice the huge poplar to the left. You must ford Deep Creek to reach the junction with Deep Creek Trail (hike 64); the Poke Patch Campsite (53) sits to the right on Deep Creek Trail. There was once a footbridge here, but all sign of it has vanished, although it may be replaced. Return as you came, or take the Deep Creek Trail to the left to Newfound Gap Road in 4.0 miles.

60 | NOLAND DIVIDE TRAIL

Distance: 11.8 miles one way
Difficulty: Moderate
Elevation loss: 4,150 feet
Season: Year-round (access road closed in winter)
Cautions: Mud holes, overgrown in places
Connections: Pole Road Creek Trail, Noland Creek Trail

Attractions: Noland Divide leads down to the Deep Creek area in a hike with one of the greatest elevation changes in the park. Camping is available at Deep Creek Campground at the trail's end.

Trailhead: The Noland Divide Trail begins at 5.8 miles on the south side of Clingmans Dome Road. New trail construction has been proposed on the north side of the road to link the Noland Divide Trail with the Appalachian Trail.

Description: Walk up a dirt road lined with thornless blackberries. At 0.4 mile the road curves left past an environmental monitoring station. At 0.5 mile, the road continues on to an old water pumping station for the Clingmans Dome rest rooms; turn left here on the Noland Divide Trail.

Although there are some ups and downs along the way, the trail generally descends along the ridge of Noland Divide. At 2.0 miles, walk out of the spruce-fir of the high elevations into a woods dominated by hemlock and rhododendron. At 3.1 miles, the trail enters a rhododendron tunnel, curves left around the ridge, and enters a second tunnel. Descend to Sassafras Gap and a junction at 3.8 miles. To the left the Pole Road Creek Trail leads 3.3 miles down to the Deep Creek Trail (hike 64), and to the right the Noland Creek Trail (hike 91) leads 9.5 miles down to Lakeview Drive out of Bryson City; continue straight ahead.

The Noland Divide Trail climbs from Sassafras Gap to skirt Sassafras

Knob on its western slope and descends to the smaller Lower Sassafras Gap, at 5.1 miles. The trail climbs until at 5.7 miles you swing left of Coburn Knob and, with a switchback left, head out Beaugard Ridge, which leads down from Noland Divide. The trail descends through a saddle and ascends to the top of a knoll at 7.6 miles. Down from this point, walk a dry, exposed ridge that provides a panoramic view south to Bryson City; the overlook is called "Lonesome Pine."

The trail follows Beaugard Ridge, passing around and over knolls with a view to the north at 8.9 miles, then finally descending toward Deep Creek. At 9.6 miles, a small cascade splashes across the path. The trail returns to a dry slope where in sunny spots you'll find blueberries in July. At 11.6 miles, reach a bottomland along a creek where the trail curves left. Cross the creek on a footlog at 11.7 miles and pass a junction with the Deep Creek Horse Trail to the left; keep straight to emerge into a parking area and the Deep Creek Horse Stables at 11.8 miles. Just beyond is the Deep Creek Road; across it lies the Deep Creek Campground.

61 | CLINGMANS DOME BYPASS AND APPALACHIAN TRAILS TO SILERS BALD

Distance: 4.9 miles one way
Difficulty: Moderate
Elevation change: 1,200 feet
Season: Year-round (access road closed in winter)
Cautions: Narrow, rocky trail
Connections: Clingmans Dome Trail, Forney Ridge Trail, Goshen Prong Trail, Welch Ridge Trail, Miry Ridge Trail

Attractions: This walk along the Smokies crest on the Appalachian Trail offers grand views. The hike includes Mount Buckley, named for Samuel B. Buckley, a well-known naturalist who explored these mountains in the 1800s. A rock outcropping there offers spectacular views on both sides of the mountain. North into Tennessee, you can see Gatlinburg in the distance. To the northeast, Mount LeConte rises above the ridge of Sugarland Mountain. South into North Carolina, Forney Ridge and Welch Ridge lead down toward Fontana Lake.

Grassy Silers Bald is rapidly shrinking. The bald is named for Jesse Siler, who once grazed cattle here. With no grazing, Silers will one day be filled in with forest. Camping is available at Double Spring Gap Shelter and Silers Bald Shelter.

Trailhead: At the end of Clingmans Dome Road, 7 miles from Newfound

Gap, park at the Forney Ridge Parking Area below Clingmans Dome.

Description: At the far end of the parking area, just at the beginning of the paved Clingmans Dome Trail to the top of the mountain, turn left down the Forney Ridge Trail on a rocky path. At 0.1 mile, reach a junction with the Forney Ridge Trail to the left; turn to the right up the Clingmans Dome Bypass Trail.

At 0.6 mile, at Mount Buckley, you reach the Appalachian Trail; to the right, the AT leads 0.3 mile to Clingmans Dome Trail (where you can descend the paved path for a 1.4-mile loop walk). To head for Silers Bald, turn left along the AT.

The trail passes through stands of hobblebush, whose white flower clusters bloom in late April and May. Descend through fir and spruce to a broad clearing on the side of the mountain at 0.9 mile that offers wide views to the southwest. The trail continues down the ridgeline, occasionally passing through grassy clearings and back into woods. The clearings sport bluets and trout lily in spring. At 2.6 miles is a junction with the Goshen Prong Trail (hike 13), which descends to the right toward Elkmont; continue straight on the AT.

In June, Clinton's lily blooms with clusters of small white flowers on long stems, and yellow bead lily blooms with clusters of yellow flowers. The trail descends again and at 3.4 miles reaches Double Spring Gap, where you'll find an AT shelter. A path in front leads down to a water source; if that one is dry in late summer, try a path behind the shelter that accesses a second source—and so the name "Double Spring."

As you ascend from the gap, notice the many beech trees that have

View from Silers Bald

slowed the spread of red spruce west of Double Spring Gap. Pass over Jenkins Knob and dip through another beech gap. After crossing an open ridge, the trail descends through a grassy area at 3.9 miles where mountain ash carry bright red berry clusters in late summer; a lone spruce stands beside the trail. Ascending, you'll have views to the north of the Fish Camp Prong watershed.

At 4.2 miles cross The Narrows, where the trail drops off the slender ridgeline only to climb back up farther down. Then begin a final ascent toward Silers Bald. At 4.5 miles the Welch Ridge Trail leads to the left (it descends to High Rocks in 6.8 miles on an old path used by farmers, probably including the Welches, to drive livestock up the mountain for summer grazing on Silers Bald); continue straight.

A steep climb tops Silers Bald at 4.9 miles. This once-open bald is now surrounded by trees, but a grassy area still crowns the summit where a rock has a metal U.S. Geological Survey marker embedded in it. At the summit, a path to the right penetrates the surrounding trees to a rocky spur on the Tennessee side of the mountains that hangs over the valley of Silers Creek, a tributary of Fish Camp Prong.

Continuing west on the AT, in another 0.3 mile descend to the Silers Bald Shelter; water is available from a spring on the Tennessee side of the mountains. The AT continues to a junction in 2.5 miles from Silers Bald with the Miry Ridge Trail (hike 14) to the right. A rugged backpack of 24.4 miles out of Elkmont ascends the Little River and Goshen Prong Trails (hike 13), crosses Silers Bald on the AT, and descends the Miry Ridge and Jakes Creek Trails.

62 | FORNEY RIDGE TRAIL

Distance: 5.7 miles one way; to Andrews Bald, 1.8 miles one way
Difficulty: Strenuous first mile, then moderate
Elevation loss: 2,400 feet; elevation gain to Andrews Bald, 570 feet
Season: Year-round (access road closed in winter)
Cautions: Rocky trail
Connections: Clingmans Dome Bypass Trail, Forney Creek Trail, Springhouse Branch Trail

Attractions: Andrews Bald offers magnificent views. Named for Andrew Thompson, who grazed cattle on the bald in the 1800s, Andrews Bald is the highest in the park, at 5,860 feet. It offers wonderful places for lying in the grass and gazing across the mountain ridges with Fontana Lake below. In June, flame azalea and Catawba rhododendron bloom orange-gold and rose-purple on the open bald. Andrews, like Gregory Bald, has been designated an experimental research subzone. These are the only two balds that the Park Service manages in order to preserve the present plant composition and the scenic values.

Trailhead: Follow the Clingmans Dome Road to its end at the Forney Ridge Parking Area.

Description: At the far end of the parking area, the Forney Ridge Trail descends to a junction at 0.1 mile with the Clingmans Dome Bypass Trail to the right, which leads up to the AT (see hike 61); turn left to stay on the Forney Ridge Trail.

Pick your way down through rocks. This trail is scheduled for renovations, so the path may not be quite so difficult when you come this way. The trail descends along Forney Ridge running down from Clingmans Dome. At 1.0 mile, level off in a saddle where the path changes from rock to dirt. At 1.1 miles the Forney Creek Trail (hike 63) leads to the right; bear left.

Climb through spruce-fir and scattered hobblebush. At 1.8 miles you'll emerge into the open grassy area of Andrews Bald. Follow the rutted path across the bald; side paths lead left to viewpoints. On the south side, the trail bears to the right along the edge of trees and becomes faint. If you lose the path, just make your way down the slope and watch for where you reenter the woods at 2.0 miles.

Descend and bear to the right across the wooded slope to a switchback

Andrews Bald

left at 2.2 miles. Hobblebush and raspberries crowd the trail. Yellow bead lily blooms in spring with pale yellow-green flowers. The trail rises to bear to the right around a knoll. In spring, new leaves of beech trees paint the scene a bright green. At 4.0 miles, Buckhorn Bald lies along the ridge, but the opening has grown up and is no longer distinguishable.

A massive oak stands in a thicket of rhododendron. Then at 4.6 miles, the trail crosses a seep where you can see the large leaves of umbrella-leaf, a relatively rare plant that grows 2 feet tall and in spring has clusters of small white flowers. At 5.0 miles, turn left around an arm of the ridge, and look through the trees to your right to see the gap where you're headed. The trail regains the descending ridgeline and drops into Board Camp Gap to end at a junction at 5.7 miles.

To the left, the Springhouse Branch Trail leads down to the Noland Creek Trail (hike 91) in 2.8 miles. To the right, the Springhouse Branch Trail descends 5.5 miles west to connect with the Forney Creek Trail (hike 63). You can take the Forney Creek Trail back to the Forney Ridge Trail, with many creek crossings, for a 20.3-mile backpack loop from the Forney Ridge Parking Area at Clingmans Dome.

63 | FORNEY RIDGE AND FORNEY CREEK TRAILS

Distance: 12.0 miles one way; to Forney Creek Cascades, 2.9 miles one way
Difficulty: Strenuous
Elevation loss: 3,900 feet
Season: Year-round (access road closed in winter)
Cautions: Numerous creek fords
Connections: Jonas Creek Trail, Springhouse Branch Trail, Whiteoak Branch Trail, Bear Creek Trail, Lakeshore Trail

Attractions: In the first 2 miles of this hike, watch for a couple of scarred openings down the slope that are probably traces left from log skidding; the Norwood Lumber Company cut trees up toward Clingmans Dome until 1925, when the area burned and the operation was abandoned. This trail descends by Forney Creek Cascades, also the site of a camp or loading area for the Norwood railroad, perhaps the end of the main line. Look for cinders, scattered cables, a grate embedded in the base of a tree. There are several fords of Forney Creek, which can be difficult in wet seasons and impossible at high water; in dry seasons, you should be able to rockhop. The hike provides a segment of the Forney Ridge/Forney Creek Loop and also descends to Fontana Lake. Camping is available at Steeltrap Campsite (68),

Upper Forney Creek Cascades

Huggins Campsite (69), Jonas Creek Campsite (70), CCC Campsite (71), and Lower Forney Campsite (74).

Trailhead: Follow the Clingmans Dome Road to its end at the Forney Ridge Parking Area.

Description: Follow the Forney Ridge Trail (see hike 62) 1.1 miles to its junction with the Forney Creek Trail on the right. The Forney Creek Trail descends in a gentle grade, still in the spruce-fir forest of the higher elevations. The trail is rocky, and seeps wet and muddy the path. Across the valley of Forney Creek, you can see Forney Ridge through the trees, but you cannot see Andrews Bald, which is on the other side.

At 1.8 miles from the trailhead, the trail switches back left and descends into the cove hardwood forest of the Forney Creek valley. At 2.3 miles, reach the edge of Forney Creek, which washes down amid a boulder-strewn creekbed. The trail does not cross here, but instead moves into the boulders and turns to the right downstream, still on this side of the creek.

Rockhop a tributary of Forney Creek at 2.8 miles; a small cascade spills over a rail wedged at the top, a leftover from the Norwood railroad. The trail switchbacks left at 2.9 miles and descends into an opening beside Forney Creek that was once a railroad camp. Walk through the camp to the edge of Forney Creek to see a grand slide; the water cascades 30 feet into a pool, spills over to skim down a smooth rock face, and gathers in another rock depression before spilling over to slide down 100 feet or more. In fall, rafting leaves shoot by in a perpetual race. Notice the strips of quartz embedded in the Thunderhead sandstone; this silicon dioxide mineral filled joints in the sandstone and then was exposed during the mountain building that exposed the rock layers.

Continue downstream on an obvious railbed. At 3.4 miles, the trail drops into the Steeltrap Campsite (68) beside Forney Creek. A path up to the right once looped around the campsite. At 3.6 miles, the trail curves to the right to cross Steeltrap Creek; scattered timbers and rockwork abutments remain

Rock wall cribbing on Forney Creek Trail

from the railroad bridge that once spanned the creek; this trail is scheduled for renovations, so some bridges may be rebuilt. Afterward, watch for rock walls below on the left that were constructed to hold up the railbed. At 3.8 miles, a small stream cuts the trail in a rocky area with the remnants of a small bridge at the far end.

The railbed cuts through low ridges, so occasionally you'll pass through troughs with high earthen berms on both sides. At 4.5 miles, just as you emerge from one of these roadcuts, the trail curves back left and descends in a second-growth forest of tall yellow poplars. The trail switchbacks to the right at 4.8 miles near Steeltrap Creek; the open area to the left was likely used by the logging trains to pull forward and then back down in order to make the turn.

Cross the gully of a small stream with the remains of a bridge and then at 5.1 miles rockhop Little Steeltrap Creek at the ruins of another bridge. At 5.3 miles, the trail swings back to the left, crosses three drainages, and then crosses back over Little Steeltrap Creek to reach the edge of Forney Creek at 5.5 miles. A causeway leads up to a bridge abutment that once supported a rail bridge. This is the first of several fords of Forney Creek; you should be able to rockhop in dry seasons. At this crossing, a small stream cascades down on the far side as Forney Creek tumbles through boulders. On the other side, continue down to cross Buckhorn Branch. If bridge timbers still span the small creek, test your weight before stepping out; better to just step down into the creek.

Rhododendrons crowd the trail, which switchbacks to the right at 6.4 miles near Chokeberry Branch, another tributary of Forney Creek. After the turn, walk along a rock wall that holds up the old railbed on your right. Through rhododendron again, switchback left and curve right to cross a small stream where the bridge timbers may still be in place. Continue straight to the edge of Forney Creek and a rockhop crossing at 6.8 miles with old stone bridge abutments.

On the other side, the Huggins Campsite (69) lies in the peninsula of land between Forney Creek and Huggins Creek, a major tributary. Soon after, cross Forney Creek again and then twice more, at 7.2 and 7.7 miles; eventually you'll ford as the creek grows larger. The trail crosses Board Camp Creek, a tributary. At 8.1 miles reach a junction with the Jonas Creek Trail (hike 94) to the right (it fords Forney Creek to the Jonas Creek Campsite, 70, which rests on the wedge of land between Forney and Jonas Creeks; there was a bridge here at one time, so it may be replaced by the time you get here); continue straight.

The Forney Creek Trail soon turns up to the left, leaving the railbed that once crossed the creek to the other side. Descend back to creek level at 9.1 miles and enter the CCC Campsite (71), the site of an old Civilian Conservation Corps camp; the rock chimney from the camp building still stands with a fireplace and mantel. At the far end, the Springhouse Branch Trail (hike 91) ascends 5.5 miles to the east to the crest of Forney Ridge. You can walk a good 20.3-mile loop down the Forney Creek Trail, up Springhouse Branch Trail, and back on the Forney Ridge Trail (hike 62).

Continue down the Forney Creek Trail to rockhop Bee Gum Branch at 9.2 miles and cross two smaller streams before turning up again to avoid another creek crossing; then return to creek level. At 10.3 miles, the trail turns up to reach a junction with the Whiteoak Branch Trail to the left (it leads to the Lakeshore Trail, hike 92, and provides a little shorter route back to Lakeview Drive, if that is your destination); turn right.

Rockhop Whiteoak Branch and continue on the Forney Creek Trail. At 11.3 miles, drop off the railbed to the right to a junction with the Bear Creek Trail (hike 94) to the left (it crosses Forney Creek on a bridge and ascends Welch Ridge); stay left to continue down the Forney Creek Trail.

At 11.8 miles, the Forney Creek Trail meets the Lakeshore Trail to the left (you can follow the Lakeshore Trail, hike 92, 2.9 miles to Lakeview Drive); continue straight ahead.

The Lakeshore Trail/Forney Creek Trail crosses Forney Creek on a bridge at 11.9 miles. The Forney Creek Trail ends at the Lower Forney Campsite (74) on the Forney Creek embayment of Fontana Lake at 12.0 miles. This campsite is accessible by boat from across the lake; it's a bit trashy with flotsam washed up along the lakeshore.

From here the Lakeshore Trail turns to the right to pass the edge of the embayment and make a long traverse to the west.

NEWFOUND GAP ROAD

From the crest of the Smokies, Newfound Gap Road descends into the North Carolina side of the park. Just down from Newfound Gap, the road makes a broad curve to the left at a pullout on the right that offers a grand view of the Oconaluftee River Valley. In the highlands, Kephart Prong, Beech Flats Prong, and Kanati Fork converge to create the Oconaluftee. The name comes from the Cherokee word *Ekwanulti,* meaning "place by the river." The river flows beside Newfound Gap Road down the mountain. At 2.1 miles from Newfound Gap (13.9 miles from the Oconaluftee Visitor Center), watch for a wide overlook on the left with parking on both ends; you can walk from either end toward the middle for outstanding views down the Deep Creek Valley.

Getting there: From the Tennessee side of the park, take Newfound Gap Road to the crest of the Smokies and cross over at Newfound Gap to descend the North Carolina side of the mountains. Several trails lead off the road on its way south.

Approaching the park from the south, take US 441 north from Cherokee into the park where it becomes Newfound Gap Road and ascends to Newfound Gap in 16 miles.

64 DEEP CREEK TRAIL

Distance: 13.6 miles one way
Difficulty: Moderate
Elevation loss: 3,000 feet
Season: Year-round
Cautions: Mud holes, stream crossings, overgrown in places
Connections: Fork Ridge Trail, Pole Road Creek Trail, Martins Gap Trail, Loop Trail, Indian Creek Trail

Attractions: This trail descends the deep valley of Deep Creek, which gathers waters in the valley between Thomas Divide and Sunkota Ridge on the east and Fork Ridge and Noland Divide on the west. This hike has plenty of campsites. Bryson Place Campsite was the site of the Bryson family cabin; Col. Thad Bryson laid out the town lots for Bryson City. A side path near the campsite leads into the bottoms along the creek, where you'll find a small memorial made of a millstone and rocks dedicated to Horace Kephart, author and park proponent. Bryson Place was a favorite spot for

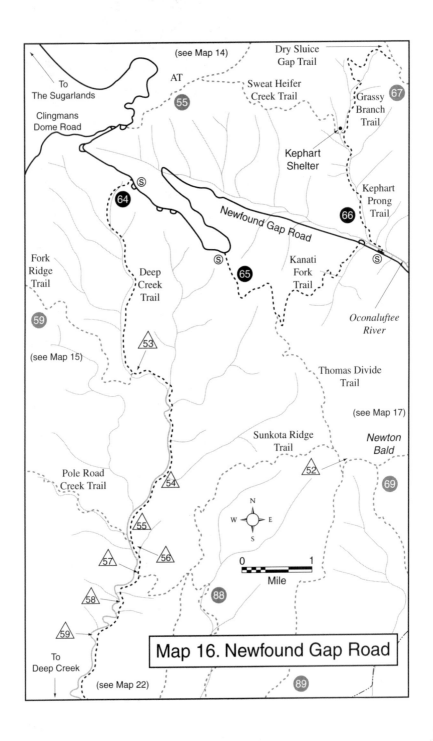

Map 16. Newfound Gap Road

Deep Creek

Kephart, who had his last permanent camp here. The memorial was erected by the Kephart Troop of the Bryson City Boy Scouts. Camping is available at Poke Patch Campsite (53), Nettle Creek Campsite (54), Pole Road Campsite (55), Burnt Spruce Campsite (56), Bryson Place Campsite (57), Nicks Nest Branch Campsite (58), McCracken Branch Campsite (59), Bumgardner Branch Campsite (60), and Deep Creek Campground.

Trailhead: The Deep Creek trailhead is on Newfound Gap Road at 1.6 miles from Newfound Gap or 14.4 miles north of the Oconaluftee Visitor Center. Hiker parking is 100 yards south of the trailhead.

Description: From the trailhead, turn down on a footpath in a lush forest of hardwoods, spruce, and rhododendron. Several switchbacks and curves help in your descent toward Deep Creek. At 1.0 mile, the trail crosses a shallow stream and turns downstream. At 1.7 miles, rockhop this tributary near its junction with Deep Creek. From here on, the trail parallels Deep Creek on the east side. Although the trail has some ups and downs, it's a steady descent. Once in these bottomlands, the trail has boggy areas that you must pass through or around.

Cross a side stream on rocks at 2.2 miles. After several more small stream crossings, descend to Poke Patch Campsite (53) at 4.0 miles and a junction with the Fork Ridge Trail to the right, which fords Deep Creek and climbs toward the Clingmans Dome Road; walk straight through the campsite to stay on the Deep Creek Trail.

185

Pass large hemlocks and at 4.7 miles cross a side stream where moss-covered rocks jut into the creek, a good place for lunch. At 4.9 miles, the trail fords Cherry Creek and later passes a rock wall on the left, crossing Beetree Creek flowing out of the rocks at 5.2 miles. The trail then moves back to a woodland environment, where it passes between two large yellow poplars at 5.6 miles.

At 5.8 miles, a side stream runs through a metal culvert under the trail (all metal culverts are slated to be replaced with more natural constructions). Just beyond, you'll see a path that leads to the left. If you go straight, you'll reach the water's edge where the creek has meandered across the trail, washing it away. By taking the side path, you climb around this area and descend to rejoin the trail at 5.9 miles. The trail crosses Nettle Creek in three branches at 6.6 miles and arrives at the Nettle Creek Campsite (54).

The Pole Road Campsite (55) lies at 7.6 miles at a junction with the Pole Road Creek Trail to the right, which crosses Deep Creek on a long footbridge and climbs to Noland Divide Trail (hike 60); just at the junction, turn on a more-used path up to the left to once more avoid the creek's uncertain edge. Regain the trail at 7.8 miles.

At 8.0 miles, pass the Burnt Spruce Campsite (56) and then cross Elliot Cove Branch on a footlog. At 8.2 miles, the trail curves left up to Bryson Place Campsite (57); a path that continues straight leads to more camping spots. At a junction in the campsite, the Martins Gap Trail (hike 88) turns left to the top of Sunkota Ridge in 1.5 miles; from this junction, the Deep Creek Trail goes straight, crosses a side creek, and passes an old house site on the right, where you can turn down to the right to the Kephart memorial.

Continuing on the Deep Creek Trail, reach the Nicks Nest Branch Campsite (58) at 8.9 miles where the trail curves left. Then cross some small streams and climb over a rise to descend to the McCracken Branch Campsite (59) at 9.3 miles. Join an old roadbed that ascends Bumgardner Ridge and then descend back to Deep Creek at the Bumgardner Branch Campsite (60) at 11.3 miles. The trail crosses Bumgardner Branch on a footlog and ascends over a ridge to a junction at 11.6 miles with the gravel Deep Creek Road, which is closed to traffic; turn left on the road to stay on the Deep Creek Trail.

At 11.9 miles pass through the Jenkins Place at a junction with the Loop Trail, which leads left over Sunkota Ridge to connect with the Indian Creek Trail (hike 86) in 1.0 mile; continue straight.

Cross a bridge over Deep Creek and pass over a rise. The Deep Creek Horse Trail leaves the road on the right to pass Juney Whank Falls (hike 87) and ends at the Deep Creek Horse Stables. Stay straight to cross another bridge over Deep Creek and a bridge over Indian Creek to a junction at 12.9 miles with the Indian Creek Trail to the left. Stay straight another 0.7 mile to the Deep Creek trailhead just north of the Deep Creek Campground.

65 | THOMAS DIVIDE AND KANATI FORK TRAILS

Distance: 4.7 miles one way
Difficulty: Moderate
Elevation loss: 2,200 feet
Season: Year-round
Cautions: Small creek crossings
Connections: Kephart Prong Trail

Attractions: This walk starts along Thomas Ridge, named for William H. Thomas, the white man who helped the Eastern Band of the Cherokees secure lands on which to live. Newfound Gap Road follows Thomas Ridge down from the crest of the Smokies to the Thomas Divide trailhead. This is a surprisingly good wildflower trail in late spring; watch for Clinton's lily, bluets, lousewort, white erect trillium, painted trillium, chickweed, and spring beauty along the ridgeline and more wildflowers down along Kanati Fork.

Trailhead: The Thomas Divide trailhead lies on the west side of the Newfound Gap Road, 3.5 miles south of Newfound Gap or 12.5 miles north of the Oconaluftee Visitor Center. To run a shuttle vehicle, drive to the Kanati Fork trailhead, 5.1 miles south on Newfound Gap Road from this point; park at the quiet walkway on the east side of the road.

Description: Climb the hill above the parking area to the Thomas Divide Trail and walk out Thomas Ridge. The trail passes over a knoll to drop through a saddle and ascend at 0.5 mile to the top of Beetree Ridge, which leads down to the right. Swing left along the narrow ridgeline covered in fine grass and tall hardwoods. At 1.0 mile bear to the right at Turkey Flyup, the highest point on Thomas Divide at 5,040 feet; this was once a good spot for hunters to flush wild turkeys. The trail descends along Thomas Ridge, with Beetree Ridge off to your right. In a gap at 1.8 miles, reach a junction with the Kanati Fork Trail on the left. The Thomas Divide Trail continues straight along the line of Thomas Ridge, eventually descending into the Deep Creek area (see hike 89); turn left onto the Kanati Fork Trail.

Descend into the Kanati Fork Valley, switching back left at 2.0 miles. This is a good trail for spring wildflowers, and in fall watch for the blue berries of blue cohosh, yellow bead lily, and Clinton's lily as well as the red berry clusters of false Solomon's seal, all mingled with blooming fall asters, white snakeroot, and an occasional gentian. Watch for a large oak on the right. Fraser magnolias scatter their conelike fruit across the trail.

At 3.1 miles, cross the first tributary drainage of Kanati Fork in a steeply descending ravine. The trail winds on down the slope, making a short, steep drop into a muddy area at 3.3 miles and then passing a small slide area at a seep.

At 3.5 miles, a large maple stands to the right where the trail turns down left. You soon cross a rocky drainage and then another tributary stream clothed in yellow jewelweed in fall. The trail switchbacks to the right to cross the same stream and switchbacks left to cross a third time. Watch for showy orchis in late April and early May and listen for Kanati Fork, which comes into sight on your right as it tumbles its way toward and eventually passes under Newfound Gap Road. The trail crosses two tributary streams and descends to the road at 4.7 miles. The parking area for the quiet walkway lies across the highway.

You can pick up the Kephart Prong Trail (hike 66) by walking south 0.4 mile down Newfound Gap Road.

66 | KEPHART PRONG AND GRASSY BRANCH TRAILS

Distance: 4.5 miles one way
Difficulty: Moderate
Elevation gain: 2,570 feet
Season: Year-round
Cautions: Narrow footbridges, creek crossings
Connections: Sweat Heifer Creek Trail, Dry Sluice Gap Trail

Attractions: This climb along Kephart Prong passes through an old CCC camp where you'll find the stone frame for the camp sign, the remains of a water fountain, and a tall stone chimney. During the 1930s the CCC had seventeen camps scattered throughout the Smokies to house the young men who constructed trails, roads, and visitor facilities for the new park. This hike also passes through a fish hatchery site. After the park was established, the Park Service continued stocking streams until 1947; here is where many of the rainbow trout were hatched. It was thought at the time these trout were needed to fill the streams left vacant by the native brook trout. As it turned out, the presence of the nonnative trout kept the brook trout from refilling the streams after the forest recovered from logging. This hike has many spring wildflowers. Camping is available at Kephart Shelter.

Trailhead: Parking is on the east side of Newfound Gap Road 9 miles south of Newfound Gap or 7.0 miles north of the Oconaluftee Visitor Center.

Description: Cross the bridge over the Oconaluftee River. Turn left and walk an old road that parallels the river and then curves to the right up Kephart Prong. At 0.2 mile, enter the old CCC camp. Large boxwood shrubs and juniper bushes mark the area. A low rock wall on the left outlines a yard or a garden. Rusting pots and utensils lie scattered around.

At 0.3 mile, the road turns left to ford Kephart Prong, but continue straight and make a sharp left to a footbridge crossing and rejoin the road on the other side of the creek. A foundation lies straight ahead in the woods, barely recognizable as a flat raised area. Turn to the right on the old roadway to pass through the fish hatchery site.

As the trail climbs steadily, watch for a structure high on the left that may have been a cistern or a holding tank. At 0.6 mile, the road fords Kephart Prong again, but a footbridge to the right takes you over the creek,

Kephart Prong Crossing

which splashes through boulders and slides through pools of cold water. At 0.8 mile you'll see old rails beside the trail; this was once a railroad bed for Champion Fibre Company. The trail once more crosses the creek on a footbridge. Continue a steady climb until the trail passes over a footbridge for the last time at 1.4 miles. Soon Sweat Heifer Creek comes in from the left to join Kephart Prong. At 2.0 miles, reach the the Kephart Shelter and the end of the Kephart Prong Trail at a junction with the Sweat Heifer Creek Trail to the left, which climbs to the crest of the Smokies to join the AT in 3.7 miles. Take the Grassy Branch Trail to the right of the shelter.

This trail becomes steeper as it ascends Richland Mountain and narrows as the railroad grade veers off to the left. At 3.0 miles cross a small tributary and then cross Lower Grassy Branch just above where Upper and Lower Grassy Branches converge to create Kephart Prong. From here enter a drier forest of overhanging laurel topped by birch, maple, and beech. At 3.4 miles the trail switchbacks right and leads up through a tunnel of rhododendron and laurel.

At 4.0 miles, the trail enters a grassy area and crosses the headwaters of Lower Grassy Branch. Watch for views on the right of the Kephart Prong Valley and Thomas Divide beyond. Reach the ridge of Richland Mountain at 4.5 miles and the end of the Grassy Branch Trail at a junction with Dry Sluice Gap Trail.

To the left Dry Sluice Gap Trail climbs Richland Mountain to connect with the AT in 1.3 miles at Dry Sluice Gap just east of Charlies Bunion (see hike 55). To the right, Dry Sluice Gap Trail descends toward the Smokemont area, a good day's outing that ends at the Smokemont Campground in another 6.9 miles (hike 67).

SMOKEMONT/ OCONALUFTEE

Smokemont Campground occupies the site of a sawmill village operated by Champion Fibre Company, the largest lumbering operation in the Smokies, controlling 93,000 acres. The small community that preceded the lumber camp was called Bradleytown for early settlers in the region. The large campground sits beside the Bradley Fork of the Oconaluftee River.

South from the campground, the Mingus Mill historic place lies on the west side of Newfound Gap Road, 0.5 mile up from the Oconaluftee Visitor Center. The 1886 turbine mill replaced an older mill that had been built here by John Jacob Mingus when he settled the region in the 1790s. The newer mill was built by Sion T. Early for Mingus's son, Dr. John Mingus. When you visit, don't miss the short walk up to the beginning of the flume that carries water to the mill; there you can cross on boards and walk a path along the millrace to the small dam and gate on Mingus Creek that divert water to the flume.

Will Messer apple house moved from Little Cataloochee Valley

At the Oconaluftee Visitor Center, you can visit other historic structures at the Mountain Farm Museum, including the John E. Davis log cabin moved from the Indian Creek area of the park, an apple house moved from Little Cataloochee Valley, and a large barn original to the site. The museum walk is also the beginning of the Oconaluftee River Trail that follows the river for 1.5 miles and ends in the town of Cherokee.

Getting there: From Cherokee on the south, take US 441 into the park where it becomes Newfound Gap Road. You'll pass a right turn on a small road that leads to Big Cove Road and then pass the end of the Blue Ridge

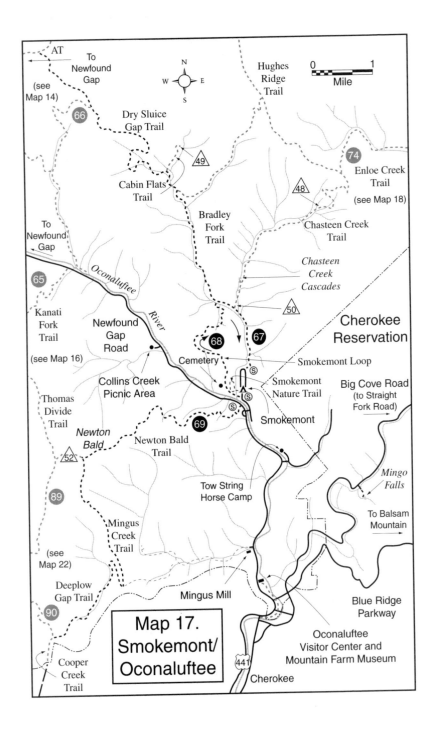

AT
To Newfound Gap
(see Map 14)
66
Dry Sluice Gap Trail
Hughes Ridge Trail
N
W   E
S
0   1
Mile
49
Cabin Flats Trail
74
Enloe Creek Trail
(see Map 18)
48
To Newfound Gap
65
Oconaluftee
River
Bradley Fork Trail
Chasteen Creek Trail
Chasteen Creek Cascades
Kanati Fork Trail
(see Map 16)
Newfound Gap Road
50
Cherokee Reservation
68   67
Collins Creek Picnic Area
Cemetery
Smokemont Loop
S
Thomas Divide Trail
Newton Bald
52
Newton Bald Trail
69
Smokemont Nature Trail
S
S
Smokemont
Big Cove Road (to Straight Fork Road)
89
Tow String Horse Camp
Mingo Falls
To Balsam Mountain
Mingus Creek Trail
(see Map 22)
Deeplow Gap Trail
90
Mingus Mill
Blue Ridge Parkway
Map 17.
Smokemont/
Oconaluftee
Oconaluftee Visitor Center and Mountain Farm Museum
441
Cooper Creek Trail
Cherokee

Parkway to reach the Oconaluftee Visitor Center on the right. Newfound Gap Road continues into the park, ascending to Newfound Gap in 16 miles. At 0.5 mile from the visitor center, a road to the west leads to Mingus Mill. At 3.2 miles, a road to the right enters Smokemont, which is 12.8 miles down from Newfound Gap. To access the campground, turn right and cross a bridge over the Oconaluftee River to an intersection. To the right, the road leads to the horse stables. Straight across and up into the woods is the beginning of the Hughes Ridge Trail, which is no longer maintained where it crosses the Cherokee Reservation, but at the trailhead you can walk 0.1 mile up to the Luftee Baptist Church, reconstructed in 1912. Turn left at the intersection to enter the Smokemont Campground.

67 BRADLEY FORK, CABIN FLATS, AND DRY SLUICE GAP TRAILS

Distance: 8.2 miles one way; to Chasteen Creek Cascades, 1.7 miles one way
Difficulty: Moderate
Elevation gain: 2,900 feet
Season: Year-round
Cautions: Muddy sections, creek crossings
Connections: Chasteen Creek Trail, Smokemont Loop, Grassy Branch Trail, Appalachian Trail

Attractions: The Bradley Fork and Dry Sluice Gap Trails connect Smokemont with the AT on the crest of the Smokies, passing a trail to Chasteen Creek Cascades. Camping is available at Smokemont Campground, Lower Chasteen Creek Campsite (50), and Cabin Flats Campsite (49).

Trailhead: In Smokemont Campground, at the beginning of a one-way loop keep right to reach the far end of the campground at a gated road for the Bradley Fork Trail.

Description: Walk up Champion Fibre's old railbed, paralleling the Bradley Fork of the Oconaluftee River. A horse trail comes in from the right to provide access for horse riders from the stables. At 0.4 mile a pumping station stands on the right and then a side road leads to the water supply for the campground; stay straight. The trail crosses a bridge over Chasteen Creek where it joins Bradley Fork and reaches a junction at 1.2 miles with the Chasteen Creek Trail to the right (that trail passes Lower Chasteen Creek Campsite, 50, and in 0.5 mile reaches a side path to the left to Chasteen Creek Cascades, a 60-foot double drop in the creekbed; see hike 74); stay straight at the junction.

Bradley Fork

Reach another junction at 1.7 miles, with the Smokemont Loop (hike 68) to the left, which crosses Bradley Fork on a narrow footbridge and loops back to the campground in 3.8 miles; continue straight up the Bradley Fork Trail.

Two bridges take you across an island in the creek to the other side at 3.0 miles. Cross back over the creek at 3.4 miles where Taywa Creek joins Bradley Fork on the right. Then at 4.1 miles where the railbed bends to the right lies a junction with the Cabin Flats Trail straight ahead; the Bradley Fork Trail turns to the right, along the road, for 3.3 miles to end at the Hughes Ridge Trail at the top of the ridge (from there you can loop back to the Smokemont Campground by turning southeast to the Chasteen Creek

Trail and turn down to link back with the Bradley Fork Trail, a hike of 15.0 miles); continue straight ahead on the Cabin Flats Trail.

The Cabin Flats Trail soon crosses Bradley Fork on a bridge and then crosses Tennessee Branch on a footbridge. At 4.4 miles is another junction, where the Cabin Flats Trail turns to the right to follow Bradley Fork to the northeast and dead-end in 1 mile at the Cabin Flats Campsite (49); take the Dry Sluice Gap Trail to the left.

Cross Tennessee Branch and its tributaries several times and then ascend the east side of Richland Mountain. Topping the ridge at 6.7 miles, ascend more gradually to a junction at 6.9 miles with the Grassy Branch Trail to the left (which leads down to the Kephart Prong Trail in 2.5 miles); continue straight.

The Dry Sluice Gap Trail reaches the AT at Dry Sluice Gap at 8.2 miles. To the left, the AT leads past Charlies Bunion (hike 55) to Newfound Gap Road in 4.4 miles. To the right, the AT continues east along a narrow ridge interrupted by a series of small knolls aptly called The Sawteeth and passes through Porters Gap to a junction with the Hughes Ridge Trail at Pecks Corner in 6.0 miles.

68 | SMOKEMONT LOOP AND BRADLEY FORK TRAILS

Distance: 5.6-mile loop
Difficulty: Moderate
Elevation change: 1,000 feet
Season: Year-round
Cautions: Long, narrow footlog, stream crossings
Connections: Chasteen Creek Trail, Smokemont Nature Trail

Attractions: This pleasant woodland walk offers a loop hike out of the Smokemont Campground. Watch for large patches of trailing arbutus; the plant hugs the ground, and so you have to turn up the leaves to see the small white or pink blossoms in spring that were once used as a perfume because of their subtle fragrance. Camping is available at Smokemont Campground.

Trailhead: In the Smokemont Campground, past the registration station, take the second left into Section B to cross the campground. On the other side, turn left. Pass the Smokemont Nature Trail on the left (it crosses Bradley Fork and makes a 0.5-mile loop over the end of Richland Mountain). Beyond the nature trail, watch for parking near the Bradley Fork bridge.

Description: Pass around a gate and cross a bridge over Bradley Fork just above its confluence with the Oconaluftee River. The trail follows a grassy roadbed until at 0.2 mile it turns right to make a gradual ascent of Richland Mountain (the road continues straight into an abandoned section of the campground).

Up the trail, watch for an unmarked side path to the left through trees and bushes that leads a few yards to the old Bradley Cemetery; several gravestones stand in the clearing.

The main trail makes several switchbacks in the climb. You reach a level area and then ascend at 1.4 miles through a field of downed chestnuts killed by blight years ago. After, watch for some large chestnut oaks. Reaching the ridgeline at 2.1 miles, wind around a point on Richland Mountain. The trail descends, passes through a gap at 2.6 miles, and heads down the northeast side of Richland Mountain with a view of Hughes Ridge and overgrown Becks Bald to the right. Pass around a hemlock knob and cross small streams at 3.5 miles and 3.7 miles.

Reaching a level with Bradley Fork, walk upstream. The trail crosses a footlog over a side stream, then at 3.9 miles turns right to cross the creek on a long, narrow footlog. On the other side is a junction with the Bradley Fork Trail (to the left it connects with Dry Sluice Gap Trail, hike 67); turn right.

Walk 1.7 miles on Bradley Fork Trail (see hike 67) back to the Smokemont Campground, passing the Chasteen Creek Trail on the way. Then follow the campground road back to the lower trailhead.

69 | NEWTON BALD, MINGUS CREEK, AND DEEPLOW GAP TRAILS

Distance: 9.8 miles one way; to Newton Bald, 4.6 miles one way
Difficulty: Moderate
Elevation change: 2,880 feet
Season: Year-round
Cautions: None
Connections: Thomas Divide Trail, Cooper Creek Trail

Attractions: Don't be disappointed, but Newton Bald is no more. The bald is overgrown with small trees, and if it were not designated on maps, you would not guess that the bald at one time stretched along this ridgeline. The semi-open knoll I found years ago had a view of the Oconaluftee River Valley to the northeast. Between my visits to this knoll, it has grown up even more, and trees have fallen to further obscure where the bald has been. It's interesting nevertheless, especially after seeing Silers, Gregory, and Andrews Balds, to witness a forest reclaiming a grassy bald. The

Newton Bald

pleasant walk along the Mingus Creek Trail has wildflowers and some of the largest surviving chestnut trees in the park. Camping is available at Smokemont Campground and Newton Bald Campsite (52).

Trailhead: At the turnoff to Smokemont Campground, park across from the campground entrance on the west side of Newfound Gap Road. Then walk north 150 yards to the trailhead. You can run a shuttle vehicle to the end of the Cooper Creek Road north from US 19 in Ela (see hike 90).

Description: The trail ascends an old roadbed through second-growth timber. At 0.2 mile, a trail on the left provides access from the horse camp on Tow String Road. At 0.3 mile, the road bends to the left (part of the horse trail network); stay to the right on a footpath that is the Newton Bald Trail.

Wind up the ridge to another junction at 0.5 mile with another trail that leads left toward the Tow String Horse Camp; turn right.

Continue a moderate climb of Newton Ridge; at 0.6 mile, round a point to look northeast across the Oconaluftee River Valley. The trail then enters a lane walled in with rhododendron and laurel and passes through a gap to continue the ascent. The trail crosses small streams, switchbacks at the head of a ravine, and climbs through another gap.

At 4.6 miles, round a bend to top a knoll at Newton Bald. At 4.7 miles, reach a junction with the Mingus Creek Trail to the left; if you are just out to see the overgrowth bald, turn around here to return to Newfound Gap Road. (The Newton Bald Trail continues straight from the junction for 0.5 mile to reach the Newton Bald Campsite, 52, a small camp in a gap with a spring 100 yards down the south slope of the mountain; ascending from the campsite another 0.1 mile, the Newton Bald Trail ends at a junction with the Thomas Divide Trail.) At the junction of the Newton Bald and Mingus Creek Trails, turn left on Mingus Creek Trail.

The trail descends a long ridge running south from Newton Bald. Watch for numerous chestnut trees, including some 6 or more inches in diameter. You'll easily recognize the lance-shaped leaves, 6 to 8 inches long with serrated edges. The chestnuts were once the dominant trees in the forests of the southern Appalachians until a fungus introduced from eastern Asia killed the mature trees in the early part of the century. But the tree is extremely hardy, and so stumps and roots continue to send up sprouts. The young saplings can survive for several years before they also succumb to the fungus.

At 5.3 miles, the trail and ridgetop meet, and the trail descends through laurel, making a straight shot down the ridgeline. Watch for the tan to red flowers of pinesap blooming in August and September; this non-green plant sticks up a few inches out of the leaf cover where it feeds off decaying matter. At 5.5 miles, the trail curves left across the ridgeline and descends the eastern slope in a series of switchbacks. Watch for tall interrupted fern; brown fertile leaflets interrupt green leaflets along the stem. In summer, you'll also see the bright orange berries of the yellow mandarin that in spring has bell-shaped yellow flowers hanging below the leaves.

The trail descends in laurel to reach a swag along the ridge at 7.1 miles and then ascends to a junction at 7.7 miles with the Deeplow Gap Trail. Straight ahead, a faint path once led 0.5 mile to the Adams Creek Road. Back to the left lies an unmaintained section of the Mingus Creek Trail that descends to a junction at 1.8 miles with an old road from the Mingus Mill Parking Area; use is no longer encouraged because it traverses the watershed for the Oconaluftee water supply. Turn to the right down the Deeplow Gap Trail.

The trail descends the west side of the ridge along the old Cooper Creek Road. At 8.3 miles, the trail reaches the edge of Cooper Creek and turns left downstream. The creek soon drops away from the trail. The two come back together where the trail crosses the creek on a footbridge at 8.7 miles. The stream channel is choked with doghobble and rhododendron. Cross two more footbridges over the creek at 9.5 miles and 9.6 miles, and reach a junction at 9.8 miles with the Cooper Creek Trail (hike 90).

To the left, Cooper Creek Road continues 0.6 mile to emerge from the park to vehicle access up from the community of Ela on US 19. To the right, the Deeplow Gap Trail (hike 90) connects with the Thomas Divide Trail (hike 89) at Deeplow Gap in 1.7 miles and the Indian Creek Trail (hike 88) in another 2.1 miles.

BALSAM MOUNTAIN

Heintooga Ridge Road up Balsam Mountain was originally, at least in part, the Suncrest Lumber Company's rail line up the mountain. Along Heintooga Ridge Road, watch for the Mile High Overlook that, at 5,250 feet, presents a panoramic vista showing nearly the entire range of the Great Smoky Mountains. Where paved Heintooga Ridge Road ends, the one-way unpaved Balsam Mountain Road (closed in winter) travels north across the western slope of Balsam Mountain, following an old railbed. It links Balsam Mountain with the Oconaluftee area via unpaved Straight Fork Road (also closed in winter) and Big Cove Road back to Newfound Gap Road. Big Cove Road passes several commercial campgrounds, including Mingo Falls Campground, where you're welcome to walk 0.2 mile up to Mingo Falls, a 200-foot slash of water streaming down a rock face (see Map 17).

Getting there: On Newfound Gap Road 0.7 mile south of the Oconaluftee Visitor Center, turn east on the Blue Ridge Parkway, which travels north 469 miles to Shenandoah National Park in Virginia. In 11.2 miles, at Wolf Laurel Gap, turn left (north) on the Heintooga Ridge Road. Coming from the east on the Blue Ridge Parkway or from Maggie Valley on US 19, where US 19 intersects the Parkway at Soco Gap, go north on the parkway 2.5 miles to reach Heintooga Ridge Road on the right. Along the road (closed in winter), you'll enter the park at 4.8 miles and reach trailheads at 5.4 miles on the left for the Flat Creek Trail and at 6.3 miles at Polls Gap on the right. From Polls Gap, continue up Heintooga Ridge Road past the Balsam Mountain Campground on the left at 8.6 miles. At a turnaround at the end of the

The Smokies, view from Mile High Overlook

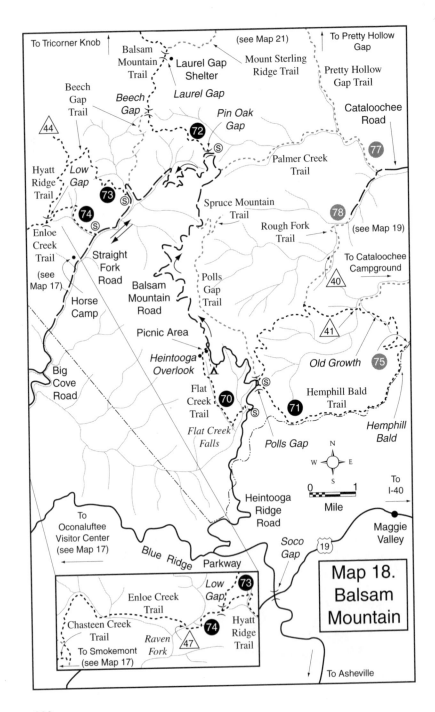

To Tricorner Knob

Balsam Mountain Trail

Laurel Gap Shelter

Laurel Gap

(see Map 21)

Mount Sterling Ridge Trail

To Pretty Hollow Gap

Pretty Hollow Gap Trail

Cataloochee Road

Beech Gap Trail

Beech Gap

Pin Oak Gap

72

Ⓢ

Palmer Creek Trail

77

44

Hyatt Ridge Trail

Low Gap

73

Ⓢ

Spruce Mountain Trail

Rough Fork Trail

78

(see Map 19)

74

Ⓢ

To Cataloochee Campground

Enloe Creek Trail

(see Map 17)

Straight Fork Road

Balsam Mountain Road

Polls Gap Trail

40

41

Old Growth

75

Horse Camp

Picnic Area

Big Cove Road

Heintooga Overlook

⛺

Hemphill Bald Trail

70

Ⓣ Ⓢ

71

Flat Creek Trail

Ⓢ

Hemphill Bald

Flat Creek Falls

Polls Gap

N
W · E
S

0 ___ 1 Mile

To I-40

Heintooga Ridge Road

Soco Gap

19

Maggie Valley

To Oconaluftee Visitor Center (see Map 17)

Blue Ridge Parkway

Map 18. Balsam Mountain

Enloe Creek Trail

Low Gap

73

Chasteen Creek Trail

Raven Fork

74

Hyatt Ridge Trail

47

To Smokemont (see Map 17)

To Asheville

road at 9 miles, the upper end of the Flat Creek Trail and the Heintooga Picnic Area are to the left; the Balsam Mountain Nature Trail also emerges on the road here, having ascended from the campground. At the end of the pavement is the beginning of the graveled one-way Balsam Mountain Road.

Continue straight on Balsam Mountain Road (closed in winter). Down this dirt road are trailheads at 5.8 miles (the Spruce Mountain Trail on the right leads 1 mile to the top of Spruce Mountain, a junction with the Polls Gap Trail to the right, and an overgrown path to the left that once led to the site of a fire tower), at 7.5 miles (the Palmer Creek Trail on the right leads 3.3 miles east to connect with the Pretty Hollow Gap Trail in Cataloochee Valley), at 8.2 miles in Pin Oak Gap (the Balsam Mountain Trail is on the right), and at 12.8 miles (the Beech Gap Trail leads 2.5 miles up to the Balsam Mountain Trail). The road then fords Straight Fork Creek. At the ford, the road becomes two-way Straight Fork Road, also unpaved and closed in winter.

Just beyond the ford, at 13 miles, on the right is the trailhead for another section of the Beech Gap Trail. On down Straight Fork Road, which parallels the Straight Fork of the Raven Fork of the Oconaluftee River, the Round Bottom Horse Camp lies in the trees on the right at 13.6 miles and the Hyatt Ridge trailhead is at 14.5 miles.

The alternative route to Straight Fork Road leads from Newfound Gap Road. At 1.3 miles south of the Oconaluftee Visitor Center, past the Blue Ridge Parkway, turn east to reach Big Cove Road in 0.2 mile. Turn left and travel through the northern part of the Cherokee Reservation. At a junction just after a bridge over Raven Fork at 8.9 miles, turn right on Straight Fork Road. In another 0.9 mile the road becomes gravel and enters the park; here the road is closed in winter. At 2.5 miles, you will reach the Hyatt Ridge trailhead on the left; the Beech Gap Trail is another 1.5 miles up the road.

70 | FLAT CREEK TRAIL

Distance: 2.6 miles one way; to Flat Creek Falls, 0.8 mile one way
Difficulty: Easy
Elevation gain: 570 feet
Season: Year-round (access road closed in winter)
Cautions: Difficult view of Flat Creek Falls
Connections: None

Attractions: This hike through a pretty woodland is one of the nicest walks in the park. At the waterfall, the narrow stream of Flat Creek runs down a twisting chute for a couple hundred feet; this is one of the longest cascades in the park. Unfortunately, there is no easy way to view Flat Creek Falls. Camping is available at Balsam Mountain Campground.

Trailhead: At 5.4 miles on Heintooga Ridge Road, you reach the trailhead for the Flat Creek Trail on the left at an unpaved pulloff beside the road. To run a shuttle vehicle, continue up Heintooga Ridge Road 3.6 miles to its end at the Heintooga Picnic Area.

Description: Drop from the road into a hardwood-rhododendron forest. The path turns left and descends to a footbridge crossing of a small stream at 0.2 mile. Then ascend over a rise and descend to a junction at Bunches Creek. A path to the right wanders to an open area that was probably a house site; turn left.

Then turn right, to cross Bunches Creek on a footlog at 0.3 mile. On the other side, a large yellow birch has a hollowed-out base. Watch for other

Flat Creek Falls

large birches as you ascend, leaving the creek and topping a ridge at 0.6 mile. Then at 0.7 mile, turn left on a 0.1-mile path that leads to Flat Creek Falls. Near the top of the waterfall a warning sign says to stay on the trail, which is intended to mean "do not take the path straight ahead," where people have bushwhacked in an attempt to get below the waterfall for a view. Instead, turn right to drop steeply to the creek and bear left to reach the top of the falls, but there is not much of a view. Upstream you can cross the creek and make your way down through bushes and over slick rocks to a couple of viewpoints. The route across the creek and down is rough and a bit dangerous, and should only be attempted by experienced hikers.

Back on the main trail, a pleasant walk takes you through a woodland of fern and grass while passing upstream along Flat Creek, a tributary of Bunches Creek. The trail crosses Flat Creek on a footbridge at 1.5 miles and again at 1.6 miles. Watch for wild geraniums in spring. Enter a forest of red spruce and cross Flat Creek again on a footbridge at 1.9 miles.

Ascending, the trail reaches a ridgeline at 2.3 miles and joins a road at 2.4 miles. To the right, the road leads into the far end of the Heintooga Picnic Area. Turn left to pass below the picnic area, which occupies a knoll. Soon reach Heintooga Overlook, which offers views northwest into the park. Then emerge on Heintooga Ridge Road at 2.6 miles. Return as you came, or take your shuttle vehicle 3.6 miles down the Heintooga Ridge Road to your right back to the Flat Creek trailhead.

71 | HEMPHILL BALD, CALDWELL FORK, AND ROUGH FORK TRAILS

Distance: 13.7-mile loop; to Hemphill Bald, 4.8 miles one way
Difficulty: Moderate
Elevation change: 2,240 feet; gain to Hemphill Bald,
420 feet
Season: Year-round (access road closed in winter)
Cautions: Steep ascents and descents
Connections: Polls Gap Trail, Cataloochee Divide Trail

Attractions: This loop route offers grand views from Hemphill Bald and penetrates old-growth forest. The trail begins at Polls Gap, named for Polly Moody, an early settler. The Polls Gap Trail to the north offers easy access to a spruce-fir highlands of the Smokies in the first 0.5 mile (beyond that, this trail needs major repair work and has been recommended for abandonment). Hemphill Bald is named for Thomas Hemphill, an early settler

Hemphill Bald

CCC fence along Cataloochee Divide

in the region who, with others, grazed cattle on the slopes of the mountain. The half of the bald within the park has since become overgrown with trees. But the other half, which is still private land, has been grazed and is open. Below, you can see Cataloochee Ranch and the adjacent ski area, started by Tom and Judy Alexander, who settled in Cataloochee Valley around 1933 to cater to people who came to fish, hike, and ride horses. As the community disbanded with the park creation, the Alexanders also left and purchased a farm just outside the park where they established the guest ranch. The Alexander family still operates the resort and recently set aside 238 acres of Hemphill Bald in an environmental easement that will save it from any future development. You're welcome to stop for lunch at a stone picnic table on the bald. Camping is available at Balsam Mountain Campground up from Polls Gap and at Caldwell Fork Campsite (41).

Trailhead: Polls Gap trailhead parking lies 6.3 miles up Heintooga Ridge Road. The Polls Gap Trail is to the far left. The Rough Fork Trail in the middle heads toward Cataloochee and is the return route of this loop. To the far right, the Hemphill Bald Trail heads southeast.

Description: The Hemphill Bald Trail begins at 5,128 feet and ascends through yellow birch, beech, mountain maple, and occasional red spruce, following an old railbed. Climb along Cataloochee Divide, the long mountain range that forms the southeast boundary of the park. As the trail travels over knolls along the ridgeline, it has more elevation change than what is indicated in the hike summary above by the overall 420-foot gain.

At a gap on Cataloochee Divide at 1.1 miles, the park boundary is marked by a split-rail fence originally built by the CCC in the 1930s. The fence extends 11 miles east to the far end of Cataloochee Divide. The trail ascends the slope below Buck Knob up to your right and descends past a rock outcrop at 1.7 miles with a view to the left of the Caldwell Fork Valley.

Drop into Maggot Spring Gap at 2.3 miles at the park boundary with the split-rail fence, and then ascend through switchbacks to the top of Sheepback Knob. Through another gap, ascend along the slope of Little Bald Knob with a dirt road outside the boundary. Descending into the next gap, look ahead to Hemphill Bald, an open area on the southeast side of the next peak.

Through Pine Tree Gap, ascend along a barbed-wire fence that has replaced the split-rail fence. Outside the park, the forest gives way to an open field. The trail reaches the top of Hemphill Bald at 4.8 miles with views to the southeast. The settlement far down the valley to the left is the Jonathan Creek community; Maggie Valley resides on the far side of the low ridge of Buck Mountain on the right. Below lies Cataloochee Ranch. Beyond stand range upon range of the mountains of

Hemphill Bald Trail

North Carolina. A peak to the left on the horizon is Cold Mountain, made famous by the recent novel of the same name by Charles Frazier. Down from Hemphill Bald, the trail passes through Double Gap and ascends to a junction at 5.5 miles with the Cataloochee Divide Trail to the right (it continues the ridgeline walk to the northeast); turn down to the left.

The Hemphill Bald Trail passes along the side of McClue Ridge and soon swings north across the upper part of Double Gap Branch Cove. The vines of Dutchman's-pipe hang from trees and in fall bury the trail in big heart-shaped leaves. Watch for big trees as you enter an old-growth forest of maples and oaks. Pass into laurel along the slope of Double Gap Ridge and curve left to continue down the hollow.

At 7.4 miles, cross a muddy creekbed with large oaks on the left and right, and pass into a hemlock woods. The trail crosses the rocky streambed of Double Gap Branch at 7.5 miles. Following the branch down the cove, reach a massive oak on the right at 7.6 miles; at 6 feet in diameter, it's one of the largest in the park. On down the trail, a massive yellow poplar stands on the left. At 7.7 miles, the trail crosses two streams of Double Gap Branch and descends into bottomland where you rockhop Double Gap Branch at 8.4 miles and reach a junction with the Caldwell Fork Trail at 8.5 miles, where the Hemphill Bald Trail ends. To the right, the Caldwell Fork Trail emerges on Cataloochee Road near Cataloochee Campground in 4.7 miles; turn left.

Continuing this loop up the Caldwell Fork Trail, cross Caldwell Fork on a footbridge and pass into the Caldwell Fork Campsite (41) at 8.8 miles. The trail then ascends from the campsite to a path on the right at 9.0 miles that leads 100 yards to the "Big Poplars," three huge yellow poplars standing in the woods. From the side trail, ascend through a poplar woods up Big Ridge to the crest of Big Fork Ridge at 9.9 miles. Continue up along the side of the ridge to the end of the Caldwell Fork Trail at a junction with the Rough Fork Trail (hike 78) at 10.2 miles. To the right, the Rough Fork Trail leads 3.0 miles down to the Cataloochee Road; turn left to complete the loop back to Polls Gap.

Ascend steeply along an old roadbed past rock outcrops as you recross the crest of Big Fork Ridge. At 11.1 miles, the trail rises to join the old railbed of the Suncrest Lumber Company that hauled timber out of this region in the early 1900s. The roadbed the trail follows up to this point may have been part of the rail line. The trail now follows this railbed to the left along the slope of Big Fork Ridge. Ascend gently, often passing between earthen berms where the rail line cut through small ridges running down from the ridge crest.

At 12.5 miles, the trail swings to the right in a broad curve. You'll then be able to see through the trees to the crest of Balsam Mountain; the notch to the left is Polls Gap. At 12.7 miles, watch for old railroad ties still embedded in the railbed. The trail continues along the slope, curving left as Big Fork Ridge joins Balsam Mountain. At 13.7 miles, pass around a gate to emerge in Polls Gap at the end of the Rough Fork Trail.

72 | BALSAM MOUNTAIN AND APPALACHIAN TRAILS TO INADU KNOB

Distance: 13.8 miles one way
Difficulty: Moderate
Elevation gain: 1,540 feet
Season: Year-round (access road closed in winter)
Cautions: Mud holes, steep climbs, briers
Connections: Beech Gap Trail, Mount Sterling Ridge Trail, Gunter Fork Trail, Snuke Den Ridge

Attractions: This trail connects the Balsam Mountain area with the AT at the Smokies crest, passing through old-growth red spruce, massive trees standing straight and tall; this is one of the finest high-country old-growth forests in the Smokies. The hike skirts Mount Yonaguska, named for the Cherokee chief who opposed removal to the west, advocated temperance among the Cherokees, and as a young man reportedly discovered Alum Cave on the side of Mount LeConte. Camping is available at Laurel Gap Shelter and Tricorner Knob Shelter. Nearby Balsam Mountain Campground can be used as a staging area the night before.

Trailhead: On the one-way Balsam Mountain Road (closed in winter), at 8.2 miles from the end of Heintooga Ridge Road, reach the Balsam Mountain Trail on the right in Pin Oak Gap.

Description: The trail ascends from the road on a path that follows an old roadbed up Balsam Mountain. Cross a couple of knolls and ascend steeply to top Ledge Bald, now overgrown, at 1.9 miles. The trail then descends a grassy slope with trillium and mayapple into Beech Gap at 2.3 miles and a junction with the Beech Gap Trail to the left, which leads 2.5 miles back to the Balsam Mountain Road; stay straight.

The trail climbs from Beech Gap through beech, maple, and luxurious grass to enter first spruce and then a fir forest. At 3.5 miles, pass over Balsam Hightop, covered in small fir trees; the fir is the "balsam" for which the mountain is named. The trail descends to Laurel Gap and the Laurel Gap Shelter at 4.1 miles; water is available down a path in front. The trail then ascends to a junction at 4.3 miles with the Mount Sterling Ridge Trail (hike 83) to the right, which leads to Pretty Hollow Gap in 4.0 miles; continue left on the Balsam Mountain Trail.

Pass along the western slope of Balsam Corner and ascend to the ridgeline of Balsam Mountain and a junction at 5.2 miles with the Gunter Fork Trail (hike 83) to the right, which leads 4.1 miles down to Big Creek; bear left.

Occasional mud holes and briers can crowd the trail. At 6.5 miles, watch for a grand view to the right down the valley of the Gunter Fork and Big Creek. At 7.2 miles, pass below Luftee Knob while staying relatively level along the ridge of Balsam Mountain. The trail gradually curves west into stands of old-growth red spruce. Walk along the slope of the mountain and then swing around Mount Yonaguska; the trail bears to the right around the peak and ascends to end at a junction with the Appalachian Trail at 10.1 miles at Tricorner Knob; here Balsam Mountain joins the main crest of the Smokies, forming three corners. The Tricorner Knob Shelter sits just 0.1 mile to the left on the AT; a small pipe delivers water from a spring just outside the shelter (farther to the west, the AT leads to Newfound Gap in 15.7 miles). At the Balsam Mountain junction, turn to the right (east) on the AT.

Cross the slope of Mount Guyot, named for Swiss geographer Arnold Guyot, who with the support of the Smithsonian Institution mapped the Smokies around 1860. At 6,621 feet, Mount Guyot is the second-highest peak in the park. The AT then descends along the ridge and circles the peak of Old Black at 12.3 miles; watch for a grand view to the northwest down the valley of Indian Camp Creek and on outside the park. Descend to cross an open, narrow ridge through Deer Creek Gap where concrete slabs set in the ground form an emergency helicopter landing site that is no longer used. Here you'll have an expansive view to the southeast of the Deer Creek Valley melding into the long valley of Big Creek. At 13.5 miles, where you step down through rocks, scraps of metal from an airplane crash lie on the right. The trail then passes Inadu Knob and reaches a junction at 13.8 miles with the Snake Den Ridge Trail (hike 46), which descends into Cosby in 5.3 miles (for a total hike of 19.1 miles, if combined with this hike).

The upper end of the Balsam Mountain Trail and the AT between Tricorner Knob and Inadu Knob can also be combined with the Low Gap Trail (hike 47), the Gunter Fork Trail (hike 83), and (for the last leg) the Snake Den Ridge Trail (hike 46) to make a fine backpack loop of 24.4 miles out of Cosby.

73 | BEECH GAP AND HYATT RIDGE TRAILS

Distance: 8.0-mile loop; with shuttle, 6.5 miles
Difficulty: Moderate
Elevation change: 2,020 feet
Season: Year-round (access road closed in winter)
Cautions: Small creek crossings, steep descents
Connections: Enloe Creek Trail

Attractions: A pleasant walk along Hyatt Ridge forms a loop with a section of Straight Fork Road. Camping is available at McGee Springs Campsite (44).

Trailhead: On the Balsam Mountain Road, after passing a trailhead for the Beech Gap Trail at 12.8 miles, ford Straight Fork to reach the second trailhead for the Beech Gap Trail at 13.0 miles; there's space for parking on the left. (The two sections of the Beech Gap Trail are joined by walking the road where it fords the creek.) Beyond the ford of Straight Fork, one-way Balsam Mountain Road becomes the two-way Straight Fork Road; you can run a shuttle vehicle 1.5 miles down the road to the trailhead for Hyatt Ridge Trail and avoid a road walk at the end of your hike. You can also reach both trailheads from Big Cove Road; Hyatt Ridge trailhead is 2.5 miles from Big Cove Road and the westerly Beech Gap trailhead is 4.0 miles.

Description: The trail climbs from the road and soon curves left up a deep side drainage. Continue in and out of coves along the slope of Hyatt Ridge. At 2.2 miles at a ridgeline, cross a gap to bear left up this spur ridge.

The trail then swings to the right through another gap at 2.6 miles and continues ascending. Hyatt Bald was once up the mountain to your right, but it has become overgrown. Reach a junction atop Hyatt Ridge at 2.9 miles where the Beech Gap Trail ends. To the right, a path leads 0.9 mile to the McGee Springs Campsite (44), with water available at the spring; turn left along the Hyatt Ridge Trail.

Walk a path that follows the ridgeline through large spruce, hemlock, and moss-covered logs. The trail eventually makes a steep descent to a junction in Low Gap at 4.6 miles with the Enloe Creek Trail (hike 74) to the right (it ascends to the Hughes Ridge Trail in 3.6 miles); turn left on the continuation of the Hyatt Ridge Trail.

The trail descends, crossing several small streams, to end at the Straight Fork Road at 6.5 miles. Walk to the left (or drive your shuttle vehicle) up the road to get back to the beginning of the Beech Gap Trail, passing the Round Bottom Horse Camp and closing the loop at 8.0 miles.

74 | HYATT RIDGE, ENLOE CREEK, CHASTEEN CREEK, AND BRADLEY FORK TRAILS

Distance: 11.2 miles one way; to Chasteen Creek Cascades, 9.5 miles one way
Difficulty: Strenuous
Elevation change: 2,600 feet
Season: Year-round (access road closed in winter)
Cautions: Steep ascents and descents, rocky trail, mud holes, stream crossings
Connections: Hughes Ridge Trail

Attractions: This combination of trails takes you over Hyatt Ridge, crosses the rushing Raven Fork, and travels over Hughes Ridge, named for Ralph Hughes, an early settler in Oconaluftee Valley. You'll then walk through isolated backcountry to Smokemont, passing Chasteen Creek Cascades. Enloe Ridge and Creek are named for Abraham Enloe, who came to the Oconaluftee Valley in the early 1800s. Camping is available at Enloe Creek Campsite (47), Upper Chasteen Campsite (48), Lower Chasteen Campsite (50), and Smokemont Campground.

Trailhead: The trailhead lies on Straight Fork Road 14.5 miles from Heintooga Ridge Road via Balsam Mountain Road. Or you can reach the trailhead via Big Cove Road. The Hyatt Ridge Trail is on the north side of the road, where you can park. To run a shuttle vehicle, drive to Smokemont

Crossing Raven Fork

Campground (see Getting There at the beginning of this chapter).

Description: The Hyatt Ridge Trail ascends from Straight Fork Road, with Hyatt Creek descending on your left. Cross the creek and top Hyatt Ridge at 1.8 miles in Low Gap (not to be confused with the Low Gap near Cosby) at a junction with the Enloe Creek Trail straight ahead. Hyatt Ridge Trail (hike 73) turns to the right; continue straight on the Enloe Creek Trail.

The trail drops down the northwest side of Hyatt Ridge. Walk past stands of large hemlock and hardwood and a couple of good views across to the next ridge. In time, you hear Raven Fork and eventually descend past large boulders to the creek at 2.8 miles. In wet seasons, Raven Fork is an impressive force of water that cascades through a rock-lined trough. A high framed bridge takes you over the creek. Just on the other side lies the Enloe Creek Campsite (47).

Chasteen Creek Cascades

Turn left downstream. At 3.0 miles, the trail ascends from the creek. Watch for a large yellow poplar on the left at 3.2 miles that yellow-bellied sapsuckers have attacked with a vengeance; this woodpecker drills parallel holes in trees and returns later to feed on sap secreted from the holes and the insects drawn to the sap.

Beyond, Enloe Creek spills down on the left to join Raven Fork below. At 3.8 miles watch for a cascading waterfall and plunge pool in the creek. Walk along a steep bank with narrow footing. At 3.9 miles, the trail crosses Enloe Creek on a footbridge. On the other side, you may have to slog through a mud patch and then ascend from the creek with more mud holes; the Enloe Creek Trail is scheduled for renovation, so the path may be in better shape when you come this way.

The trail parallels Enloe Creek as it skirts the northern end of Enloe Ridge. At 4.5 miles turn from the creek and climb Hughes Ridge. Watch for large spruce and hemlock at 4.9 miles. After a couple of switchbacks, gain Hughes Ridge at 5.4 miles at a junction with the Hughes Ridge Trail (to the right it leads 4.7 miles to the AT on the crest of the Smokies); turn left.

Walk 0.5 mile down to a junction with the Chasteen Creek Trail on the right. Straight ahead, the Hughes Ridge Trail once led to the Smokemont Campground, but the trail crosses a part of the Cherokee Reservation that is now closed; turn to the right on the Chasteen Creek Trail.

Steeply descend the southwest side of Hughes Ridge. At 6.5 miles, the trail crosses the head of a ravine and switchbacks left to cross it again. At

7.2 miles the downhill is relentless. The grade eases up a bit as the trail joins an old railbed, but it's still downhill and quite rocky. At 7.8 miles, pass the Upper Chasteen Campsite (48). Just beyond, a branch of Chasteen Creek flows under the road on its way down to join Bradley Fork. The trail now gradually descends with better footing while paralleling the creek on the right. At 9.5 miles, watch for the double-slide of Chasteen Creek Cascades. Keep going downhill to a sharp right turn onto a side path that leads past hitching rails to the cascade.

Continue downhill on the old railroad grade, formerly a spur off the main line of the Champion Fibre Company railway that ran along Bradley Fork. At 9.8 miles, the trail crosses Chasteen Creek on a wide bridge and passes the Lower Chasteen Creek Campsite (50) on your left. The trail descends to end at a junction at 10.0 miles with the Bradley Fork Trail. To the right, the trail goes up 2.9 miles to Cabin Flats Trail (hike 67); turn left to go 1.2 miles to the Smokemont Campground.

CATALOOCHEE VALLEY

The Caldwells (originally Colwells) were the first whites to settle in Cataloochee Valley. Henry Colwell purchased 100 acres in 1814, but it was not until sometime in 1834–36 that his son James Colwell, grandson Levi Colwell, and another man, Young Bennett, built two log cabins and settled on the land. George and Polly Palmer arrived in the valley in 1838 and a

Palmer Chapel

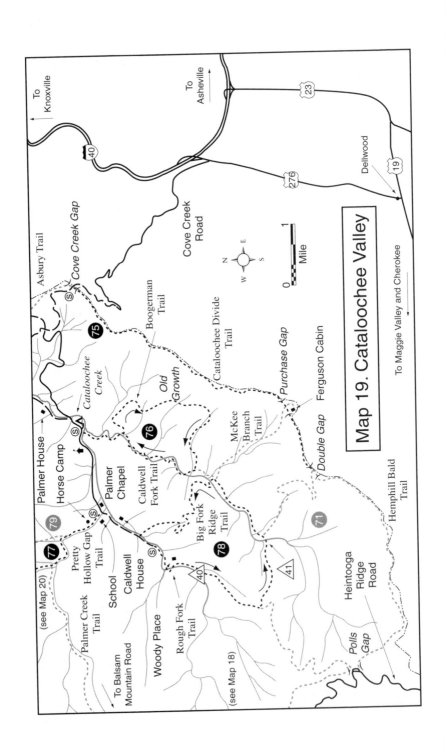

Map 19. Cataloochee Valley

year later built a two-room log cabin with a dogtrot between. Their son Fayte and grandson Jarvis modernized and added to the Palmer House.

The main part of the community, sometimes referred to as "Big Cataloochee," consisted of 765 people in 137 households in 1900; the combined population of Big and Little Cataloochee was over 1,200. The two together made up the largest community in the park area, twice the population of Cades Cove.

Cataloochee Valley contains several other historic structures. The Will Messer Barn was brought from Little Cataloochee and reconstructed beside the ranger station, which was the Hub and Maude Caldwell house. The Palmer Chapel, built in 1902 with a bell tower added in 1929, faces away from the road because it fronted a lane that ran along Palmer Creek; Mary Ann Palmer gave the land for the church. The Beech Grove School was built in 1901. Just down the road from the school, a footbridge across Rough Fork to the left accesses a walled-in spring that was the drinking water for the schoolchildren. The Caldwell House, a white frame house, was completed in 1906 by Hiram Caldwell, grandson of James and son of Levi, the first settlers in Cataloochee; the barn across the road was built by Hiram's son Eldridge Caldwell in 1923.

Getting there: From I-40, 80 miles southeast of Knoxville or 30 miles west of Asheville, take the Waynesville/Maggie Valley exit to US 276. Almost immediately turn northwest on Cove Creek Road. From Oconaluftee, take US 19 east from Cherokee, through Maggie Valley, and at Dellwood turn north on US 276 to Cove Creek Road on the left. The road passes

Caldwell House

through the Cove Creek community and winds up the mountain, changing from pavement to gravel; the road, which is old Hwy. 284, will eventually be paved to the park boundary. At 5.9 miles enter the park at Cove Creek Gap, where there is a trailhead and parking for a couple of vehicles. At 7.4 miles there is a four-way intersection: to the right, a gated road was a proposed access that was never completed and now dead-ends at the park boundary; straight ahead, Hwy. 284 leads to Big Creek in 16 miles; turn left on a paved road to drop into Cataloochee.

At 7.7 miles, a short trail from a parking area climbs to a rock overlook of the valley. At 10.3 miles the road crosses a bridge over Cataloochee Creek; watch for a pullout on the left where you can pick up a booklet guide to the valley. Soon after, a sharp turn to the right leads 0.5 mile to the Palmer House, which has an information and exhibit room where you can learn about Cataloochee. Past the turn the campground is on the left at 10.6 miles; shortly after lies a trailhead for the Caldwell Fork Trail.

The road continues into the valley, passing the Messer barn and ranger residence. In another mile, the road becomes gravel where the Palmer Chapel stands to the left. The road forks at 12.3 miles; the main route goes to the left, and the fork to the right is a trailhead for the Pretty Hollow Gap Trail. Turn left at the fork and continue down the valley, crossing a bridge over Palmer Creek, passing the Beech Grove School on the right, and then following the Rough Fork. The road crosses a bridge over Shanty Branch and passes the Caldwell house and barn. You reach the end of the road and a trailhead for the Rough Fork Trail at 13.3 miles from US 276.

75 | CATALOOCHEE DIVIDE TRAIL

Distance: 6.4 miles one way; to Cataloochee Valley
Overlook, 1.2 miles one way
Difficulty: Moderate
Elevation gain: 970 feet
Season: Year-round
Cautions: Ascents and descents along the ridge
Connections: Asbury Trail, McKee Branch Trail, Hemphill
Bald Trail

Attractions: Cataloochee Divide offers occasional views into Cataloochee Valley and into North Carolina to the south. It was called *Gad-a-lu-tsi* by the Cherokees, meaning "fringe standing erect" or "standing in ranks," most likely referring to trees appearing to stand in line along the ridge. The divide possesses some of the largest oak trees in the park. These trees remain

View from Cataloochee Divide

because commercial logging did not occur in much of the Cataloochee area. In Cove Creek Gap, the Asbury Trail leads north to Mount Sterling Gap along a route used by Francis Asbury, a Methodist bishop and circuit-riding preacher who served the communities of the southern Appalachians around 1800. Maintained by the Boy Scouts of America, this unofficial trail does not appear on park maps. Camping is available at nearby Cataloochee Campground.

Trailhead: At Cove Creek Gap, where you enter the park 5.9 miles from US 276, there is parking for a couple of vehicles at the trail's beginning.

Description: From Cove Creek Gap, the Cataloochee Divide Trail heads left (southwest), ascending while paralleling the boundary of the park. The boundary is marked by a split-rail fence constructed by the CCC in the 1930s. In some places, sections have been replaced over the years. Where it is broken down, it's likely to be the original fence.

Along Cataloochee Divide there is much up and down as the trail crosses the northwest slope of the mountain and drops into gaps in the ridgeline. At 0.4 mile the trail passes through the first of the gaps and ascends, passing a large oak tree on the right at 0.5 mile. This tree marks the beginning of an oak forest that contains massive trees, mostly red oaks, scattered at intervals along the ridge.

Gooseberry Knob

At 1.2 miles, an overlook of Cataloochee Valley opens on the right. The view is framed by trees, and a short log offers a resting place. In the fall, you'll look down on a sea of red and yellow leaves.

At 1.4 miles, a gate in the boundary fence leads to a development of house lots outside the park. A large oak standing in a break in the boundary fence on the left at 1.6 miles has a massive limb that curls over the trail. Another gap in the fence at 2.1 miles marks an open area and a view southeast into North Carolina. As you continue up the ridge, watch for young chestnut trees that have not yet been affected by the chestnut blight.

Farther up the ridge, a dirt road runs on the other side of the fence, outside the park; you'll see this road occasionally as you continue up the trail. At 2.4 miles, a massive oak stands between the trail and the fence; basswoods, yellow birches, and maples are here too. There's another view left into the North Carolina mountains and then you pass a tilted rock outcrop on the left.

Somewhere along this next section, a hiker's shelter will be built on the left on private property by the owners of The Swag, a country inn that borders the park farther up the trail. You'll be able to take a rest here or get in out of the rain.

The trail then passes over a high point on Cataloochee Divide and descends along the fence line into Purchase Gap at 4.6 miles, where there's a four-way junction; the McKee Branch Trail to the right descends into Cataloochee Valley (the trail passes more large oaks and a house site with broken-down chimney and foundations and crosses McKee Branch twice to reach the Caldwell Fork Trail, hike 76, in 2.3 miles; there you can turn right to get to the Cataloochee Campground in another 3.2 miles). In Purchase Gap, a path to the left goes through the boundary fence and leads downhill, then right, to the Ferguson Cabin, a two-room home with a dog-trot between, rebuilt of old logs after the original burned (this tract of over 500 acres was donated to the park in 1999). The Cataloochee Divide Trail continues straight through Purchase Gap.

You reach a repaired section of the boundary fence at 5.3 miles at a corner of property belonging to The Swag. Ascend steeply to top another high point, locally called "Gooseberry Knob," at 5.5 miles. Hitching rails stand on the right and a gateway on the left leads out to an open area on the side of the hill where the inn has benches; hikers are welcome to stop. The trail then descends into a gap and moves up beside The Swag, built of old logs for a rustic look (meals and lodging are by reservation only; if you call ahead to have lunch there or to pick up a gourmet pack lunch, you can leave a car at The Swag for a shuttle).

The trail continues past the lodge and cabins, making a steep ascent to top a lower knoll and then descending into Double Gap at 6.4 miles to end at a junction with the Hemphill Bald Trail.

Straight ahead, the Hemphill Bald Trail leads up to panoramic views from Hemphill Bald (hike 71); to the right, it drops off Cataloochee Divide to connect with the Caldwell Fork Trail in 3.0 miles.

76 | CALDWELL FORK AND BOOGERMAN TRAILS

Distance: 7.4-mile loop
Difficulty: Moderate
Elevation change: 1,300 feet
Season: Year-round
Cautions: Mud holes and footbridges on Caldwell Fork Trail
Connections: None

Attractions: George and Polly Palmer settled in Cataloochee in 1838; by the time their great-grandson Robert was born, a community had been established in the valley. Robert was a shy boy, and on the first day of school, when asked his name, he ducked his face into his arms on the desk and replied, "The Booger Man." The nickname stuck into adulthood, and he emphasized his image by growing his hair and beard long and living apart from the rest of the community. In the seclusion of the forest, Robert Palmer built his home high on the mountainside now traversed by the Boogerman Trail. With the Caldwell Fork Trail, the Boogerman Trail forms a loop through old-growth forest spared the lumberman's saw due to Robert Palmer's protection, and so for nearly all of the Boogerman Trail's distance you'll walk among big hemlocks and yellow poplars. Camping is available at Cataloochee Campground.

Trailhead: Just past the Cataloochee Campground, the Caldwell Fork Trail begins on the left. There's room for a vehicle or two to park just past the trailhead, but you might also park at the campground and walk to the trailhead.

Description: Begin by crossing Palmer Creek on a long footbridge. The trail bears to the right to follow an old roadbed through a bottomland

Tree cavity on Boogerman Trail

along the Caldwell Fork; Palmer Creek and Caldwell Fork join to form Cataloochee Creek just before the campground. At 0.5 mile, reach a fork with a path to the left, which is for horses to ford Caldwell Fork; hikers go right.

Ascend to a view of where the creek makes a right-angle turn after running into hard rock at the base of the rise. Take care walking across the slanted rock if it is wet. The trail then descends to creek level, where the horse trail rejoins. Then cross Caldwell Fork on a footbridge at 0.7 mile; horses ford to the left. At 0.8 mile, reach a junction with the Boogerman Trail to the left; the Caldwell Fork Trail continues straight ahead, your return route; turn left onto the Boogerman Trail.

Hop a small stream and ascend into large trees. The trail climbs, following an old roadbed, to pass around a point and descend to cross Palmer Branch over an old bridge at the house site of Robert Palmer at 2.3 miles. Then ascend from the cove and curve right to climb to a low gap on Den Ridge at 2.5 miles and ascend along a rail fence.

The trail crosses small streams and then dips to cross Sag Branch at 3.0 miles. A wagon wheel may still lie on the right. The trail then ascends steeply over a ridge at 3.2 miles and descends, passing large chestnut oaks, black gum, and prone chestnut logs. Across a small stream, pass through an old gateway that has only the side posts remaining. The trail then skirts a long rock wall on the right that's 3 feet high and 2 feet thick. Pass large poplars, one with a cavity you can walk into.

At 4.0 miles, the trail crosses Snake Branch and follows an old roadbed downstream to cross back over the branch. The trail passes a small waterfall and then fence posts between road and creek. At 4.4 miles, the remains of a log building lie to the right, and then you cross Snake Branch again. The trail climbs from the creek over a rise to a house site on the left that had a root cellar. At 4.6 miles the Boogerman Trail ends at another junction with the Caldwell Fork Trail; to the left the Caldwell Fork Trail reaches a junction with the Big Fork Ridge Trail (hike 78) in 0.4 mile; turn right to complete the loop back to the campground.

Cross a footbridge over Snake Branch and follow Caldwell Fork downstream to cross on a footbridge at 4.8 miles. Horses must ford; so at each crossing, a horse trail moves down to a ford and the hiker trail rises to a footbridge. Cross two small tributary streams on footbridges.

Then at 5.2 miles, a footbridge takes you over a side channel of Caldwell Fork onto an island and a second footbridge brings you back. Soon after, cross a footbridge to the other side. At 5.8 miles, cross the creek again on a footbridge and then walk over a short footlog that spans a muddy area. Afterward, cross five footbridges over Caldwell Fork in quick succession. Then crossing the fifteenth footbridge, over Palmer Branch, return to the junction with the beginning of the Boogerman Trail on the right at 6.6 miles; keep straight to cross one more footbridge over the creek and return to the trailhead at 7.4 miles.

77 | PRETTY HOLLOW GAP TRAIL

Distance: 5.3 miles one way
Difficulty: Moderate
Elevation gain: 2,440 feet
Season: Year-round
Cautions: Steady climb
Connections: Little Cataloochee Trail, Palmer Creek Trail, Mount Sterling Ridge Trail, Swallow Fork Trail

Attractions: This trail gives access to Little Cataloochee and connects Cataloochee Valley with the trails out of the Big Creek area. Near the trailhead is the homesite of Turkey George Palmer, who was known for trapping wild turkeys in a pen; he was the son of Jesse Palmer, brother of Fayte, and the father of Robert "Boogerman" Palmer. Camping is available at Cataloochee Campground and Pretty Hollow Campsite (39).

Trailhead: From the Cataloochee Campground, continue into Cataloochee Valley, and where the road forks (the main route goes to the left to cross Palmer Creek), turn to the right to the Pretty Hollow Gap trailhead.

Description: Walk around the gate and up the old road. At 0.2 mile, a horse camp on the right occupies the homesite of Turkey George Palmer. Pass another gate and ascend upstream along Palmer Creek on the left. Over a rise, reach a junction at 0.8 mile with the Little Cataloochee Trail (hike 79) to the right (the Pretty Hollow Gap and Little Cataloochee Trails, combined with the Long Bunk, Mount Sterling, and Mount Sterling Ridge Trails, make a grand loop of 15.6 miles, passing through Little Cataloochee Valley); stay straight on the old road.

Cross a bridge over Davidson Branch at 0.9 mile. At 1.3 miles reach a junction with the Palmer Creek Trail on the left (it immediately crosses Pretty Hollow Creek on a footbridge and follows Palmer Creek west to the Balsam Mountain Road); stay straight.

Parallel Pretty Hollow Creek upstream to the Pretty Hollow Campsite (39) at 1.7 miles on the right. Beyond the camping area the old road fades into a trail as it ascends Pretty Hollow. At 2.8 miles cross the creek on a footbridge where the water slips down a small winding slide. The confluence of Cooks Creek lies to your left.

Continuing upstream, the trail passes through a hemlock wood and at 3.0 miles squeezes between blocks of stone on the left and the creek on the right. Emerge to another footbridge crossing of the creek. Soon after another crossing at 3.3 miles, a small stream spills down from the left. The trail then turns up the Onion Bed Branch of Pretty Hollow Creek to pass through a stand of large hemlocks, cross the branch at 3.6 miles, and turn back toward Pretty Hollow Creek. Watch for a huge hemlock on the right as the trail makes a broad curve to the left and resumes the ascent. The tall rampart of Indian Ridge stands on the other side of the valley. Pass from cove hardwood forest to spruce intermingled with beech and yellow birch, and ascend into Pretty Hollow Gap where the trail ends on Mount Sterling Ridge at 5.3 miles.

Straight ahead, the Swallow Fork Trail (hike 82) descends to the Big Creek Trail in 4.0 miles. To the left, the Mount Sterling Ridge Trail (hike 83) leads 4.0 miles to the Balsam Mountain Trail. To the right, the Mount Sterling Ridge Trail leads 1.9 miles to the Mount Sterling fire tower (hike 82) and a junction with the Baxter Creek Trail (hike 84), which also leads down to Big Creek.

78 ROUGH FORK, CALDWELL FORK, AND BIG FORK RIDGE TRAILS

Distance: 9.3-mile loop
Difficulty: Moderate
Elevation change: 1,200 feet
Season: Year-round
Cautions: Mud holes, stream crossings, steep climb
Connections: Hemphill Bald Trail, McKee Branch Trail

Attractions: These three trails loop through big-tree country. The Rough Fork Trail passes the Woody Place, a white frame house enclosing a log cabin built sometime before the Civil War by Jonathan Woody; the house was enlarged after 1900 by his son Steve Woody. Camping is available at Cataloochee Campground, Big Hemlock Campsite (40), and Caldwell Fork Campsite (41).

Trailhead: Near the end of the Cataloochee Road, you'll see the Big Fork Ridge Trail on the left, which is your return route. At the end of the road is the Rough Fork trailhead.

Description: The Rough Fork Trail heads out on the old road that parallels Rough Fork, gradually ascending. At 0.5 mile cross Rough Fork on a

Big Poplars, Caldwell Fork Trail

footbridge, and then cross twice more to reach the Woody Place at 1.0 mile; a springhouse sits to the right near the house. At 1.2 miles watch for a grove of large hemlocks and yellow poplars on the left and then two good examples of trees standing on their roots, having grown on rotting logs now gone. The trail crosses Hurricane Creek, a tributary of Rough Fork, at 1.4 miles; the Big Hemlock Campsite (40) lies to the right on the point of land between the two creeks.

The trail ascends more steeply while Rough Fork moves off to your right. In a small gap at 2.7 miles on Little Ridge, watch for a couple of tall chestnut snags. Ascend along the ridgeline toward the crest of Big Fork Ridge to a junction with the Caldwell Fork Trail at 3.0 miles. The Rough Fork Trail continues straight to Heintooga Ridge Road (hike 71), emerging in Polls Gap in 3.5 miles; turn left on the Caldwell Fork Trail.

Descend through hemlock, oak, and yellow poplar. At 3.3 miles, the trail passes over the crest of Big Fork Ridge in a swag where large oaks stand in a hemlock wood. Then descend the slope of Big Ridge, which runs down from Big Fork Ridge. The trail descends into a poplar forest. A side trail left at 4.2 miles leads 100 yards to the "Big Poplars," three huge yellow poplars, the largest about 20 feet in circumference. Continue descending to pass through the Caldwell Fork Campsite (41) beside Caldwell Fork at 4.4 miles. The camp consists of several alcoves in the forest. Cross Caldwell Fork on a footbridge and ascend to a junction at 4.7 miles with the Hemphill Bald Trail to the right (hike 71); continue straight.

At 4.8 miles, rockhop Double Gap Branch and cross other small streams while descending along Caldwell Fork. At 6.2 miles, just before a junction, watch for a steep path to the right that leads to two graves marked with fieldstones, two valley men killed by marauders during the Civil War. Then reach the junction with the McKee Branch Trail to the right (in 2.3 miles it reaches Purchase Gap on the Cataloochee Divide Trail, hike 75); stay straight.

In another 100 yards reach another junction, with the Big Fork Ridge Trail; the Caldwell Fork Trail (hike 76) continues straight (in 3.2 miles it reaches the Cataloochee Campground); turn left down the Big Fork Ridge Trail.

After crossing Caldwell Fork on a footbridge, the trail then passes through a bottomland and ascends Rabbit Ridge, topping the ridge at 7.3 miles and following it up to Big Fork Ridge. At 7.6 miles the trail passes over the ridge and descends. At 8.9 miles, notice a spring beside the trail and a more open forest, probably a field. At 9.1 miles pass an old homesite on the left. At 9.3 miles, the trail crosses Rough Fork on a footbridge and emerges on the Cataloochee Road. Turn left and walk a short distance to return to parking.

LITTLE CATALOOCHEE

Little Cataloochee Baptist Church

As the population grew in Cataloochee, the community spread over Noland Mountain to the north into Little Cataloochee Valley. Jack Vess and his wife, Elizabeth, daughter of George Palmer, were probably the first to come, arriving about 1854. Then Daniel J. Cook and his wife, Harriett, daughter of Levi Colwell, settled on Coggins Branch. Will Messer married one of Dan and Harriett Cook's daughters, Rachel, in 1894; they succeeded in establishing a thriving farm in Little Cataloochee, which eventually included the Cook place as well.

As the community developed, apple growing became a principal occupation and lasted through the early 1900s. At the old Dan Cook Place stand the tall stone foundations of an old apple house that was used to store apples for the winter and before hauling them to market. The valley also contains the Hannah Cabin, a log house built around 1864, and the Little Cataloochee Baptist Church, a white frame construction built in 1889 that is still the site of reunions.

Getting there: From I-40, 80 miles southeast of Knoxville or 30 miles west of Asheville, take the Waynesville/Maggie Valley exit to US 276. Almost immediately turn northwest on Cove Creek Road. From Oconaluftee,

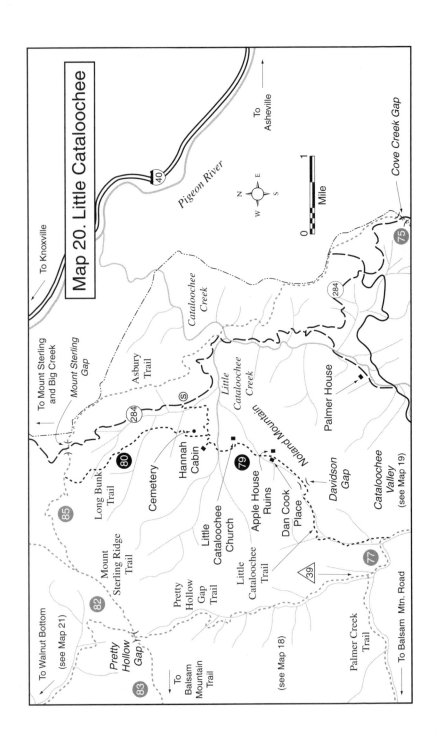

Map 20. Little Cataloochee

take US 19 east from Cherokee, through Maggie Valley, and at Dellwood turn north on US 276 to Cove Creek Road on the left. The road, which is old Hwy. 284, passes through the Cove Creek community and winds up the mountain, changing from pavement to gravel. At 5.9 miles from US 276 enter the park at Cove Creek Gap, and at 7.4 miles reach a four-way intersection: to the right, a gated road dead-ends at the park boundary; to the left a paved road drops into Cataloochee; straight ahead, Hwy. 284 leads to Big Creek in 16 miles. Continue straight toward Big Creek on old Hwy. 284.

In 2.3 miles from the intersection, the road turns right to continue toward Big Creek and a road straight ahead drops down into Big Cataloochee in 2.0 miles, passing the Palmer House and reaching the Cataloochee Campground (this is the way to come from Cataloochee Valley); turn right on Hwy. 284. The road descends to cross a bridge over Cataloochee Creek next to a hydrological station at Asbury Crossing, where the Asbury Trail crosses the creek. The road crosses a smaller bridge over Little Cataloochee Creek and ascends, eventually reaching a gated road at 5.9 miles that drops off to the left into Little Cataloochee. A couple of vehicles can park beside the road. Hwy. 284 continues to Big Creek in another 9.4 miles, following the approximate route of the old Cataloochee Turnpike.

79 | LITTLE CATALOOCHEE TRAIL

Distance: 5.2 miles one way; to Hannah Cabin, 1.0 mile one way; to Little Cataloochee Baptist Church, 2.0 miles one way; to Cook Place, 2.8 miles
Difficulty: Moderate
Elevation change: 1,000 feet
Season: Year-round
Cautions: Creek crossings, muddy sections on the back side
Connections: Long Bunk Trail, Pretty Hollow Gap Trail

Attractions: In this hike through Little Cataloochee, you'll see remains of the once-thriving settlement.

Trailhead: You can access the Little Cataloochee Trail on the Pretty Hollow Gap Trail (hike 77), but if you're mainly interested in the old structures remaining in the valley, enter along the gated road on Hwy. 284, 5.9 miles from the four-way intersection down from Cove Creek Gap. A couple of vehicles can park beside the road.

Description: Descend steeply on the old road into Little Cataloochee Valley. At 0.2 mile the road curves left and crosses a bridge over Correll Branch at 0.3 mile. Then ascend from the creek to reach a junction at 1.0 mile

Cook Apple House

with the Long Bunk Trail (hike 80) on the right, which leads 3.7 miles north to the Mount Sterling Trail (hike 85); stay straight.

The road winds down to a steep path at 1.2 miles that leads up to the John Jackson Hannah Cabin. Continue descending to cross Little Cataloochee Creek on a bridge at 1.5 miles in the former community of Ola, named after Will and Rachel Messer's daughter Viola. Look for fence posts and rock walls left from the settlement. The road winds uphill from the Little Cataloochee crossing. Watch for a rock-walled spring to the right at 1.6 miles. At a ridgetop at 2.0 miles, the Little Cataloochee Baptist Church stands on the left. A cemetery lies down the hill in front of the church.

The road descends to cross Coggins Branch, a tributary of Little Cataloochee Creek, which runs under the road in a culvert at 2.2 miles. Open fields to the left have a few apple trees remaining from the orchards that once graced the mountain slopes. In fall, hanging red apples lure you off the trail. Ascending, reach the site of the Dan and Harriet Cook Place on the right at 2.8 miles. To the left stand the tall stone foundations of the old apple house. To the right, the Cooks' 1850s cabin stood here until 1975, when it had become so damaged it was dismantled and the materials put into storage. With donated funds, the park service reconstructed the cabin in 1999.

The road continues up the hollow of Coggins Branch, becoming less like a road. As you ascend, watch for rock walls of the Will Messer Farm, which included the old barn that was relocated to Big Cataloochee and an apple house that was moved to the Mountain Farm Museum next to the Oconaluftee Visitor Center. The trail continues steeply up the hollow to curve right and then left along the slope of Short Bunk. Top the ridge at Davidson Gap at 3.2 miles. Noland Mountain, which separates Little Cataloochee from Big Cataloochee, stands to your left.

Leaving Little Cataloochee Valley, descend from the gap on an unusually steep trail that can be quite muddy. Notice on the right the end of a rock wall that parallels the old road as it continues down the mountain. Cross a small stream and pass over a rise where a path to the right leads to the remains of a log cabin. The trail follows Davidson Branch downhill, a tributary of Palmer Creek. At 3.8 miles, you must walk in the shallow water for several yards and then cross Davidson Branch three times as you curve left down the valley.

Rockhop Davidson Branch for the last time at 4.5 miles and then cross a smaller stream. The trail then crosses Little Davidson Branch at 5.1 miles and ends at a junction with the Pretty Hollow Gap Trail (hike 77) at 5.2 miles.

To the left, the Pretty Hollow Gap Trail emerges in Cataloochee Valley in 0.8 mile; to the right, the trail ascends to Pretty Hollow Gap on Mount Sterling Ridge in 4.5 miles.

80 | LONG BUNK TRAIL

Distance: 4.7 miles one way
Difficulty: Moderate
Elevation gain: 1,150 feet
Season: Year-round
Cautions: Small stream crossings
Connections: Little Cataloochee Trail, Mount Sterling Trail

Attractions: This trail connects Little Cataloochee with Mount Sterling, passing the Hannah Cemetery and many large oak trees. The Long Bunk Trail ascends an old road along the lower slope of Long Bunk, a ridge running southeast from Mount Sterling. The peculiar name perhaps came from its resemblance to a bed, or bunk. But it might also refer to a stack of logs that was loaded on railcars during lumbering operations. A stack was called a "bunk"; it was a "long bunk" if longer than 16 feet, or a "short bunk" if shorter.

Trailhead: Begin at the Little Cataloochee trailhead on old Hwy. 284.

Description: Walk 1.0 mile on the Little Cataloochee Trail (hike 79) to the junction with the beginning of the Long Bunk Trail and turn right. At 1.2 miles the Hannah Cemetery lies on the right, bounded by a wire fence and yucca plants. The road soon passes an open area on the right that was an old homesite. Cross over a small stream and swing to the right around the upper end, passing a huge branched oak, partly dead, that likely stood in the yard of the house.

The trail continues along the slope of the mountain, gradually ascending. The valley of Correll Branch of Little Cataloochee Creek lies to the right. Cross several drainages and muddy areas until you near Correll Branch and ascend, sometimes steeply. At 3.4 miles, pass through a sawed gap in a large chestnut log that lies across the trail. Soon after, the trail crosses an upper branch of the creek and then another; watch for a large yellow birch at the first crossing and a large basswood at the second.

The trail ascends along a huge chestnut log, and you'll see other chestnut logs lying in the forest, victims of the chestnut blight that struck the Smokies decades ago. At 3.6 miles watch for a large oak standing in a curve to the right. Pass more large oaks, including a giant on the right at 4.0 miles and an old oak on the left at 4.1 miles with a huge cavity in its base. The trail crosses more drainages along the lower slope of Mount Sterling and ascends to a gap to end at a junction with the Mount Sterling Trail (hike 85) at 4.7 miles.

To the left, it's 1.8 miles to the top of Mount Sterling Ridge. To the right the Mount Sterling Trail reaches Mount Sterling Gap on old Hwy. 284 in 0.5 mile. (The Long Bunk Trail can be combined with the Mount Sterling, hike 85, Mount Sterling Ridge, hike 82, Pretty Hollow Gap, hike 77, and Little Cataloochee, hike 79, Trails for a good backpack loop of 17.6 miles, including the hike up to the Mount Sterling Fire Tower and back.)

BIG CREEK

The remote area of Big Creek offers a chance to enjoy the national park away from the possibly large crowds along the main thoroughfares and at popular trailheads. The campground is for tent camping only, and trails out of the area form two of the best backpack loops in the park.

Getting there: On I-40, 60 miles east of Knoxville or 50 miles west of Asheville, take the Waterville exit and cross a bridge over the Pigeon River. On the other side bear left to stay on the main road. The Appalachian Trail descends from the right to join the road, crosses the river bridge, and continues north. Soon you reach the Walters Plant of the Carolina Power and Light Company, where you cross from Tennessee into North Carolina. The road crosses two bridges over Big Creek and at 1.7 miles becomes gravel and passes through the Waterville community. At 2.3 miles you will reach an intersection in the community of Mount Sterling. To the right, a dirt road leads up to Davenport Gap in 1.3 miles, where the road becomes paved Hwy. 32, which con-

Big Creek

tinues another 11.4 miles to Cosby. The gap is where the AT exits the park.

Straight through the intersection in Mount Sterling, the Big Creek Ranger Station stands on the right in 0.3 mile. Continue down the Big Creek Road, crossing a bridge over Chestnut Branch. Pass a horse camp to the left and the Big Creek trailhead on the right at 0.7 mile from the ranger station. Continue on, passing the entrance for a group camp on the left and ending at picnic area parking and Big Creek Campground to the right at 0.8 mile.

To the left at the intersection in the community of Mount Sterling, old Hwy. 284 heads to the Mount Sterling trailhead. It's a rough, winding, up-hill road that can be negotiated by cars but is a little jarring. At 1.0 mile bear right where a left fork heads downhill. Enter the park at 4.2 miles. Just after, a Forest Service road turns left into Pisgah National Forest, which

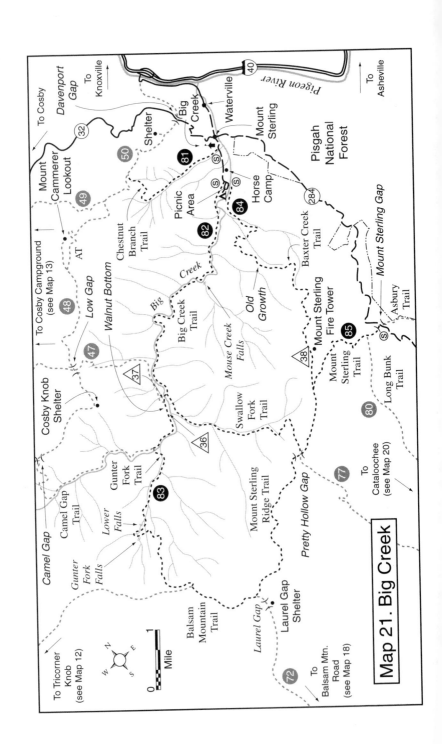

Map 21. Big Creek

borders the park. At 5.8 miles, in a broad curve to the left, Mount Sterling Creek flows under the road in a huge culvert. Then at 6.9 miles, reach Mount Sterling Gap and the trailhead. The road continues on to Cataloochee in another 9.1 miles.

81 | CHESTNUT BRANCH TRAIL

Distance: 2 miles one way
Difficulty: Moderate
Elevation gain: 1,500 feet
Season: Year-round
Cautions: Boggy areas, stream crossings
Connections: Appalachian Trail

Attractions: This pleasant walk provides a route to Mount Cammerer from the North Carolina side of the mountains. Camping is available at Big Creek Campground.

Trailhead: Park at the Big Creek Ranger Station and walk 60 yards farther down the road to the trailhead on the right, just before the road crosses Chestnut Branch.

Description: While paralleling Chestnut Branch upstream, the trail follows an old roadbed that once served lumbering operations and later led to a farming community up the hollow. On this lower section of the trail, pass through several muddy areas. The trail levels off where a small stream flows along the right side of the trail and then begins a gradual climb into a hardwood forest with small hemlocks. Step across a small side stream and at 0.7 mile enter a clearing that was a homesite, now taken over by small trees. There's a low rock wall on the right, fragments of tubs, and, in spring, blooming daffodils.

The trail then passes close to Chestnut Branch as the path enters a rhododendron woods and climbs above the creek with switchbacks right and left. To your left, watch for views of Mount Sterling Ridge through the trees across Big Creek Valley. Walk across a drier south-facing slope with laurel more abundant. The trail then enters a rhododendron thicket and crosses a small stream at 1.4 miles and another that may be nonexistent in dry weather. At 1.6 miles, the trail enters a hollow and bears right to ascend the side of Mount Cammerer Ridge. At the ridge top at 2.0 miles, the trail ends at an intersection with the AT.

To the right, you can reach the Davenport Gap Shelter in 1.1 miles and Davenport Gap itself in 1.9 miles at the park boundary. To the left, the AT leads up Mount Cammerer past a junction with the Lower Mount Cammerer

Trail (hike 49) at 3.0 miles and on up to the Mount Cammerer Lookout at 5.9 miles (see hike 50).

82 | BIG CREEK, SWALLOW FORK, AND MOUNT STERLING RIDGE TRAILS

Distance: 10.9 miles one way; to Mouse Creek Falls, 2.0 miles one way; to Walnut Bottoms, 5.0 miles one way
Difficulty: Strenuous
Elevation gain: 4,100 feet
Season: Year-round
Cautions: Rocky, steep ascent, mud holes
Connections: Pretty Hollow Gap Trail, Mount Sterling Trail, Baxter Creek Trail

Attractions: This combination of trails ascends to the Mount Sterling Fire Tower and forms a segment of two of the best backpacking loops in the park. Big Creek Trail follows an old road used by the CCC in the 1930s; it generally follows the railbed for the logging train of the Crestmont Lumber Company, which logged this part of the Smokies before the park was established. Walnut Bottom, which this route passes through, was a way station on this rail line. The views from the steps of the fire tower are some of the best in the park—Mount Cammerer to the north, Mount Guyot to the west, Balsam Mountain to the southwest, and Cataloochee Valley, backed by Cataloochee Divide, to the south. Since the park does not maintain the tower for observation purposes, take care if you climb the stairs, and go at your own risk. Camping is available at Big Creek Campground, Lower Walnut Bottom Campsite (37), Upper Walnut Bottom Campsite (36), and Mount Sterling Campsite (38).

Trailhead: Drive to the end of the Big Creek Road at the picnic area and park. Walk back up the road to the Big Creek trailhead.

Description: The trail follows the old road that makes a gradual ascent along Big Creek, aptly named, for it is big and wide. The stream spills through huge gray boulders, also scattered uphill to the right; such large boulders were brought down the mountainside during the last ice age. Mount Sterling Ridge to the left towers over the Big Creek Valley.

A side path on the left at 0.1 mile leads down to the campground. At 1.4 miles, a path drops left to a spillway in the creek where several chutes of water spout over a ledge. Then at 1.5 miles another path on the left leads down to a forked spillway and a deep, blue-green pool called Midnight Hole, a great place for a dip on a hot summer day.

At 2.2 miles, a path leads to a view of Mouse Creek Falls, a 40-foot cascade where Mouse Creek stair-steps into Big Creek. Then at 2.4 miles, cross Big Creek on a bridge with a large pool downstream. On the other side, the raised bed of an old railroad spur leads up from the left and joins the road, which now swings right.

The road ascends to Brakeshoe Springs at 3.0 miles, which trickles down the rock wall on your left; an engine brakeshoe was found here for many years. At 4.3 miles, the trail crosses a side creek, passes through Flint Rock Cove Creek on a concrete ford, and reaches a junction with Swallow Fork Trail to the left at 5.0 miles. To camp, continue straight on Big Creek Trail, crossing Big Creek on a bridge into Walnut Bottom and the Lower Walnut Bottom Campsite (37); just beyond, the Upper Walnut Bottom Campsite (36) accommodates horses. (The Big Creek Trail ends at 5.5 miles at the Camel Gap Trail, which leads in 4.0 miles to the AT.) Turn left on the Swallow Fork Trail to continue this hike.

Begin a long ascent of Mount Sterling Ridge. The trail is a footpath, but probably the route of a spur rail-bed. The trail crosses two small side streams and then parallels Swallow Fork on your right, a tributary of Big Creek.

Mount Sterling Fire Tower

Cross Swallow Fork on a footbridge at 6.0 miles, rockhop McGinty Creek at 6.2 miles, and continue up along Swallow Fork to cross another small tributary at 7.0 miles. Then leave Swallow Fork and pass upstream along another tributary and cross it at 7.6 miles. From here up, a steep climb with a couple of switchbacks brings you to a four-way junction in Pretty Hollow Gap on Mount Sterling Ridge at 9.0 miles. The gap has grassy areas and in spring an expanse of spring beauties. The Pretty Hollow Gap Trail (hike 77) leads straight down the other side of the ridge into Cataloochee Valley; to the right, the Mount Sterling Ridge Trail heads 4.0 miles to the Balsam Mountain Trail (hike 83); turn left on the Mount Sterling Ridge Trail.

Ascend through spruce-fir forest, dark and cool. At 10.4 miles in an open grassy area, reach a junction with the

Mount Sterling Trail (hike 85) to the right (it descends a road for 2.3 miles to old Hwy. 284); continue straight.

In another 0.5 mile reach the summit of Mount Sterling, where you'll find the Mount Sterling Campsite (38) and the Mount Sterling Fire Tower, built by the CCC in the 1930s. Camping spots lie in front of the fire tower and to the left of the trail in the woods.

Straight ahead, the Baxter Creek Trail (hike 84) leads 6.2 miles back down to Big Creek, creating a 17.1-mile backpack loop that's one of the most enjoyable. The water source for the campsite is 0.4 mile down this trail.

83 | BIG CREEK, GUNTER FORK, BALSAM MOUNTAIN, AND MOUNT STERLING RIDGE TRAILS

Distance: 15.0 miles one way; to Gunter Fork Falls, 7.9 miles one way
Difficulty: Strenuous
Elevation gain: 3,850 feet
Season: Year-round
Cautions: Creek fords, long ascent
Connections: Swallow Fork Trail, Low Gap Trail, Camel Gap Trail, Pretty Hollow Gap Trail

Attractions: This route combined with the eastern end of the Mount Sterling Ridge and Baxter Creek Trails makes a 23.1-mile backpack, one of the finest in the park. Along the Gunter Fork Trail, the hike passes a small falls dropping into a pool on Gunter Fork and later a long cascading fall of water. Camping is available at Big Creek Campground, Upper Walnut Bottom Campsite (36), Lower Walnut Bottom Campsite (37), and Laurel Gap Shelter.

Trailhead: Drive to the end of the Big Creek Road at the picnic area and park. Walk back up the road to the Big Creek trailhead.

Description: Hike the Big Creek Trail (hike 82) 5.0 miles to the junction with the Swallow Fork Trail to the left; continue straight.

The Big Creek Trail crosses Big Creek on a bridge and enters Walnut Bottom with the Lower Walnut Bottom Campsite (37) among streamside hemlocks. Just beyond the campsite is a junction with the Low Gap Trail (hike 47) to the right (it leads over the mountain to the Cosby Campground in 5.4 miles); continue straight to pass the Upper Walnut Bottom Campsite (36), which accommodates horses.

The Big Creek Trail then ends at 5.5 miles at a junction with the Camel

Gap Trail, which continues straight ahead along Big Creek. At 6.0 miles reach a junction with the Gunter Fork Trail to the left (the Camel Gap Trail continues straight to curve north and ascend to the AT at Camel Gap in 4.1 miles); turn left.

In a few yards the Gunter Fork Trail fords Big Creek. Most of the year you'll get your feet wet and sometimes the water will be too high to attempt a crossing. If you cannot cross, go back and hike up the Swallow Fork Trail as an alternative route to Pretty Hollow Gap (see hike 82).

After the ford, hike through bottomlands filled with rhododendron and reach a ford of Gunter Fork above its confluence with Big Creek at 6.2 miles; you'll likely get wet here as well. The trail then heads up Gunter Fork to a crossing of a tributary stream at 6.5 miles and to another ford of Gunter Fork at 7.0 miles. Then swing away from the creek, but come back to another ford at 7.4 miles. After the crossing, step over a tributary and continue upstream.

At 7.6 miles, watch for where the trail curves left at a bank above the stream; here you can scramble down to the creek to where the water slides down a crack in the rocks and spills into a blue-green pool. From this Lower Gunter Fork Falls, the trail heads left uphill along a bluff to once more ford the creek at 7.8 miles. Then rockhop a small tributary and swing left to ford the creek again at the foot of Gunter Fork Falls at 7.9 miles. Gunter Fork drops 25 feet and then descends a grand slide down the rock face for 30 yards or more before gliding into the pool at your feet.

Make your last ford at 8 miles, crossing an upper branch of Gunter Fork. The trail then begins a long ascent of Balsam Mountain. At 8.4 miles, switchback to the right at a rocky point with views left of Sevenmile Beech Ridge, which runs down from Big Cataloochee Mountain standing at the junction of Balsam Mountain and Mount Sterling Ridge.

The trail passes through massive hemlocks and curves to the right up a spur ridge, following an old Indian trail that led over Balsam Mountain. Ahead you can see the crest of the mountain with the peaks of Balsam Corner and Big Cataloochee to the left. Up and up,

Crossing Big Creek

you finally reach the ridgeline of Balsam Mountain where the Gunter Fork Trail ends at a junction with the Balsam Mountain Trail at 10.1 miles. To the right on the Balsam Mountain Trail (hike 72), it's 4.9 miles up to the AT at Tricorner Knob; turn left down the Balsam Mountain Trail.

At 11.0 miles reach Laurel Gap and a junction with the Mount Sterling Ridge Trail to the left. The Laurel Gap Shelter lies another 0.2 mile straight

Upper Gunter Fork Falls

ahead down the Balsam Mountain Trail. Turn left on the Mount Sterling Ridge Trail, which travels along the southeast slope of the ridge, passing below Big Cataloochee Mountain and a knob known as Big Butt, referring to an abruptly ending ridge rather than someone's anatomy. The trail stays fairly level along Mount Sterling Ridge, which links Big Cataloochee with Mount Sterling, eventually drop into Pretty Hollow Gap at 15.0 miles, with a four-way junction.

To the left, the Swallow Fork Trail (hike 82) leads down to the Big Creek Trail, forming a shorter hike. To the right, the Pretty Hollow Gap Trail (hike 77) descends into Cataloochee Valley. Straight ahead, the Mount Sterling Ridge Trail continues to a junction with the Mount Sterling Trail (hike 85) and the Baxter Creek Trail (hike 84). You can return along the Baxter Creek Trail for a 23.1-mile loop back to the Big Creek trailhead.

84 | BAXTER CREEK TRAIL

Distance: 6.2 miles one way; to old-growth forest, 2.8 miles one way
Difficulty: Strenuous
Elevation gain: 4,100 feet
Season: Year-round
Cautions: Steep ascent, stream crossings
Connections: Big Creek Trail, Mount Sterling Ridge Trail, Mount Sterling Trail

Attractions: This trail passes the former lumber company town of Crestmont, which was also the site of a CCC camp; there's a curious stone structure that may have been part of a gateway and, nearby, a massive stone chimney standing among trees. For a time, the trail follows Baxter Creek, named for Steven Baxter, who once lived in the area. This route climbs from cove hardwood forest through spruce-fir forest of the higher elevations to the Mount Sterling Fire Tower, a shorter walk to the summit of Mount Sterling than the route in hike 82, if you're out to just see the fire tower and return. But if you want to walk a loop, the Baxter Creek Trail combines with the Big Creek, Swallow Fork, and Mount Sterling Ridge Trails (hike 82) to make a great 17.1-mile backpacking loop. You can also make a longer backpack of 23.1 miles using the Gunter Fork and Balsam Mountain Trails (hike 83). Camping is available at Big Creek Campground and Mount Sterling Campsite (38).

Trailhead: Drive to the end of the Big Creek Road at the picnic area and park.

Description: Walk down through the picnic area, cross Big Creek on a

Crestmont chimney

metal footbridge, and turn right, following Big Creek upstream. At 0.2 mile, the trail rises away from the creek to a massive rock wall and swings right to cross a small tributary stream. At 0.3 mile, a side trail to the right enters the site of Crestmont; bearing to the right and down a slope, you'll find the massive stone chimney.

The main trail approaches Baxter Creek, flowing down Mount Sterling Ridge to join Big Creek. The trail then curves left to begin a relentless climb to the summit of Mount Sterling. In spring, crested dwarf iris line the trail. At 0.7 mile, rockhop Baxter Creek and continue ascending past occasional large yellow poplars.

The trail crosses a small stream and at 1.3 miles turns away from Baxter Creek to the right. In spring, notice the white-blooming stonecrop growing on almost every rock and boulder in sight. At 1.7 miles, rockhop a tributary of Baxter Creek.

Pass a large hemlock on the left at 2.8 miles and enter an old-growth woods. Large hemlocks reach into the higher elevations, and at 3.9 miles large spruce intermingle with the hemlock; eventually the hemlock give way to the spruce.

At 4.4 miles the trail reaches Mount Sterling Ridge and switchbacks right. The Big Branch Trail to the left once also led up from the Big Creek Picnic Area, but has long been abandoned. The Baxter Creek Trail climbs along the ridge as it leads to the summit of Mount Sterling. This is the prettiest part of the trail, just a path through the woods, lined with fern and Clinton's lily, passing among gray boulders draped in moss amid a dense spruce-fir forest gently humming with a cool breeze.

At 5.8 miles, a side trail to the right leads to a water source for those spending the night on the mountain. At 6.2 miles, emerge into a clearing where the Baxter Creek Trail ends and the Mount Sterling Fire Tower crowns the summit. Take care if you climb the steps for the views. On your right lies the Mount Sterling Campsite (38).

Straight ahead, the Mount Sterling Ridge Trail leads down an old road in 0.5 mile to a junction with the Mount Sterling Trail (hike 85), which turns left down to old Hwy. 284 in 2.3 miles. The Mount Sterling Ridge Trail (hike 82) continues down the ridge to Pretty Hollow Gap.

85 | MOUNT STERLING TRAIL

Distance: 2.3 miles one way
Difficulty: Moderate
Elevation gain: 1,950 feet
Season: Year-round
Cautions: Steady ascent, rocky sections
Connections: Asbury Trail, Long Bunk Trail, Mount Sterling Ridge Trail

Attractions: This trail provides a short but steep route to the Mount Sterling Fire Tower.

Trailhead: Drive old Hwy. 284 to Mount Sterling Gap, 6.9 miles from the intersection in the community of Mount Sterling. There's room to park along the road. (The Asbury Trail on the left follows the boundary of the park to Cove Creek Gap above Cataloochee.)

Description: To the right, the Mount Sterling Trail heads up an old road. There's little relief from the steady ascent up Mount Sterling Ridge. Watch for a large oak tree on the right at 0.2 mile. The trail then parallels a powerline running up to the radio equipment mounted on the old fire tower atop Mount Sterling. For a short stretch at 0.3 mile, you can see directly up the mountain to the tower. At 0.5 mile, reach a junction with the Long Bunk Trail (hike 80) to the left (it leads south to Little Cataloochee); stay straight.

Watch for more large oaks as you continue the ascent. Soon switchback right and at 1.0 mile enter a hemlock woods. The trail curves back left and soon ascends along a drier south-facing slope of laurel and pine. At 1.7 miles climb into the cooler spruce zone and cross under the powerline as you see it for the last time along the trail.

At 2.0 miles, the trail crosses a more open area with a low rock wall on the right where the old road has been cut into the side of the mountain. A small spring in wet weather washes the trail. Then climb more steeply. The trail makes a broad curve and reaches the crest of Mount Sterling Ridge and ends at a junction with the Mount Sterling Ridge Trail at 2.3 miles. The junction lies in an open, grassy area that is great for laying out lunch and soaking up the sun. To the left, the Mount Sterling Ridge Trail (hike 82) leads 1.4 miles down to Pretty Hollow Gap; turn right to ascend 0.5 mile to the Mount Sterling Campsite (38) and the Mount Sterling Fire Tower. If you're camping on the summit, it's 0.4 mile down the Baxter Creek Trail (hike 84) to water.

DEEP CREEK

The area of Deep Creek at the southern boundary of the park was the location of the ancient Cherokee town of Kituhwa, perhaps the first Cherokee village. In addition to calling themselves the Principal People, the Cherokees were known as the *Ani-Kituhwa,* the "people of Kituhwa."

Now Deep Creek is home to outdoor recreationists. The large Deep Creek Campground has shaded campsites. Hiking trails lead to three waterfalls. And here where Deep Creek flows out of the park to join the Tuckasegee River, the stream is popular for trout fishing, and at the height of summer crowds ride the creek on large inner tubes, which can be rented at establishments that border the park.

Getting there: From Asheville take I-40 west, and exit onto US 23/74 west to Bryson City. From the Oconaluftee Visitor Center on Newfound Gap Road, head south into the town of Cherokee and in 3.5 miles turn right on US 19 to reach Bryson City in 10 miles. From the south, take US 441 to US 74 and turn west to Bryson City. From Fontana Village, take Hwy. 28 east to US 19/74 and turn east to Bryson City.

Once in Bryson City from any direction, turn north on Everett Street to cross the Tuckasegee River and pass through town. On the other side of

Indian Creek Falls

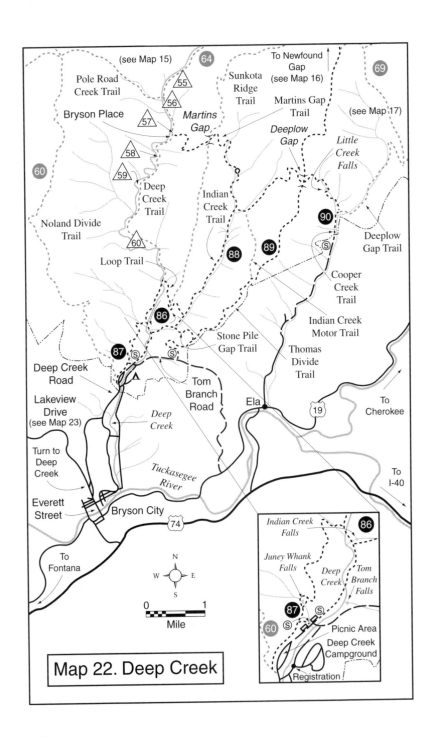

Map 22. Deep Creek

town, turn right at a sign directing you toward Deep Creek. Immediately turn left, and in 1.4 miles from Everett Street make another left. In another 0.5 mile, enter the park. Shortly after, the campground lies on the right and the Noland Divide trailhead (hike 60) is on the left. Continuing on the Deep Creek Road, pass the picnic area, after which the road becomes gravel. Past a newer parking area on the left, enter a second parking area at the end where the road is gated at the Deep Creek trailhead. Near the end of the Deep Creek Road, the Tom Branch Road turns east to the Thomas Divide trailhead (hike 89) 1.2 miles east of Deep Creek Campground. Tom Branch Road then becomes Galbraith Creek Road before connecting with US 19 between Bryson City and Cherokee.

From there, you can turn left (east) on US 19 and travel to the community of Ela, between Cherokee and Bryson City. In Ela, turn north on Cooper Creek Road. At 1.4 miles, the paved road becomes gravel. Stay right at a fork. At 3.4 miles, you will reach a trout farm where you can park for the Cooper Creek Trail (hike 90) if you ask permission.

86 | DEEP CREEK, INDIAN CREEK, AND LOOP TRAILS

Distance: 4.2-mile loop; to Tom Branch Falls, 0.2 mile one way; to Indian Creek Falls, 0.7 mile one way
Difficulty: Easy
Elevation change: 560 feet
Season: Year-round
Cautions: None
Connections: Stone Pile Gap Trail, Sunkota Ridge Trail

Attractions: This introductory hike to the Deep Creek area passes two waterfalls and wildflower displays in spring. These trails include the remains of roads left from a planned Indian Creek Motor Nature Trail; some work was done in the 1970s, but objections to building roads in the park caused the project to be abandoned. In summer, people crowd Deep Creek in inner tubes, walking back up the trail to put in again. These roads are also open for bicycling. Camping is available at Deep Creek Campground.

Trailhead: Begin at the Deep Creek trailhead, past the campground, at the end of the road where it is gated.

Description: Walk up the road that follows Deep Creek on your right. In 0.2 mile, Tom Branch Falls cascades 75 feet into Deep Creek on the other side. Cross Deep Creek on a bridge at 0.3 mile at one of the deep pools for which the stream gets its name. The trail then begins a steeper climb.

Tom Branch Falls (David Cann)

Watch for wildflower displays in spring—wild geranium, phlox, rue anemone, trillium, bishop's cap, foamflower, toothwort, showy orchis. At 0.7 mile, reach a junction with the Indian Creek Trail to the right. The Deep Creek Trail, the return route, continues north; turn right onto the Indian Creek Trail, which is also an old road.

In 200 feet, a side path on the left drops to Indian Creek Falls, a broad cascade of 60 feet on Indian Creek. Soon after, cross Indian Creek on a bridge. Watch for long stretches of crested dwarf iris in late April. At 1.2 miles, reach another junction, with the Stone Pile Gap Trail (hike 89) on the right (it climbs to Thomas Divide in 0.9 mile); continue straight.

At 1.5 miles, reach a junction with the Loop Trail. The Indian Creek Trail continues straight ahead to connect with the Deeplow Gap Trail (hike 90) and the Martins Gap Trail (hike 88); turn left on the Loop Trail.

Ascend Sunkota Ridge. The name comes from a Cherokee word for apple; apple trees once grew on the ridge. The footpath climbs steadily with a small creek on the left. Watch for a rock wall forming a terrace on the left at a house site. At 2.0 miles, top Sunkota Ridge and reach another junction, with the Sunkota Ridge Trail turning north to Thomas Divide in 8.6 miles; stay straight on the Loop Trail.

Descend across the ridge slope, crossing several small streams before bottoming out at 2.5 miles in an open area that was the Jenkins Place and a junction with the Deep Creek Trail. To the right the Deep Creek Trail climbs toward Newfound Gap Road (hike 64); turn left.

The road crosses a bridge over Deep Creek and passes over a low rise. The Deep Creek Horse Trail coming in from the right leads to the stables at the Noland Divide trailhead (hike 60); stay left.

Cross Deep Creek again on a bridge and then cross Indian Creek on a bridge to close the loop at 3.5 miles at the junction with the Indian Creek Trail to the left; stay straight to return to the Deep Creek trailhead at 4.2 miles.

87 | JUNEY WHANK FALLS AND DEEP CREEK HORSE TRAILS

Distance: 0.9 mile one way; Juney Whank Falls, 0.2 mile one way
Difficulty: Moderate
Elevation gain: 100 feet
Season: Year-round
Cautions: Narrow footbridge at base of falls
Connections: Deep Creek Trail

Attractions: This steep route takes you to a waterfall on Juney Whank Branch. Junaluska Whank lived in the area and is thought to be buried nearby; called "Juney," he was named for the Cherokee chief Junaluska. Camping is available at Deep Creek Campground.

Trailhead: Past the Deep Creek Campground, reach a newer parking area on the left and a second parking area at the end where the road is gated. The trail begins on the left between the two parking areas.

Juney Whank Falls

Description: Walk up the path with Juney Whank Branch on your right flowing down to pass under the road and empty into Deep Creek. Where the trail bends to the left, a path heads up along the creek—this is a rough passage that is not recommended. Stay left to climb steeply to a junction at 0.1 mile with the Deep Creek Horse Trail. To the left it leads 0.3 mile to the stables at the Noland Divide trailhead (hike 60); turn right on the Deep Creek Horse Trail.

Climb to a junction with a footpath that drops off to the right; take this side trail to descend to the base of Juney Whank Falls at 0.2 mile. The slender stream of water dances down a rock face, passes under a footbridge, and cascades steeply down the hollow. Across the narrow footbridge, the path rises to rejoin the Deep Creek Horse Trail, which crossed the branch above the falls. To the left, the Deep Creek Horse Trail circles above the falls and reconnects with your way in. To the right, the Deep Creek Horse Trail connects with the Deep Creek Trail; bear right.

Just beyond, another path drops off to the right in a gully that descends to the Deep Creek Trail; stay to the left on the horse trail.

Ascend to top a ridge at 0.5 mile. The trail then descends to Hammer Branch, a tributary of Deep Creek. Follow the stream down to ford the branch and walk out to a junction with the Deep Creek Trail at 0.9 mile.

To the left, the Deep Creek Trail leads to the Loop Trail and beyond. To the right, pass the junction with the Indian Creek Trail and reach the trailhead in another 0.8 mile.

88 | DEEP CREEK, INDIAN CREEK, AND MARTINS GAP TRAILS TO BRYSON PLACE

Distance: 7.3 miles one way
Difficulty: Moderate
Elevation change: 1,600 feet
Season: Year-round
Cautions: None
Connections: Stone Pile Gap Trail, Loop Trail, Deeplow Gap Trail, Sunkota Ridge Trail

Attractions: Two possible loop hikes out of the Deep Creek area incorporate these trails. The route intersects the Deep Creek Trail at Bryson Place, the site of Horace Kephart's camp. Camping is available at Deep Creek Campground and Bryson Place Campsite (57).

Trailhead: Begin at the Deep Creek trailhead, past the campground, at the end of the road where it is gated.

Description: Walk up the Deep Creek Trail to the Indian Creek Trail at 0.7 mile, and turn right. On the Indian Creek Trail, past Indian Creek Falls, cross Indian Creek on a bridge and pass a junction at 1.2 miles with the Stone Pile Gap Trail on the right (hike 89) and a junction at 1.5 miles with the Loop Trail on the left (hike 86).

The Indian Creek Trail continues straight ahead, ascending the old road while paralleling the cascading creek on your right. At 2.2 miles, a side path to the left leads up to the Laney Cemetery. The main trail/old road crosses Indian Creek on bridges at 2.9 miles and 3.4 miles. Just before the second crossing, a side trail leads up to the Queen Cemetery. Make one more crossing of Indian Creek on a bridge just before a junction at 3.6 miles with the Deeplow Gap Trail (hike 90) to the right (it ascends to Thomas Divide); continue straight.

The road crosses Indian Creek on a bridge at 3.9 miles. Pass spreads of crested dwarf iris beside the trail and cross again at 4.2 miles. The road then passes over Estes Branch and reaches a turnaround at the end of the road at 4.3 miles. At the upper part of the loop, turn off left onto the Martins Gap Trail.

At 4.5 miles, cross Indian Creek twice on footbridges as you continue upstream. The trail crosses Indian Creek on a footbridge for the last time at 4.9 miles. Then begin an ascent of Sunkota Ridge with a switchback left. The trail climbs through two more switchbacks. Then follow a small stream on your right into the head of a cove, where you switchback left onto an old roadbed to complete the ascent to a junction at Martins Gap at the top of Sunkota Ridge at 5.8 miles. To the right, the Sunkota Ridge Trail ascends Sunkota Ridge to connect with the Thomas Divide Trail (hike 89) in 4.8 miles. To the left, the Sunkota Ridge Trail ascends from Martins Gap and then descends to the Loop Trail in 3.8 miles. (Looping back to the trailhead from Martins Gap along the Sunkota Ridge, Loop, and Indian Creek Trails forms a hike of 11.6 miles.) Stay straight on the Martins Gap Trail.

Descend the west side of Sunkota Ridge to a junction with the Deep Creek Trail at 7.3 miles at Bryson Place Campsite (57), where the Martins Gap Trail ends.

To the right, the Deep Creek Trail continues to Newfound Gap (hike 64). To the left, the Deep Creek Trail returns to the Deep Creek trailhead in 5.4 miles (for a total hike of 12.7 miles). Just to the left on the Deep Creek Trail, turn off on a side path to the right to reach the stone Kephart memorial, marking the site of Horace Kephart's last permanent camp.

89 | STONE PILE GAP AND THOMAS DIVIDE TRAILS TO NEWFOUND GAP ROAD

Distance: 14.8 miles one way
Difficulty: Moderate
Elevation gain: 2,760 feet
Season: Year-round
Cautions: Overgrown in places
Connections: Indian Creek Motor Trail, Deeplow Gap Trail, Newton Bald Trail, Sunkota Ridge Trail, Kanati Fork Trail

Attractions: This route leads along Thomas Ridge to Newfound Gap Road, providing several connections for loop hikes. Camping is available at Deep Creek Campground and Newton Bald Campsite (52).

Trailhead: Begin at the Deep Creek trailhead at the end of the Deep Creek Road where it is gated. You can also use a trailhead 1.2 miles east from Deep Creek Campground on Tom Branch Road, which begins near the end of the Deep Creek Road. To run a shuttle vehicle to the trailhead on Newfound Gap Road, see hike 65.

Description: Walk up the Deep Creek and Indian Creek Trails 1.2 miles to the beginning of the Stone Pile Gap Trail (hike 86). Turn right off the Indian Creek Trail, dropping to a footbridge crossing of Indian Creek and climbing Thomas Ridge, or "Thomas Divide," as it's also known. Top the ridge at 2.1 miles and reach a junction with the Thomas Divide Trail. This southern end of the trail is an old road that was part of the abandoned Indian Creek Motor Nature Trail. To the right, it leads 1.1 miles to the Tom Branch Road trailhead. Turn left (north).

Walk up the old roadbed along Thomas Ridge. At 4.2 miles, reach another junction, with the Indian Creek Motor Trail straight ahead (the route reaches the Deeplow Gap Trail in 2.1 miles); turn right off the road onto the Thomas Divide Trail, a footpath.

Almost immediately, turn left to continue your ascent of Thomas Ridge. At 5.0 miles walk through one of the largest displays of wild geranium in the park; blooms of pink to purple cover the slopes in spring. The trail passes over knolls on Thomas Ridge while gradually gaining elevation. Then make a long descent into Deeplow Gap, which is deep and low, at 6.6 miles, and reach a four-way junction. To the left, the Deeplow Gap Trail (hike 90) leads down to the Indian Creek Trail (hike 88) for a 12.3-mile loop hike back to the Deep Creek Campground. To the right, the Deeplow Gap Trail descends to the Cooper Creek Trail. Go straight to follow the Thomas Divide Trail as it continues north.

The trail hugs the right side of the ridge until you gain the ridgeline at 7.2 miles. At a rock outcrop at 7.9 miles, look to the south through the trees to the seemingly endless mountains beyond the park in the Nantahalla National Forest. Ascend over two peaks and at 9.7 miles reach a junction with the Newton Bald Trail (hike 69) straight ahead (it leads to the Newton Bald Campsite, 52, and in 0.6 mile the Mingus Creek Trail); go left on the Thomas Divide Trail.

The trail drops off to another junction at 10.1 miles with the Sunkota Ridge Trail to the left (the Sunkota Ridge Trail bears left along Sunkota Ridge to Martins Gap, where trail connections lead back to Deep Creek for a backpack loop of 20.7 miles); stay straight on the Thomas Divide Trail.

The trail ascends to eventually drop through Tuskee Gap at 11.0 miles, pass over Nettle Creek Bald, which is no longer open, at 12.5 miles, and ascend to a junction at 13.0 miles with the Kanati Fork Trail (hike 65) to the right; continue straight along the Thomas Ridge Trail. The trail swings by Turkey Fly-up and reaches Newfound Gap Road at 14.8 miles.

90 | COOPER CREEK AND DEEPLOW GAP TRAILS

Distance: 4.4 miles one way; to Little Creek Falls, 1.4 miles one way
Difficulty: Moderate
Elevation change: 1,290 feet
Season: Year-round
Cautions: Creek crossings
Connections: Thomas Divide Trail, Indian Creek Trail

Attractions: This route provides short access to Little Creek Falls, a 90-foot cascade that skips down a rock wall with a 60-degree slant to then splash on down the mountain. Beyond, the trail passes through Deeplow Gap on

Little Creek Falls

Thomas Divide. This hike can be part of a long loop over Newton Bald.

Trailhead: Drive to the community of Ela on US 19, between Bryson City and Cherokee, and turn north on Cooper Creek Road. At 1.4 miles the paved road becomes gravel. Stay to the right at a fork. At 3.4 miles, you'll reach a trout farm where you can park if you ask permission. You can run a shuttle vehicle to the Deep Creek trailhead.

Description: Continue by walking up the road, bearing to the right into the woods along Cooper Creek. Up the rocky road, pass around a gate at the park boundary and continue now on the Cooper Creek Trail; a few buildings stand off to the right on Cherokee Reservation land. At 0.3 mile, slog through a wet section of the road next to the creek. Then stay straight as a branch of the road curves to the right through the creek to an open area and a shed. At 0.6 mile, cross Little Creek above its confluence with Cooper Creek and walk up to where the Cooper Creek Trail ends at a junction with the Deeplow Gap Trail. To the right, the Deeplow Gap Trail follows the old Cooper Creek Road up to the Mingus Creek Trail (hike 69); turn left onto the Deeplow Gap Trail.

Cross two side streams and at 1.0 mile bear left to cross Little Creek on a footbridge. Head downstream but then switchback to the right to continue up through wildflowers in the spring to the cascading Little Creek Falls at 1.4 miles. The trail crosses the creek on a footbridge below the falls; notice the large yellow buckeye tree standing on the other side of the creek.

Soon after the falls, the trail switchbacks left to climb above the waterfall and ascend along Little Creek, which is covered in leucothoe, or doghobble. Cross Little Creek on a footbridge at 1.8 miles and ascend through switchbacks to a four-way junction in Deeplow Gap at 2.3 miles. To the left, the Thomas Divide Trail (hike 89) leads to Stone Pile Gap Trail for access to the Deep Creek trailhead in 6.6 miles. To the right, the Thomas Divide Trail leads up to Newton Bald and a connection with the Mingus Creek Trail (which, with the other end of the Deeplow Gap Trail, hike 69, makes a loop of 11.7 miles). Stay straight on the Deeplow Gap Trail.

Descend the west side of Thomas Ridge. At 2.7 miles, the trail turns left and continues down into a hemlock woods that has several large trees. Reach an old roadbed at 3.4 miles and turn down left, crossing several streams in a hardwood forest with ferns and iris. The old road drops to a junction with a more obvious road at 4.2 miles. To the left, the Indian Creek Motor Trail follows the abandoned Indian Creek Motor Nature Trail route, connecting with the Thomas Divide Trail in 2.1 miles. Turn right to stay on the Deeplow Gap Trail.

The road crosses Georges Branch on a bridge and ends at a junction with the Indian Creek Trail at 4.4 miles. To the left, the Indian Creek Trail connects with the Deep Creek Trail and reaches the trailhead in another 3.6 miles; to the right, the Indian Creek Trail continues up to Martins Gap (hike 88).

LAKEVIEW DRIVE

Fording Forney Creek

When the Tennessee Valley Authority built its Fontana Dam on the Little Tennessee River in the early 1940s, old Hwy. 288 along the north bank of the river was flooded. Since this was during World War II, resources were not available to rebuild the road above the lake waters. Instead TVA, in what has since been termed the "1943 agreement," bought the 44,000 acres north of the lake and south of what was then the park boundary and turned the land over to the Department of Interior to be included in the park, with the Department of Interior to rebuild a Northshore Road sometime in the future. The National Park Service actually completed 5.7 miles by 1968 before it became obvious the road was not really necessary. This completed section is now Lakeview Drive, which provides access to a remote area of the park. The uncompleted road remains an obstacle to park preservation, because those in North Carolina who still hold out for some compensation from the 1943 agreement have so far effectively blocked wilderness designation for the park.

Getting there: From Asheville take I-40 west, and exit onto US 23/74 west to Bryson City. From the Oconaluftee Visitor Center on Newfound Gap Road, head south into the town of Cherokee; in 3.5 miles, turn right on US 19 to reach Bryson City in 10 miles. From Fontana, take Hwy. 28 east to US 19/74 and turn east to Bryson City. From the south, take US 441 to US 74 and turn west to Bryson City.

Once in Bryson City from any direction, drive north on Everett Street past the turn to Deep Creek. The road curves west, becoming Lakeview

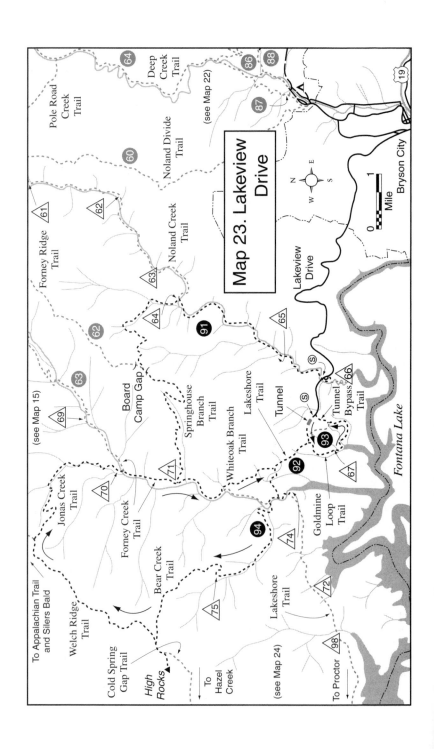

Map 23. Lakeview Drive

Drive and entering the park at 3.0 miles. You will reach the Noland Creek trailhead parking on the left at 8.0 miles and the Lakeshore trailhead at the end of the road at 8.7 miles.

91 | NOLAND CREEK AND SPRINGHOUSE BRANCH TRAILS

Distance: 12.5 miles one way
Difficulty: Moderate
Elevation change: 2,200 feet
Season: Year-round
Cautions: Creek crossings
Connections: Noland Divide Trail, Forney Ridge Trail, Forney Creek Trail

Attractions: This combination of trails can be part of a backpacking loop connecting Noland Creek with Forney Creek. The walk along cascading Noland Creek is one of the prettiest streamside hikes in the park. Camping is available at Lower Noland Creek Campsite (66), Bearpen Branch Campsite (65), Mill Creek Campsite (64), and CCC Campsite (71).

Trailhead: Noland Creek trailhead parking lies on the left on Lakeview Drive in 8.0 miles from Bryson City. To avoid a road walk at the end of the hike, run a shuttle vehicle up to the end of the road in 0.7 mile.

Description: From the parking area, walk a small paved road to the left that drops from Lakeview Drive. After a steep descent, reach a junction with the Noland Creek Trail on an old road. To the left, the trail crosses four bridges over Noland Creek in the 1.0 mile to the creek's embayment on Fontana Lake, where you'll find the Lower Noland Creek Campsite (66). Turn right, upstream, on Noland Creek Trail.

Pass under the Lakeview Drive bridge where a gravel road on the right leads back up to the highway. The trail soon crosses Noland Creek on a bridge. At 1.6 miles the road curves to the right where a side trail to the left leads up to the Bearpen Branch Campsite (65) along Bearpen Branch, which flows under the road at this junction. At 2.1 miles, the creek flows through large slabs of rock in the creekbed, a good spot for lunch. Pass through a pine forest and cross Noland Creek on bridges at 2.2 and 2.8 miles. Just across the second bridge, an old road leads left, but stay right. Cross Noland Creek again on bridges at 4.0 and 4.2 miles and reach a junction with the Springhouse Branch Trail in Solola Valley. The Mill Creek Campsite (64) lies in this former community. (Straight ahead, the Noland Creek Trail continues up the old roadway 4.8 miles to the Noland Divide Trail, hike 60, at Sassafras Gap, passing the Jerry Flats [63], Upper Ripshin [62], and Bald Creek [61] Campsites). Turn left on the Springhouse Branch Trail.

Join Mill Creek in shallow water for a few yards and then ascend an old road. The trail passes a former house site and crosses Mill Creek on a foot-bridge at 4.8 miles. Then walk through another once-settled area with rock walls, rusted wash basins, and remains of a chimney.

The trail follows Springhouse Branch upstream. At 5.4 miles, curve left to cross the headwaters of the branch and ascend to top a ridge at 6.1 miles leading down from Forney Ridge; curve to the right along the ridgeline. Cross to the left slope and descend to Board Camp Gap on Forney Ridge and a junction at 7.0 miles with the Forney Ridge Trail (hike 62) to the right (it leads 5.7 miles to the Forney Ridge Parking Area at the end of Clingmans Dome Road); continue straight on the Springhouse Branch Trail.

Climb from the gap to follow Forney Ridge south before a switchback right drops off the ridgeline. At 9.3 miles, parallel Bee Gum Branch down-stream and curve to the right along a dry slope that affords views of Forney Creek Valley. At 12.2 miles the trail switchbacks left and right and descends to a small stream crossing to end at a junction with the Forney Creek Trail at 12.5 miles, where you'll find the CCC Campsite (71). Here stands a large intact chimney; a bathtub sits on the ground.

To the right, the Forney Creek Trail (hike 63) connects with the Forney Ridge Trail down from Clingmans Dome Road, a good 20.3-mile backpack. To the left, the Forney Creek Trail leads along Forney Creek to a junction in 1.2 miles with the Whiteoak Branch Trail to the left, which in 2.0 miles joins the Lakeshore Trail (hike 92) to the left, which leads out to Lakeshore Drive in another 1.9 miles; from the road you can either take a shuttle vehicle back to the Noland Creek trailhead, or walk the road 0.7 mile back to the trailhead for a round trip of 18.3 miles.

92 | LAKESHORE TRAIL TO FONTANA LAKE

Distance: 3.1 miles one way
Difficulty: Moderate
Elevation change: 600 feet
Season: Year-round
Cautions: A tunnel
Connections: Tunnel Bypass Trail, Goldmine Loop Trail,
Whiteoak Branch Trail, Forney Creek Trail

Attractions: This section of the Lakeshore Trail travels through an aban-doned highway tunnel and serves to connect several trails while providing

Lakeshore Trail tunnel

access to camping on Fontana Lake at Lower Forney Campsite (74).

Trailhead: Follow Lakeview Drive from Bryson City 8.7 miles to where the road is gated. The Tunnel Bypass Trail lies on the left; parking is on the right.

Description: Going straight up the road, soon enter a tunnel that was to be part of the Northshore Road, sometimes affectionately called "the road to nowhere." The tunnel extends for about 150 yards; by the time you reach the center it is quite dark, but you can still see the light at both ends. After the tunnel, the pavement ends and the Lakeshore Trail becomes a footpath following the road cut.

At 0.5 mile reach a junction with the Tunnel Bypass Trail on the left (it leads back to Lakeview Drive); stay straight. The trail then curves to the right to another junction, with the Goldmine Loop Trail (hike 93) descending to the left; stay straight on the Lakeshore Trail.

The trail winds along the slope of a ridge. At 1.1 miles, the trail penetrates a cove and climbs to the right over the ridge. Descend to a shallow creek crossing at 1.5 miles. The trail continues down to a junction at 1.9 miles with the Whiteoak Branch Trail to the right (it leads to the Forney Creek Trail, hike 63, in 2.0 miles); stay left.

The trail descends through a clearing with a pile of stones on the right at a house site. At 2.1 miles, the trail crosses the shallow stream you crossed above, descending along an old roadbed that once led to the house site. At a fork in the road, turn to the right down to an old log bridge over a small stream. The road forks again; turn left to continue west. Descend to a junction at 2.9 miles with the Forney Creek Trail on an old railbed of the Norwood Lumber Company beside Forney Creek (to the right the Forney Creek Trail leads up toward Clingmans Dome); stay left on the Lakeshore Trail, which follows the other end of Forney Creek Trail down Forney Creek.

The trail crosses the creek on a bridge at 3.0 miles and reaches the Lower Forney Campsite (74) on the Forney Creek embayment of Fontana Lake at 3.1 miles.

You can also reach this campsite from across Fontana Lake, by taking a boat from the Almond Boat & RV Park west of Bryson City on Hwy. 28. From the campsite the Lakeshore Trail curves to the right to continue along the north shore of Fontana Lake for 21.7 miles to Hazel Creek (hike 96), along the way passing campsites 72 (boats only), 98, 76, 78 (boats only), 77, and 81.

93 | GOLDMINE LOOP AND TUNNEL BYPASS TRAILS

Distance: 3.8-mile loop
Difficulty: Moderate
Elevation change: 500 feet
Season: Year-round
Cautions: Creek crossing
Connections: Lakeshore Trail

Attractions: This short, pleasant walk through lowlands passes homesites, one of which still has an intact chimney. Camping is available at Goldmine Branch Campsite (67).

Trailhead: Follow Lakeview Drive from Bryson City 8.7 miles to where the road is gated. The Tunnel Bypass Trail (which is the return route) lies on the left; parking is on the right.

Description: Walk straight ahead 0.6 mile on the Lakeshore Trail (hike 92) to the junction with the Goldmine Loop Trail; take this trail to the left. The trail drops steeply through laurel and blueberry and bears to the right down to a junction with an old road at 0.9 mile. Turn left down the roadbed as it parallels Goldmine Branch on the right.

At 1.0 mile, a chimney remaining from an old cabin stands to the right in a clearing. The road passes through a rhododendron tunnel. At 1.4 miles watch for a spring on the left once lined with bricks that are now scattered around the small pool of water. The trail leaves the roadway and ascends to the left but then returns. At 1.8 miles reach a junction with a side trail to the left that leads 0.2 mile up to the Goldmine Branch Campsite (67), a flat area beside Hyatt Branch, a tributary of Goldmine Branch; bear to the right on the main trail.

Cross Hyatt Branch with a small waterfall to the right. The old roadway reaches the edge of an embayment at 2.1 miles where Goldmine Branch enters Fontana Lake. The trail turns up left, crosses a small stream, and parallels Tunnel Branch to the right, another tributary of Goldmine Branch. Ascend along Tunnel Branch and at 2.5 miles pass another clearing, likely a house site. The trail swings right to reach the ridgeline and continues up to end at a junction at 3.3 miles with the Tunnel Bypass Trail.

To the left, the Tunnel Bypass Trail serves to bypass the abandoned tunnel and connects with the Lakeshore Trail in 1.6 miles; turn right. Cross the slope of the ridge, pass through a gap at 3.6 miles, and return to Lakeview Drive at 3.8 miles.

94 | BEAR CREEK, WELCH RIDGE, AND JONAS CREEK TRAILS

Distance: 23.5-mile loop; to High Rocks, 9.9 miles one way
Difficulty: Strenuous
Elevation change: 3,100 feet
Season: Year-round
Cautions: Long ascent, numerous creek fords
Connections: Tunnel Bypass Trail, Goldmine Loop Trail, Whiteoak Branch Trail, Springhouse Branch Trail, Lakeshore Trail, Forney Creek Trail

Attractions: This backpack loop offers the shortest access to High Rocks, the site of an old fire tower at 5,188 feet. Only the foundation of the tower remains; still, you'll have an expansive view to the south of Fontana Lake. The walk along Welch Ridge is fairly level among luxuriant grass, masses of fern, and gnarled trees. Down along Jonas Creek, the campsite at the confluence with Forney Creek is one of the nicest in the park. Camping is available at Poplar Flats Campsite (75), Jonas Creek Campsite (70), and CCC Campsite (71).

Trailhead: Follow Lakeview Drive from Bryson City 8.7 miles to where the road is gated; parking is on the right.

Description: Follow the Lakeshore Trail to the Forney Creek Trail in 2.9 miles (see hike 92), passing connections with the Goldmine Loop and Whiteoak Branch Trails. At the junction, turn to the right up the Forney Creek Trail (hike 63).

In 0.5 mile reach a junction at 3.4 miles with the Bear Creek Trail to the left. Straight ahead, the Forney Creek Trail continues to Clingmans Dome Road; turn left to take the Bear Creek Trail.

The trail crosses a wide bridge over Forney Creek and follows an old spur railbed that ran off the main line along Forney Creek. At 3.6 miles, cross a bridge over Bear Creek above its junction with Forney Creek. At 3.9 miles, the trail bears left as the old railbed heels to the right where it crossed a bridge over Welch Branch and then crossed back at a switchback left up-hill. This swing in the railbed was necessary for the logging train to make the turn downhill.

The trail ascends over a low ridge to curve to the right up the drainage of Bear Creek. Cross the creek on bridges at 5.2 and 5.4 miles. At 6.1 miles, bear right up to Poplar Flats Campsite (75) beside Bear Creek. There's a picnic table and a level area for tents.

The trail turns to the right in the campsite to continue ascending on a railbed that is more rutted and rocky. Wind to the top of Jumpup Ridge at 6.6 miles; the path is steep. Bear left to ascend along the ridge as it leads toward Welch Ridge. Watch for flame azalea and mountain laurel blooming in spring.

Continue up to an indistinct meeting of Jumpup Ridge with Bald Ridge, and curve left up Bald Ridge to make a final steep ascent to the top of Welch Ridge, where the Bear Creek Trail ends at a junction at 9.2 miles with the Welch Ridge Trail. To the left, the Welch Ridge Trail leads to High Rocks and the Cold Spring Gap Trail; to the right it leads to the Jonas Creek Trail.

For a 1.4-mile round-trip hike to High Rocks, turn left along the Welch Ridge Trail. In 0.3 mile, a side trail to the right leads 0.4 mile up to the site of the fire tower. To the right stands the old watchman's cabin, built of logs covered with shake shingles; out back, a cistern collected water. (The Welch Ridge Trail continues down from High Rocks 0.5 mile to the Cold Spring Gap Trail, which leads 3.6 miles west to the Hazel Creek Trail, hike 96.)

From the junction with the Bear Creek Trail, turn right (northeast) on the Welch Ridge Trail. It ascends from the gap to pass to the left of ˉˉarwallow Bald at 9.5 miles. At 10.1 miles, a walled-in spring on the right has water spouting out of a pipe that runs on down the mountain to become Hawk Ridge Branch. Then pass below Hawk Knob and Mount Glory.

Welch Ridge Trail remains on a fairly level grade, passing knobs along the ridgeline, one side or the other. Walk through rhododendron thickets, stands of cinnamon and New York ferns, thornless blackberries, and thick grass where the sun penetrates areas with fewer trees. Watch for gnarled oaks and yellow birches growing along the ridge, big around but not very tall, hugging the ground on what is, at times, a cold and windswept ridge.

The trail passes west to east through a gap and descends to a junction with the Jonas Creek Trail at 13.2 miles. To the left, Welch Ridge Trail continues to Silers Bald and the AT; turn to the right on the Jonas Creek Trail.

The trail descends along Yanu Ridge, separating the drainages of Yanu Branch to the left and Scarlett Ridge Creek to the right. The ridge becomes quite narrow, with exposed rock in laurel and rhododendron.

High Rocks watchman's cabin

At 14.2 miles, the trail curves left and descends off the northern slope of the ridge. At 14.9 miles, reach Yanu Branch; the trail curves to the right to continue downstream, staying above the creek. Pass large yellow poplars. Water seeps from under a low overhang at 15.3 miles. Soon after, descend through several switchbacks to a level with Yanu Branch, which you rockhop at 15.9 miles below a cascade in the stream. The trail continues downstream to a shallow crossing at 16.0 miles of Little Jonas Creek above the confluence of Yanu Branch, and then follows Little Jonas Creek down the mountain.

Reach Jonas Creek at 16.3 miles, where you must ford to the other side above the confluence of Little Jonas Creek. You might as well go ahead and get your feet wet, because you'll make several wet crossings as the trail follows Jonas Creek down the mountain. This trail is scheduled for renovation in the near future, so you might find footbridges, or at least easier crossings, when you come this way. Ford Jonas Creek again at 16.4 and 16.6 miles. Then at 16.7 miles, the creek has taken over the trail; you must walk down the streambed, hugging the left bank for about 30 yards.

The trail stays on the left side of the creek for a time but then fords Jonas Creek again at 17.0 and 17.1 miles. The trail rises above the creek to eventually drop into the Jonas Creek Campsite (70) at 17.4 miles. This is a beautiful campsite resting in the peninsula of land between Jonas Creek on your right and Forney Creek on the left—flat, open areas, rocks to sit on, plenty of water. Pass straight through camp to ford Forney Creek, or perhaps make a new footbridge crossing; the Jonas Creek Trail ends at a junction with the Forney Creek Trail on the other side. To the left, the Forney Creek Trail (hike 63) climbs 8.1 miles to Clingmans Dome; turn to the right on the Forney Creek Trail.

The trail passes downstream along Forney Creek. In the CCC Campsite (71) at 18.4 miles it is joined by the Springhouse Branch Trail (hike 91) to the left; continue straight.

Reach another junction at 19.6 miles, with the Whiteoak Branch Trail to the left. To the right the Forney Creek Trail crosses Whiteoak Branch and continues down along Forney Creek; turn left onto Whiteoak Branch Trail.

The trail climbs along Whiteoak Branch to cross the stream at 19.7 miles and ascend over a gap and descend to a junction with the Lakeshore Trail (hike 92) at 21.6 miles. To the right, the Lakeshore Trail reconnects with the Forney Creek Trail in 1.0 mile; turn left to return to the trailhead on Lakeview Drive at 23.5 miles.

FONTANA/TWENTYMILE

In the early 1940s, aluminum was needed for America's airplanes in World War II. So in 1941, the federal government proposed building a dam on the Little Tennessee River to supply the great amounts of electricity needed to produce aluminum at ALCOA's nearby plant in southeastern Tennessee. From 1942 till 1945, the Tennessee Valley Authority, a federal agency, constructed the 480-foot-high Fontana Dam. To house the workers, TVA constructed the community of Fontana, which today is a resort village in these remote mountains of eastern North Carolina. The name came from a lumber milltown of the Montvale Lumber Company, which logged the Eagle Creek watershed; the site of the original town of Fontana is now under the lake of the same name.

Getting there: From the east, head west on US 74. At 8.8 miles from Bryson City, turn right on Hwy. 28. At 30.5 miles, you'll come to a T junction; to the right, Fontana Dam has a trailhead for the Appalachian and Lakeshore Trails at road's end in 2.3 miles; to the left, Hwy. 28 passes Fontana Village to reach the Twentymile Ranger Station trailhead in 7.0 miles.

Pumphouse at Proctor sawmill

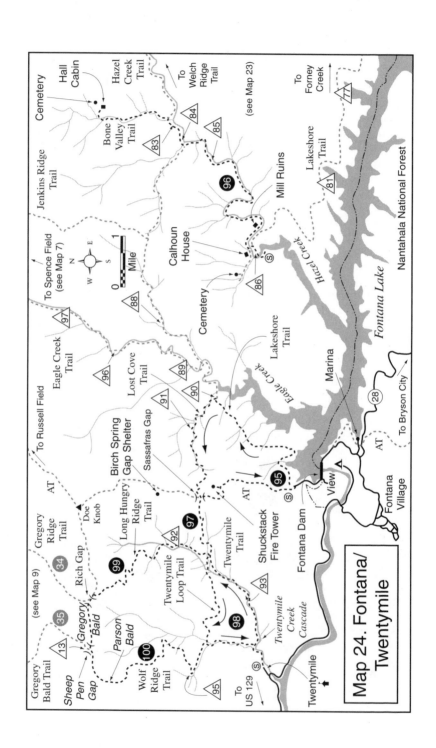

Map 24. Fontana/Twentymile

From the west, head southeast on US 129. In 10.4 miles past the Abrams Creek access, pass the Parson Branch Road exit from Cades Cove, and at 15.1 miles turn left on Hwy. 28. The Twentymile Ranger Station lies on the left at 18 miles. At 23.1 miles cross a bridge over the Little Tennessee River; pass the turnoff on the left for the Fontana Campground, stay on the highway up the hill past Fontana Village on the right, and reach the intersection for the top of the dam at 25 miles. Stay straight on the road to the top of the Fontana Dam; you'll pass the marina to the right and the stables on the left. Before the dam, the AT comes from the right to join the road. Past the visitor center on the left, cross over the dam at 26.2 miles, and on the other side, turn to the right for the trailheads at the end of the road at 27.3 miles.

There's also a trailhead at Proctor on Hazel Creek, which has no road access. You can reach it on foot, with long hikes over the crest of the Smokies from the Tennessee side, or from the east or west on the Lakeshore Trail. Or you can take a boat across from the Fontana Marina. From the road onto the top of Fontana Dam, turn right to descend the hill to the marina dock at the lake's edge. How far the boat can take you up Hazel Creek depends on the level of the lake. Wherever you're let off, you'll walk a dirt road that leads up Hazel Creek to Proctor.

95 | LAKESHORE, LOST COVE, AND APPALACHIAN TRAILS TO SHUCKSTACK

Distance: 12.0-mile loop; to Shuckstack Fire Tower, 3.5 miles one way via the AT
Difficulty: Strenuous
Elevation change: 2,100 feet
Season: Year-round
Cautions: Creek fords, steep ascents
Connections: Eagle Creek Trail, Twentymile Trail

Attractions: This combination of trails loops by the Shuckstack Fire Tower for expansive views. For a short hike to the Shuckstack Fire Tower, you can walk up the AT from the trailhead for a steep 3.5-mile one-way climb. Camping is available at Fontana Campground, Lost Cove Campsite (90), and Upper Lost Cove Campsite (91).

Trailhead: Drive the Fontana Dam Road past the visitor center on the left and across the dam to the end of the road, 2.3 miles from Hwy. 28. The AT emerges on the left.

View north from Shuckstack

Description: Head straight on the Lakeshore Trail, which goes down a road overrun by grass. At the end of the road, descend into a cove with Fontana Lake on your right. At 0.7 mile the trail turns upstream to rockhop Payne Branch.

From here the trail follows the route of old Hwy. 288, which was abandoned when Fontana Lake was created. Along the old roadway, you'll find the remains of a car at 1.2 miles and in an open grassy area another car skeleton and car parts lying about. At 1.6 miles another car is overturned against a tree.

At 2.0 miles, the trail turns left to leave the roadbed and ascend over Shuckstack Ridge, running down from Shuckstack Mountain on Twentymile Ridge. The trail from here is a series of ups and downs, crossing parallel ridges, including Snakeden Ridge at 4.2 miles, with small streams in the coves between. The trail switchbacks right and left to descend to a junction at 5.2 miles at Lost Cove Creek. To the right, the Lakeshore Trail turns to follow the Lost Cove Trail 0.2 mile to a left turn into the Lost Cove Campsite (90) on the embayment of Eagle Creek. (The Lakeshore Trail passes through the campsite to ford Lost Cove Creek and continue northeast; a segment of the Lakeshore Trail may eventually be built to extend east along the lake to connect with Proctor; see hike 96.) At the junction, turn left and follow the Lost Cove Trail upstream.

In the next 0.5 mile ford the creek seven times. The trail then curves left through the Upper Lost Cove Campsite (91) at 6.3 miles and continues to follow Lost Cove Creek while ascending Twentymile Ridge. The trail descends to a junction with an old road and bears right to continue following Lost Cove Creek, crossing it and its small tributaries several times on the way up. At 7.2 miles, the trail cuts across the head of Lost Cove Creek and climbs steeply through switchbacks to reach a four-way junction in Sassafras Gap on Twentymile Ridge at 8.3 miles. Straight ahead, the Twentymile Trail descends 4.7 miles to the Twentymile Ranger Station; to the right, the AT leads to the crest of the Smokies at Doe Knob in 3.1 miles; turn left on the AT.

Ascend to a junction at 8.6 miles where the AT continues right; take a side trail to the left, which leads 0.1 mile to the Shuckstack Fire Tower. The chimney, foundations, and cistern of the old watchman's cabin still sit beside the fire tower, constructed by the CCC in 1932. You can climb the tower steps for one of the finest views in the park, but take care. You do so at your own risk since the tower is not maintained for observation purposes. To the south, Twentymile Ridge extends to the right, and Snakeden Ridge lies to the far left; Shuckstack Ridge ahead runs down toward Fontana Lake. To the north stands the main crest of the Smokies, Gregory Bald to the left and Clingmans Dome to the far right.

From the Shuckstack summit, continue south on the AT, descending steeply along Shuckstack Ridge. The trail passes below the peak of Little Shuckstack and out a finger ridge to the south. Switchback left at 8.8 miles and continue descending. At 11.8 miles the trail swings around a large oak and drops off the ridgeline back to the road and trailhead at 12.0 miles.

96 | LAKESHORE, HAZEL CREEK, AND BONE VALLEY TRAILS

Distance: 7.8 miles one way
Difficulty: Easy
Elevation gain: 480 feet
Season: Year-round
Cautions: Somewhat rocky
Connections: Lakeshore and Hazel Creek Trails lead out of the area

Attractions: This piece of the Lakeshore Trail wanders through the old lumber town of Proctor and provides access to Bone Valley and the wilderness of Hazel Creek. The former community of Proctor was named for Moses Proctor, who settled on Hazel Creek in 1830, having come from Cades Cove by crossing the mountain through Ekaneetlee Gap. Others arrived, and by 1886 a community was established, though for years Proctor was not much more than the post office. Then after the turn of the century, the W. M. Ritter

Lumber Company came to harvest trees on a grand scale. The Southern Railway arrived at the mouth of Hazel Creek in 1907 to haul lumber out of the mountains. The Ritter Company completed a sawmill in 1910 and began cutting trees. In the 18 years Ritter operated, the company harvested trees all the way to the Smokies crest near Silers Bald. Proctor grew to a population of 1,000 and included a doctor, dentist, train depot, cafe, barber shop, and movie theater. When the Ritter Company left in 1928, the area reverted to a farming community. When TVA began construction on Fontana Dam, the 44,000 acres north of the proposed lake that included Proctor became part of the national park; 1,200 families left this north-shore area, and Proctor became a ghost town. Camping is available at Proctor Campsite (86), Sawdust Pile Campsite (85), Sugar Fork Campsite (84), and Bone Valley Campsite (83).

Trailhead: Take a boat from the Fontana Marina across the lake to Proctor (call ahead to let them know you're coming; if you're camping, you can register at the sign-up station above the marina).

Description: Wherever the boat can let you off, walk a dirt road that leads up Hazel Creek, named for the hazelnut shrubs that grow along the stream. At about 0.5 mile, the Proctor Campsite (86) lies on the left, a large camp beneath white pines that's a popular base from which to explore the area. Continue up the road to a junction with the Lakeshore Trail at 0.6

Embarking from Fontana Lake at Hazel Creek

mile in Proctor. Straight ahead on the Lakeshore Trail, a small concrete bunker and scattered bricks mark the site of the Ritter Office and Commissary; soon the trail turns to the right and heads east toward Forney Creek Trail (hike 92). The overgrown street continues straight; it once crossed the creek on a bridge, now gone. At the Lakeshore Trail junction, turn left and cross the creek on a new bridge to join the major part of the town on the other side at a junction with Calico Street.

To the left stands a house built in 1928 that was later the home of Granville Calhoun, a descendent of John C. Calhoun, U.S. Secretary of War and Vice President in the early 1800s. Granville once took Horace Kephart on a bear hunt, as recounted in Kephart's *Our Southern Highlanders*. You can explore past the Calhoun House over a hill and then up a second hill to reach a steep side path to the right that leads up to the Proctor Cemetery in 0.5 mile. This was the site of the Moses Proctor cabin; Moses and his wife, Patience Rustin, are buried there along with many other residents of Proctor.

At the junction at Calico Street, turn right. The roadway joins the old railbed of the Smoky Mountain Railway that Ritter built up Hazel Creek. At 1.0 mile, watch for a makeshift path to the left that leads across an earthen berm to the ruins of a kiln where lumber was quickly dried with heat. When the land was purchased for the park, the houses and structures were torn down or burned, except for the Calhoun house, but the brick and concrete ruins of this structure remain. The berm you walked to the kiln was the lower end of a log pond. When logs were brought in from the mountains, they were caked with mud from being dragged down the mountain slopes and needed to be washed before they were sent into the mill. Also, floating logs were more easily moved from one location to another.

On up the trail, walk along the edge of the pond to where the sawmill stood at the upper end. The ghostly ruins, mostly broken down, stand in the woods. The curious domed structures on the corners most likely housed valves and pumps for controlling the water flow in the pond.

Continue up the old railbed along Hazel Creek, a noted trout fishing stream; Granville Calhoun stocked the stream with rainbow trout when he lived on the creek. At 1.7 miles, pass an old gauge house that measured water flow. The roadway enters a more open area at 1.8 miles, the site of North Proctor, a small community that housed African-American workers.

At 2.0 miles, the roadway crosses a bridge over Hazel Creek and then again at 2.9 miles. The Sawdust Pile Campsite (85) rests on a narrow stretch of land between the trail and the creek at 3.7 miles. Cross another bridge over the creek at 4.9 miles. When you cross again at 5.2 miles, stop to look at the surrounding rocks, which look like giant blocks of Swiss cheese. The holes are caused by pebbles settling into depressions in the rock and swirling around and around with the current to grind circular cavities. At 5.3 miles, reach a junction with the Hazel Creek Trail. The Lakeshore Trail continues uphill to the left to circle back toward Fontana Dam, passing the

Drying kiln at Proctor

Jenkins Ridge and Eagle Creek Trails; turn right on the Hazel Creek Trail.

The trail crosses a low bridge spanning Haw Gap Branch to the Sugar Fork Campsite (84), nestled between Haw Gap Branch and Hazel Creek. The trail continues uphill along an old roadway, passing the Bone Valley Campsite (83) at 6.0 miles and crossing a bridge over Bone Valley Creek to a junction with the Bone Valley Trail to the left. The Hazel Creek Trail turns right to penetrate the vast wilderness on the North Carolina side of the Smokies, connecting with the Cold Spring Gap and Welch Ridge Trails (hike 94); turn left up the Bone Valley Trail.

The trail heads north up Bone Valley, fording the creek four times and reaching the Hall Cabin at 7.8 miles. This was the second home of the Jesse Crayton Hall family, who came to the valley in 1877. Nearby was the site of the Kress Lodge, built by the Kress Department Store family as a private resort; the building burned in 1960. To the north a path leads to the Hall

Cemetery. Bone Valley got its name when a herd of cattle that had been taken to the mountain crest for grazing in early spring became caught in a late snowstorm in 1888. The herd left the mountaintop in search of shelter but was trapped in the valley and froze to death. The bones of the cows could be seen for several years afterward.

97 TWENTYMILE AND APPALACHIAN TRAILS TO SHUCKSTACK

Distance: 5.1 miles one way; to Twentymile Cascade, 0.6 mile one way
Difficulty: Moderate
Elevation gain: 2,700 feet
Season: Year-round
Cautions: Long ascent
Connections: Wolf Ridge Trail, Twentymile Loop Trail, Long Hungry Ridge Trail, Lost Cove Trail

Attractions: The road this hike follows was once the railbed for the Kitchens Lumber Company, which logged the area of Twentymile Creek. The

Twentymile Creek Cascade

railbed was later improved to provide access to the Shuckstack Fire Tower. At Twentymile Creek Cascade, the creek stair-steps down a drop in the creekbed; the last step is a broad rock slide where the water slips into a pool. Camping is available at Twentymile Creek Campsite (93).

Trailhead: Follow Hwy. 28 to Twentymile and turn up a gravel road past the ranger station to a parking area.

Description: Walk up the gravel road while paralleling Twentymile Creek on your right. At 0.4 mile, the confluence of Moore Springs Branch with Twentymile Creek is barely noticeable amid thick rhododendron. The trail follows Moore Springs Branch upstream and at 0.5 mile crosses the branch on a bridge to a junction with the Wolf Ridge Trail (hike 100) to the left; turn to the right on the Twentymile Trail.

The trail once more parallels Twentymile Creek. At 0.6 mile, a short side trail leads down to Twentymile Creek Cascade; continue straight up the old railbed. Cross Twentymile Creek on bridges at 1.5 and 1.7 miles before reaching the Twentymile Creek Campsite (93) at 1.8 miles. Beyond the campsite, cross the creek on a bridge again.

At 2.1 miles the trail crosses a bridge over a tributary stream and at 2.4 miles a bridge over Twentymile Creek; on the far side, watch for a small cascade in the creekbed and then a long water slide. At 2.5 miles, cross a bridge over the stream once more and follow a tributary creek upstream to a four-way junction at 3.0 miles at Proctor Field Gap, named for Jake Proctor, who settled the area. Straight ahead is the Long Hungry Ridge Trail (hike 99), which leads up the mountain to the Smokies crest; to the left, the Twentymile Loop Trail (hike 98) turns west; bear right to continue on the Twentymile Trail.

The trail continues steeply up the mountain following the old roadbed that provided access to the fire tower atop the peak of Shuckstack Mountain. The road narrows and becomes a rocky, sometimes eroded trail. At 3.3 miles, rockhop Proctor Branch, a tributary of Twentymile Creek; an old culvert fills half the rocky channel across the road.

The road winds its way up the mountain. At 3.7 miles, curve left on a drier, south-facing slope where you can see across the valley of Proctor Branch to Twentymile Ridge, which runs down from Shuckstack. At 4.5 miles, where the trail swings right, look ahead above the treeline for your first view of the Shuckstack Fire Tower standing atop the ridge. Curve back left and soon you'll have a better view through the trees to the right. The trail then ascends to a junction with the Appalachian Trail at Sassafras Gap at 4.7 miles. To the left, the AT ascends the mountain past the Birch Spring Gap Shelter in 0.8 mile to the Gregory Bald Trail (hike 35) in 3.1 miles. Straight ahead, the Lost Cove Trail (hike 95) descends 3.1 miles to the Lakeshore Trail. Turn right on the AT to get to the fire tower.

In 0.3 mile ascend to a junction along the ridge at 5.0 miles. To the right, the AT continues to Fontana Dam in 3.4 miles; turn left.

Follow a rocky 0.1-mile path that shifts up to the Shuckstack Fire Tower

atop the mountain peak at 5.1 miles. Take care if you climb the tower steps
for views.

98 | TWENTYMILE, TWENTYMILE LOOP, AND WOLF RIDGE TRAILS

Distance: 7.3-mile loop
Difficulty: Moderate
Elevation change: 1,300 feet
Season: Year-round
Cautions: Creek fords, overgrown sections
Connections: Long Hungry Ridge Trail

Attractions: This trail combination offers a circuit walk over the lower
slope of the mountains, passing Twentymile Creek Cascade and wander-
ing along Moore Springs Branch, which cascades down along the return
part of the hike. Camping is available at Twentymile Creek Campsite (93).

Trailhead: Follow Hwy. 28 to Twentymile and turn up a gravel road
past the ranger station to a parking area.

Description: Hike up the Twentymile Trail (hike 97) to the junction at
0.5 mile with the Wolf Ridge Trail on the left (the return route for this loop)
and continue to the right on the Twentymile Trail. Pass Twentymile Creek
Cascade at 0.6 mile and Twentymile Creek Campsite (93) at 1.8 miles, then
reach a four-way junction in Proctor Field Gap at 3.0 miles. To the right, the
Twentymile Trail (hike 97) continues up to the AT near the Shuckstack Fire
Tower in 1.7 miles; straight ahead, the Long Hungry Ridge Trail (hike 99)
heads up the mountain to the Smokies crest; turn left on the Twentymile
Loop Trail.

The footpath winds down to cross Proctor Branch at 3.1 miles. Turn
downstream and walk a low ridge that stands between Proctor Branch on
the left and Twentymile Creek on the right. The trail soon winds down the
end of the ridge to a ford of Twentymile Creek at 3.5 miles; the creek runs
into a rock wall on the right and turns left to pass in front of you.

Up from the creek, pass along a tributary to bear left and make a rockhop
crossing at 3.6 miles. The trail then climbs, crossing Long Hungry Ridge, which
leads down from the Smokies crest. At 4.7 miles, the trail ascends through a
gap and descends to a ford of Moore Springs Branch at 5.7 miles with a small
cascade upstream. At 5.8 miles, walk up to a junction with the Wolf Ridge
Trail, where the Twentymile Loop Trail ends. To the right, the Wolf Ridge
Trail (hike 100) ascends to the AT at Sheep Pen Gap; turn left to complete the loop.

Soon rockhop Dalton Branch, a tributary of Moore Springs Branch, and then ford the main branch four times; the last two crossings have collapsed footbridges that may be repaired when you come this way. A footbridge at a fifth crossing at 6.5 miles still spans the creek. Watch for several slides in the creek until you close the loop at the junction with the Twentymile Trail at 6.8 miles. Turn right to cross the bridge over Moore Springs Branch and walk the 0.5 mile back to the parking area at 7.3 miles.

99 | TWENTYMILE AND LONG HUNGRY RIDGE TRAILS TO GREGORY BALD

Distance: 8.2 miles one way
Difficulty: Strenuous
Elevation gain: 3,300 feet
Season: Year-round
Cautions: Stream crossings, steady climb
Connections: Twentymile Loop Trail, Gregory Ridge Trail

Attractions: This hike can be combined with the Wolf Ridge Trail (hike 100) to make one of the outstanding loop backpacks in the park. Long Hungry Ridge got its name when a group of hunters became stranded in a snowstorm and nearly starved before getting off the mountain. Camping is available at Twentymile Creek Campsite (93), Upper Flats Campsite (92), and Sheep Pen Gap Campsite (13).

Trailhead: Follow Hwy. 28 to Twentymile and turn up a gravel road past the ranger station to a parking area.

Description: Follow the Twentymile Trail (hike 97) past a junction with the Wolf Ridge Trail (hike 100) at 0.5 mile, Twentymile Creek Cascade at 0.6 mile, and Twentymile Creek Campsite (93) at 1.8 miles, to reach a four-way junction in Proctor Field Gap at 3.0 miles. To the right, the Twentymile Trail (hike 97) continues up to the AT at Sassafras Gap; to the left, the Twentymile Loop Trail (hike 98) crosses to Wolf Ridge Trail; go straight ahead on the Long Hungry Ridge Trail.

The trail initially follows a spur railbed that descends to cross Proctor Branch at 3.2 miles and parallels Twentymile Creek upstream. Cross two small tributaries where there were once short bridges, but only the spanning beams remain. The trail curves through the Upper Flats Campsite (92) at 4.3 miles to a rockhop of Greer Branch. Then walk up to a rockhop of Twentymile Creek at 4.6 miles. An old train car wheel may still lie to the left.

The trail leaves the railbed and climbs steeply, paralleling Rye Patch Branch. Cross a small stream and then Rye Patch Branch at 4.9 miles. The trail climbs steeply with several switchbacks to top Long Hungry Ridge at

6.9 miles at Rye Patch, a swatch of grass surrounded by trees. The trail makes a right turn here to follow the ridge to the crest of the Smokies at 7.6 miles and a junction with the Gregory Bald Trail (hike 35). To the right the Gregory Bald Trail reaches the AT in 2.0 miles; turn left.

Pass the Gregory Ridge Trail (hike 34) to the right at 7.7 miles (it leads down to Cades Cove); stay straight. The trail ascends to cross Gregory Bald at 8.2 miles, where you'll have grand views and blooming azalea in late June.

In another 0.5 mile, you can connect with the Wolf Ridge Trail (hike 100) in Sheep Pen Gap at the Sheep Pen Gap Campsite (13) and loop back to the Twentymile trailhead for a total of 15.6 miles.

100 | WOLF RIDGE TRAIL TO GREGORY BALD

Distance: 7.4 miles one way; to Parson Bald, 6.2 miles one way
Difficulty: Moderate
Elevation gain: 3,300 feet
Season: Year-round
Cautions: Creek crossings, steady ascent
Connections: Twentymile Loop Trail

Attractions: This trail ascends to Parson Bald on its way to the Smokies crest. In the early 1800s, crowds once gathered here for revivals, and so the name "Parson," although some say it was named for Joshua Parson, who in 1829 helped build a turnpike that ran along the Little Tennessee River to the west. This hike can be combined with the Long Hungry Ridge Trail (hike 99) and Twentymile Trail (hike 98) to form a great backpacking loop. Camping is available at Dalton Branch Campsite (95) and Sheep Pen Gap Campsite (13).

Trailhead: Follow Hwy. 28 to Twentymile and turn up a gravel road past the ranger station to a parking area.

Description: Follow Twentymile Trail (hike 97) 0.5 mile to the bridge crossing of Moore Springs Branch and a junction with the Wolf Ridge Trail on the left. To the right, the Twentymile Trail continues to Proctor Field Gap; turn left onto Wolf Ridge Trail.

The trail ascends an old railbed along Moore Springs Branch on your left. The creek contains numerous spillways and slides. At 0.8 mile the trail crosses Moore Springs Branch on a long footbridge. Cross again at 0.9 mile and at 1.0 mile, but you'll have to rockhop or ford where the bridges have collapsed, unless they have been replaced. Ford again at 1.2 and 1.4 miles, rockhop Dalton Branch, a tributary of Moore Springs Branch, and reach a junction at 1.5 miles with the Twentymile Loop Trail to the right (it leads 2.8 miles to the Twentymile Trail); curve left to stay on the Wolf Ridge Trail.

Parallel Dalton Branch on your left. Ascend to a sharp right turn at the Dalton Branch Campsite (95) at 2.5 miles and begin an ascent of Wolf Ridge, named for the gray wolf that once roamed the Smokies. At 3.4 miles, the trail crosses a small stream that falls steeply to your right. Cross another small stream at 3.7 miles and ascend to pass left around a point as you move to the other side of Wolf Ridge. Now parallel a small stream up a hollow to the ridgeline at 3.8 miles.

From here up, ascend along the ridge through several switchbacks and sharp curves. At 6.2 miles, the trail emerges onto Parson Bald, an open area of grass and shrubs. The trail then descends from the summit of Parson Bald, reentering the forest but still with luxuriant grass on the forest floor. Reach Sheep Pen Gap at 6.9 miles and connect with the Gregory Bald Trail at the Sheep Pen Gap Campsite (13). Straight ahead, the Gregory Bald Trail (hike 35) leads down to Sams Gap on the Parson Branch Road out of Cades Cove; turn to the right on the Gregory Bald Trail, which leads up to Gregory Bald at 7.4 miles. You can continue east for another 0.5 mile to a junction in Rich Gap with the Gregory Ridge Trail (hike 34), which descends to the left toward Cades Cove. In another 0.1 mile the Long Hungry Ridge Trail (hike 99) leads to the right, looping back to the Twentymile trailhead for a total of 15.6 miles. Straight ahead the Gregory Bald Trail leads to Doe Knob and a junction with the AT.

SELECTED REFERENCES

Adams, Paul J. *Mt. LeConte*. Knoxville: Holston Printing Company, 1966.
  Edgar, Kevin, ed.

Appalachian Trail Guide to Tennessee–North Carolina. 11th edition. Harpers
  Ferry, W. Virginia: Appalachian Trail Conference, 1995.

Brewer, Alberta, and Carson Brewer. *Valley So Wild, A Folk History*.
  Knoxville: East Tennessee Historical Society, 1975.

Brewer, Carson. *A Wonderment of Mountains, The Great Smoky Mountains*.
  Knoxville: Tenpenny Publishing, 1981.

Bush, Florence Cope. *Dorie, Woman of the Mountains*. Knoxville: The
  University of Tennessee Press, 1992.

Campbell, Carlos C. *Birth of a National Park in the Great Smoky Mountains*.
  Knoxville: The University of Tennessee Press, 1960.

Coggins, Allen R. *Place Names of the Smokies*. Gatlinburg, Tenn.: Great
  Smoky Mountains Natural History Association, 1999.

Davis, Hattie Caldwell. *Cataloochee Valley, Vanished Settlements of the Great
  Smoky Mountains*. Alexander, N.C.: WorldComm, 1997.

DeLaughter, Jerry. *Mountain Roads & Quiet Places*. Gatlinburg, Tenn.:
  Great Smoky Mountains Natural History Association, 1983.

Dunn, Durwood. *Cades Cove, The Life and Death of a Southern Appalachian
  Community, 1818-1937*. Knoxville: The University of Tennessee Press,
  1988.

Finger, John R. *The Eastern Band of Cherokees, 1819–1900*. Knoxville: The
  University of Tennessee Press, 1984.

Frome, Michael. *Strangers in High Places, The Story of the Great Smoky
  Mountains*. Knoxville: The University of Tennessee Press, 1980.

Great Smoky Mountains National Park. *Trails Rehabilitation Guide for 1999,
  Environmental Assessment*. Gatlinburg, Tenn.: Great Smoky Mountains
  National Park, 1999.

Harris, Ann G. "Great Smoky Mountains National Park," in *Geology of
  National Parks*, pp. 261–271. 2d ed. Dubuque, Iowa: Kendall/Hunt
  Publishing, 1977.

Houk, Rose. *Exploring the Smokies*. Gatlinburg, Tenn.: Great Smoky
  Mountains Natural History Association, 1994.

———. *Great Smoky Mountains National Park, A Natural History Guide*.
  New York: Houghton Mifflin, 1993.

Hutson, Robert W., et al. *Great Smoky Mountains Wildflowers*. Northbrook,
  Ill.: Windy Pines Publishing, 1995.

Kephart, Horace. *Our Southern Highlanders*. Knoxville: The University of
  Tennessee Press, 1922.

King, Duane H., ed. *The Cherokee Nation, A Troubled History*. Knoxville:
  The University of Tennessee Press, 1979.

King, Philip B., et al. *Geology of the Great Smoky Mountains National Park, Tennessee and North Carolina*, Geological Survey Professional Paper. Washington, D.C.: U.S. Government Printing Office, 1968.

Luther, Edward T. *Our Restless Earth*. Knoxville: The University of Tennessee Press, 1977.

National Park Service. *At Home in the Smokies*. Washington, D.C.: U.S. Department of Interior, 1984.

———. *Great Smoky Mountains*. Washington, D.C.: U.S. Department of Interior, 1981.

Oliver, Duane. *Hazel Creek from Then Till Now*. Maryville, Tenn.: Stinnett Printing, 1989.

Schmidt, Ronald G., and William S. Hooks. *Whistle Over the Mountains, Timber, Track & Trails in the Tennessee Smokies*. Yellow Springs, Ohio: Graphicom Press, 1994.

Shields, A. Randolph. *The Cades Cove Story*. Gatlinburg, Tenn.: Great Smoky Mountains Natural History Association, 1977.

Stevenson, George B. *Trees of the Great Smoky Mountains National Park*. Gatlinburg, Tenn.: Great Smoky Mountains Natural History Association, 1967.

Stupka, Arthur. *Trees, Shrubs, and Woody Vines of the Great Smoky Mountains National Park*. Knoxville: The University of Tennessee Press, 1964.

———. *Notes on the Birds of Great Smoky Mountains National Park*. Knoxville: The University of Tennessee Press, 1963.

Trout, Ed. *Historic Buildings of the Smokies*. Gatlinburg, Tenn.: Great Smoky Mountains Natural History Association, 1995.

Weals, Vic. *Last Train to Elkmont*. Knoxville: Olden Press, 1993.

APPENDIX: ADDRESSES AND PHONE NUMBERS

Great Smoky Mountains National Park
107 Park Headquarters Road
Gatlinburg, TN 37738
423-436-1200
www.nps.gov/grsm
Campground reservations: 800-365-CAMP;
http://reservations.nps.gov
Backcountry Reservation Office: 423-436-1231
Trail map: www.nps.gov/carto/RDF/GRSMmap.pdf

FOR ENVIRONMENTAL EDUCATION PROGRAMS AND FIELD COURSES AND HIKING

Great Smoky Mountains Institute at Tremont
Great Smoky Mountains National Park
9275 Tremont Road
Townsend, TN 37882
423-448-6709
www.nps.gov/grsm/tremont.htm

Great Smoky Mountains Hiking Club
P.O. Box 1454
Knoxville, TN 37901

Smoky Mountain Field School
The University of Tennessee Community Programs
600 Henley Street, Suite 105
Knoxville, TN 37996-4110
423-974-0150
www.ce.utk.edu/Smoky/default.htm

FOR PUBLICATIONS

Appalachian Trail Conference
P.O. Box 807
Harpers Ferry, WV 25425-0807
304-535-6331

Great Smoky Mountains Natural History Association
115 Park Headquarters Road
Gatlinburg, TN 37738
423-436-0120
www.nps.gov/grsm/bookstor.htm

FOR BOAT SERVICE

Almond Boat & RV Park
1165 Almond Boat Park Road
Bryson City, NC 28713
704-488-6423

Fontana Village Resort
P.O. Box 68
Fontana Dam, NC 28733
800-849-2258 or 704-498-2211
Marina: ext. 277

FOR ACCOMMODATIONS

Cherokee Visitor Center
P.O. Box 460
Cherokee, NC 28719
800-438-1601

Fontana Village Resort
P.O. Box 68
Fontana Dam, NC 28733
800-849-2258 or 704-498-2211

Gatlinburg Chamber of Commerce
P.O. Box 527
Gatlinburg, TN 37738
800-568-4748

LeConte Lodge
250 Apple Valley Road
Sevierville, TN 37862
423-429-5704

Maggie Valley Chamber of Commerce
P.O. Box 87
Maggie Valley, NC 28751
800-785-8259

Pigeon Forge Department of Tourism
P.O. Box 1390
Pigeon Forge, TN 37868
800-251-9100

Swain County Chamber of Commerce (Bryson City)
P.O. Box 509
Bryson City, NC 28713
800-867-9246 or 828-488-3681

Townsend Visitors Center
7906 East Lamar Alexander Parkway
Townsend, TN 37882
800-525-6834

INDEX

ABOUT THE AUTHOR

Russ Manning began his career as a science writer, but for the past ten years has devoted his attention to travel and outdoor subjects. With his wife and hiking companion, Sondra Jamieson, he has co-authored several books about the Southeast, including *The Best of Shenandoah National Park: A Guide to Trails and the Skyline Drive; Trails of the Big South Fork National River and Recreation Area: A Guide for Hikers, Bikers, and Horse Riders;* and *Tennessee's South Cumberland: A Hiker's Guide to Trails and Attractions.* He has also written over 200 articles for such magazines as *Outside, Backpacker, The Tennessee Conservationist, Appalachia,* and *Environmental Ethics.*

THE MOUNTAINEERS, founded in 1906, is a nonprofit outdoor activity and conservation club, whose mission is "to explore, study, preserve, and enjoy the natural beauty of the outdoors . . . . " Based in Seattle, Washington, the club is now the third-largest such organization in the United States, with 15,000 members and five branches throughout Washington State.

The Mountaineers sponsors both classes and year-round outdoor activities in the Pacific Northwest, which include hiking, mountain climbing, skitouring, snowshoeing, bicycling, camping, kayaking and canoeing, nature study, sailing, and adventure travel. The club's conservation division supports environmental causes through educational activities, sponsoring legislation, and presenting informational programs. All club activities are led by skilled, experienced volunteers, who are dedicated to promoting safe and responsible enjoyment and preservation of the outdoors.

If you would like to participate in these organized outdoor activities or the club's programs, consider a membership in The Mountaineers. For information and an application, write or call The Mountaineers, Club Headquarters, 300 Third Avenue West, Seattle, Washington 98119; (206) 284-6310.

The Mountaineers Books, an active, nonprofit publishing program of the club, produces guidebooks, instructional texts, historical works, natural history guides, and works on environmental conservation. All books produced by The Mountaineers are aimed at fulfilling the club's mission.

Send or call for our catalog of more than 300 outdoor titles:

The Mountaineers Books
1001 SW Klickitat Way, Suite 201
Seattle, WA 98134
1-800-553-4453

mbooks@mountaineers.org
www.mountaineersbooks.org

Other titles you may enjoy from The Mountaineers:

100 CLASSIC HIKES IN™ WASHINGTON: North Cascades, Olympics, Mount Rainier & South Cascades, Alpine Lakes, Glacier Peak,
Ira Spring & Harvey Manning
A full-color guide to Washington's finest trails. The essential classic for hiking this picturesque state, including maps, photos, and full details you need to plan the perfect trip.

100 HIKES IN™ SERIES: These are our fully detailed, best-selling hiking guides with complete descriptions, maps, and photos. Chock-full of trail data, safety tips, and wilderness etiquette.
100 HIKES IN™ WASHINGTON'S ALPINE LAKES, 2d ed.
100 HIKES IN™ WASHINGTON'S GLACIER PEAK REGION: THE NORTH CASCADES, 3d ed.
100 HIKES IN™ WASHINGTON'S NORTH CASCADES NATIONAL PARK REGION, 2d ed.
100 HIKES IN™ WASHINGTON'S SOUTH CASCADES AND OLYMPICS, 3d ed.
100 HIKES IN™ THE ALPS, 2d ed.
100 HIKES IN™ ARIZONA
100 HIKES IN™ NORTHERN CALIFORNIA
100 HIKES IN™ CALIFORNIA'S CENTRAL SIERRA AND COAST RANGE
100 HIKES IN™ THE INLAND NORTHWEST
100 HIKES IN™ OREGON
120 HIKES ON™ THE OREGON COAST

ANIMAL TRACKS OF THE SOUTHEAST: Book and poster,
Chris Stall
Information on more than 40 animals common to this region. This pocket-size guide contains life-size drawings of footprints and information on size, sounds, habitat, diet, and patterns of movement.

EVERYDAY WISDOM: 1001 Expert Tips for Hikers,
Karen Berger
Expert tips and tricks for hikers and backpackers selected from one of the most popular *Backpacker* Magazine columns. A one-stop, easy-to-use collection of practical advice, time-saving tips, problem-solving techniques, and brilliant improvisations shows hikers how to make their way, and make do, in the backcountry.

BACKCOUNRTY MEDICAL GUIDE, Second Edition,
Peter Steele, M.D.
A pocket-size, comprehensive medical guide for backcountry emergencies. Explains what to include in your first-aid kit and covers all types of injuries from major to minor.